JEWISH SPIRITUALITY AND SOCIAL TRANSFORMATION

JEWISH SPIRITUALITY AND SOCIAL TRANSFORMATION

HASIDISM AND SOCIETY

EDITED BY
PHILIP WEXLER

A PUBLICATION OF
THE INSTITUTE OF JEWISH
SPIRITUALITY AND SOCIETY

A Herder & Herder Book
The Crossroad Publishing Company
New York

A Herder & Herder Book
The Crossroad Publishing Company
www.crossroadpublishing.com

© 2019 by Philip Wexler.

Crossroad, Herder & Herder, and the crossed C logo/colophon are registered trademarks of The Crossroad Publishing Company.

All rights reserved. No part of this book may be copied, scanned, reproduced in any way, or stored in a retrieval system, or transmitted, in any form or by any means, electronic, mechanical, photocopying, recording, or otherwise, without the written permission of The Crossroad Publishing Company. For permission please write to rights@crossroadpublishing.com.

In continuation of our 200-year tradition of independent publishing, The Crossroad Publishing Company proudly offers a variety of books with strong, original voices and diverse perspectives. The viewpoints expressed in our books are not necessarily those of The Crossroad Publishing Company, any of its imprints or of its employees, executives, or owners. Although the author and publisher have made every effort to ensure that the information in this book was correct at press time, the author and publisher do not assume and hereby disclaim any liability to any party for any loss, damage, or disruption caused by errors or omissions, whether such errors or omissions result from negligence, accident, or any other cause. No claims are made or responsibility assumed for any health or other benefits.

The text of this book is set in 12/15 Adobe Garamond Pro.

Composition by Rachel Reiss.
Cover design by Sophie Appel.
Cover artwork by Lesley Friedman.

Library of Congress Cataloging-in-Publication Data
available upon request from the Library of Congress.

ISBN 978-0-8245-9947-8 paperback
ISBN 978-0-8245-9946-1 cloth
ISBN 978-0-8245-9948-5 ePub
ISBN 978-0-8245-9949-2 mobi

Books published by The Crossroad Publishing Company may be purchased at special quantity discount rates for classes and institutional use. For information, please e-mail sales@crossroadpublishing.com.

CONTENTS

Acknowledgments ix

Introduction xi
PHILIP WEXLER

SECTION I: HASIDISM, SOCIETY, AND SOCIAL SCIENCE

1. The Institute of Jewish Spirituality and Society 3
   PHILIP WEXLER, Hebrew University of Jerusalem
   (Professor Emeritus)

2. On Mystical Sociology and Turning Judaism Outward 17
   DON SEEMAN, Emory University

3. Mysticism and the Quest for Universal Singularity—
   Post-Subjective Subjectivity and the Contemplative
   Ideal in Habad 37
   ELLIOT R. WOLFSON, University of California, Santa Barbara

4. Habad Hasidism and the Mystical Reconstruction
   of Society 59
   ELI RUBIN, Chabad.org

SECTION II: HABAD IN THEORY AND PRACTICE

5. Chassidic Prayer and Society 81
   NAFTALI LOEWENTHAL,
   University College London

6. Modest Dress: The Rules, The Controversies, and the Experiences   99
KATE MIRIAM LOEWENTHAL,
Royal Holloway, University of London (Professor Emeritus)

7. Education as Life: Reflections from the Field by a Chabad *Shlucha* on a College Campus   113
RIVKAH SLONIM, Rohr Chabad Center for Jewish Student Life at Binghamton University

8. Touch of Gray: Aging as Spiritual Completion in the Thought of the Lubavitcher Rebbe   125
SHAUL WERTHEIMER, Chabad on Campus of Queens

SECTION III: LAW, LITERATURE, AND MYSTICISM

9. Demonization and Transformation: Legal and Kabbalistic Myths of Self and Other   139
NATHANIEL BERMAN, Brown University

10. Walter Benjamin's Modern-Mystical Theory of Youth   163
YOTAM HOTAM, University of Haifa

SECTION IV: MEDITATION, MORALITY, AND THE SELF: HABAD AND MUSAR

11. Contemplation, Meditation, and Metaphysics in Second-Generation Habad   185
JONATHAN GARB, Hebrew University of Jerusalem

12. The Road from Religious Law (Halakha) to the Secular: Constructing the Autonomous Self in the Musar Tradition and Its Discontents   203
SHAUL MAGID, Indiana University, Bloomington

SECTION V: JEWISH SPIRITUALITY AFTER MODERNITY: DEATH AND RENAISSANCE

13. Holocaust Memories and Memories of Depression: The Influences of My Parents on My Scholarship in the Sociology of Education   225
ALAN SADOVNIK, Rutgers University, Newark

14. Jewish Spirituality in Israel as Lived Religion: A New Perspective for the Study of Contemporary Jewish Life   245
RACHEL WERCZBERGER, Ariel University

Notes on Contributors   265

ACKNOWLEDGMENTS

I would like to thank Rabbi Menachem Schmidt for his support for the vision of the Institute of Jewish Spirituality and Society and for this specific conference. For their financial support, I thank George Rohr, Meir Moss, and Ari Chitrik.

Eli Rubin was key in the design of this conference, and he remains an increasingly valuable partner in our work. Chana Colin coordinated the conference and made it happen, and smoothly. She also helped me in tracking down authors and ensuring that they submitted their publications on time.

I want to thank especially all the participants in the conference, which was held over the course of three days at a retreat center in Briarcliff Manor, New York, and of course, those who went on to contribute their papers to this publication.

Thanks to our unfailing editor, Chris Myers, for his patience and practical wisdom.

INTRODUCTION
Philip Wexler

Even before the Inaugural Conference of the Institute of Jewish Spirituality and Society, where earlier versions of these papers were first presented, I had been working for some years on the relationship between mysticism and society, particularly Jewish mysticism (Wexler, 1996, 2000, 2007, 2013; Wexler & Garb, 2012). In Jerusalem, where I moved in 2000 to learn how to read original texts, it was Hasidic adepts, especially Habad Hasidim, who made themselves readily available to teach me—to "learn with" me, as they say—in reading work in their lineage, and beyond, both in Hebrew and Yiddish.

The focus on Hasidism is neither gratuitous nor a historical, educational convenience. It was, as I write in the first essay in this volume, the press from wider crises in modern Western culture and in academic social science that drew me to the pedagogical openness of these Hasidic teachers. Needless to say, even before my time in Jerusalem, I learned theory and practice in other traditions, within and beyond Judaism. Further, at the Hebrew University, I was privileged to be at the core of critical literature in religion. It was, however, the pertinence of the ideas and practices of Hasidism to contemporary social issues and social analytical problems that led me to the meeting between Hasidism and sociology. Well "beyond the crisis" in sociology, there is an extended search for alternative explanatory discourse, both in popular and academic languages and traditions. "Mystical sociology," which is directly engaged by several of the papers herein, is an attempt to show how

Hasidic ideas, as part of a more general "inner worldly mystical" movement of ideas and practices, better address practical and explanatory failings than hegemonic social arrangements and key ideas in modern social science.

As I argue in the opening chapter, neither Hasidism nor I, nor Jewish mysticism, am alone in this effort, which occurs within a variety of cultural and religious traditions. It is not currently popular to think epochally, or in terms of civilizational changes, or academic paradigm shifts that seem to originate outside of professional, university communities. Yet we know that there is an existential and intellectual quest to go beyond the agon of modernity and post-modernity, toward the revitalization of old worlds, the inversion of present premises, and the quest to be "out of this world," even in the powerful, digitalized, highly capitalized new colonialism of interplanetary habitation and settlement. The "religious turn," and within that the "Hasidic turn"—which is a major, everyday force in American congregational Jewish life (as well as in the broader cultural and intellectual sense)—belongs to that hunger for revitalization at every level of meaning and expression.

Don Seeman sympathetically takes up this argument and, without dissenting from a commonality in practice, modifies it from a position of empirical, anthropological knowledge of Hasidism. Theoretically, for an anthropologist and ethnographer of everyday life and social suffering, Seeman is temperate in his distantiation from macro and historical sociology. For his engagement with the epistemological issues and contradictions of his discipline, he favors an existential, phenomenological anthropology as a jumping-off point of analysis in the struggles of immediate social practice. He accomplishes all of this without losing awareness that the Hasidic–social theory engagement is rooted in the unhappiness and injustice of contemporary everyday life, and without neglecting to bring particular ethnographic data on Habad Hasidism to the fore and juxtaposing that with larger paradigmatic and cultural questions.

Elliot Wolfson is one of the rare philosophical, hermeneutical scholars of Jewish mysticism willing to take seriously the social

Introduction xiii

aspect of mysticism in society, and particularly Hasidism, as did Scholem, and also Idel, as Wolfson notes, in the various statements of "kabbalah become ethos." Beyond that, however, Wolfson recognizes that the "mystical sociology" effort is neither an outsider's undifferentiated appropriation of sociology, nor a more typical sociological reductionism, a sociologism, that is less differentiated and, in his language, more "general" or "universal," than the more "nuanced" work of a cosmic interactionism and an entry into the lived and theorized dynamics of mystical sociality.

Wolfson's own contribution in his essay lies both at the general level—to offer a more mutually implicative, constitutive understanding of the individual-collective relationship of sameness and difference—and at the more specific or "particular" level, in that he explores the dual meanings of "contemplation" in textual excerpts from the Habad Hasidic lineage. He wants to avoid the usual polarizing tendency of those conceptual stereotypes and instead show how universal and particular forms of contemplation are represented and what they mean for a non-binary, non-essentialist understanding of being, both of the supernal and in human interrelationality.

Eli Rubin does that, too, living with the differences, the analytical subtleties, and the tensions, as do both Seeman and Wolfson. But he works from a very different starting point. Rubin comes out of a lifelong immersion in Habad Hasidic ideas, practices, and schooling. His scholarship works from the inside out, and he displays his virtuosity in the reading of classical texts in the Habad lineage. Not content to remain behind closed or even sectarian doors, Rubin engages with secular, academic scholarship, as well as with university scholars in Jewish studies. His first and last points of reference are the Habad texts, and, not unlike other scholars, the focus is generally (though not exclusively) on Tanya and the writings and transcribed talks of the Seventh Lubavitcher Rebbe, Rabbi Menachem Mendel Schneerson.

Rubin's relative independence from academic tribalism frees him from taking sides, so that he is able to appreciate the metaphysical, anti-historical, philosophical phenomenology of Elliot Wolfson, and, at the same time, the Durkheimian sociologism of Randall Collins, modified by my less insistent sociology. He aims to combine these three threads into a "socio-mystical" approach to salient phenomena such as prayer, love, and charity that are central in the classical Habad texts. Aiming to keep one foot in the ontological and the other in the sociological domain, he returns to the texts, rooted in their transcendental commitments.

Naftali Loewenthal is also deeply rooted inside Habad Hasidism, though he has straddled the academic fence for many years in his foundational work on early Hasidism. He also emphasizes classical Habad texts in his essay, though with a focus on contemplative prayer. What can we learn from these teachings, he asks, for the "Chassidic community, Jewish society beyond the Chassidic community, and also for general society"? The focus on contemplation becomes a lens for Loewenthal's deeper exposition of the basic assumptions of Habad Hasidism on creation, being, energy, and the importance of the Hebrew letters. Not unlike Rubin, he ends with the Lubavitcher Rebbe's engagement in the contemporary social world and his emphasis on social issues, particularly education. Here the oft-cited "activism" of "the Rebbe" is brought into play, as well as his work in mobilizing collective action for societal transformation.

Kate Miriam Loewenthal takes the Habad analytical path even more specifically into contemporary issues of social practice, with a comparative analysis of women's dress in Habad, but also in Islam and beyond. She explores the values of "modest dress" as part of Hasidic modesty, or "tznius" generally, asking how it serves the interests of women, but also provides an antidote to a wider objectification of gender identities and the body. In an extensive drawing of the domains and implications of modesty in women's dress, she explores "fashion" in modesty and reflects on whether the rise of the Internet has contributed to highlighting the competitive aspect of fashion and wonders whether "modesty has become cool." But it is the role of modest dress in fostering spiritual sensitivity and awareness for women that is, generally, Loewenthal's more enduring interest.

Introduction

Rivkah Slonim's paper, "Education as Life," clearly details the interspersion of theory and practice in Habad Hasidism. The "education question" looms large in the Habad social movement, and perhaps its most notable and extensive innovation is the creation of a broad-based, relatively decentralized network of "shluchim," as well as (in the Hebrew feminine plural) "shluchot," or emissaries. Slonim relates the story of an early beginning of the work of the "Shlucha" on an American university campus, detailing both the feelings of the experience and the variegated tasks entailed in the role. Hers is a rare look at the everyday life of educational work in Habad, and the vividness of the descriptions of practice could lead the curious outsider to miss the serious theoretical, theological, and metaphysical points that this pioneering Shlucha shares in her account. It is at once a "reflection from the field" of a "college campus" and a meditation on the binaries and interplay of transcendence and immanence as Habad teachings on creation, everyday life, and education. Slonim brings the philosophical exploration of the teachings back to the teaching itself—the work of the educator—and what she has to say about formal and informal education and the importance of modeling and character education is far more comprehensive than the understated initial account of her "life in the field."

Shaul Wertheimer takes the Habad practical interest back to the text, in Judaism more generally, but particularly in the thought of the Seventh Lubavitcher Rebbe. Interestingly, Wertheimer mentions only in passing his own practical work as a Habad emissary in nursing and old-age homes, emphasizing instead the Rebbe's views on aging. Here there is an almost peevish expression in the Rebbe's teachings, as expressed in his disapproval of the whole notion of retirement and of age—specific definitions of productivity and accomplishment. In addition to the critique of current practices and attitudes toward retirement, the Rebbe emphasized, as Wertheimer puts it, "the positive side of retirement." More than that, there is a normative valuation of aging as "positive" that should also be represented in the self-definitions of the elderly. Here, too, the higher value is the "spiritual," and aging can be viewed as "spiritual maturity." Again, the spiritual insight returns to social practice, and Wertheimer cites the establishment of schools for seniors, academies for teaching Torah, that were an additional element of the Habad interest in social practice and change.

Nathaniel Berman's paper and Yotam Hotam's paper, while they might be connected to Hasidism through its roots in Kabbalah and mysticism broadly, both engage the more theoretical aspects of mysticism. Berman, however, offers a parallel between the logic of law and of Kabbalah, showing how both articulate myths of the self-other relation. In Kabbalah, the emergence of the divine from the demonic is discussed by Berman in his interpretations of the Kabbalistic, foundational Zohar. In parallel, he argues that the self-determination of alienated peoples in overarching state regimes can be seen in post–World War I international law emphasizing the self-determination of alienated minorities as a "national self" and the expression of "ethno-nationalities." There is, as it were, an emergence here too of the divine though secular and collective self, from an identity-erasing, demonic, institutionally enshrined state. Both the mystical and the national dynamics of the self-other relation find some unity in Berman's closing reflection on the work of Gershom Scholem, who "brings together, with startling eloquence, these two discourses…": the Kabbalist and the nationalist.

Yotam Hotam's paper is an investigation of another sort of Kabbalist, indeed: Walter Benjamin, Gershom Scholem's friend and correspondent, a secular theorist of German literature who tried to bridge not so much nationalism and Jewish mysticism but Marxism and the Kabbalah, which he learned from Scholem, into a transcendentally oriented, social cultural critique. And, I would say, it was a good time for it, historically. Benjamin wanted to get beyond literalist temporal thinking for a mystical, though historically embedded, "now time" of an eternal, real present. If, on the one hand, he had Scholem pulling him out of his own background in German Romanticism, he had, on the other, Brecht giving him

Introduction xvii

Marxist ideas that he could apply not only to a mystically modified understanding of history, but also to art and literature.

Hotam takes Benjamin at an earlier stage, a quarter-century before he took his own life while escaping from Nazi persecution. This was Benjamin's apprenticeship to the charismatic German theorist of education and of the special power and promise of youth, which is Hotam's emphasis in his paper: the ideal of youth, as in itself a new "voice of the spirit," like Benjamin's "now time," a time heralding eternity. Benjamin's view of a true youth education that is creative and erotic follows Wedekind, though long before Benjamin was caught in the mythical dialectic that Berman describes, between the political, of Brecht, and the mystical, of Scholem.

Jonathan Garb's paper resonates with Naftali Loewenthal's emphasis on the importance of contemplation in the Habad lineage. Garb takes a controversy between two figures in early Hasidism, the so-called Mittler Rebbe and Aharon Horovitz of Starosseloje, as an initial instance of Hasidic texts devoted to contemplation/meditation, while he dwells on the exemplary texts, en route, and offers his own original translations. Garb's facility to intellectually live in both the Hasidic and academic conceptual worlds is on display here in his review of the critical literature on this early, second generation of Habad Hasidism. His discussion includes both the critical Jewish scholarship and more general theories of the phenomenology of mysticism—notably, as he quotes Steinbock, the "verticality of religious experience." En route, he reviews the scholarship of Louis Jacobs, Rachel Elior, Elliot Wolfson, Dov Schwartz, Shmuel Ehrenfield, and, in an intriguing footnote, David Zori.

Garb raises methodological points about the value of "cross-Hasidic comparison," highlighting his wider commitment to the value of comparative method both within Jewish studies and beyond. The substantive controversy seems to move around the locus of the divine and the direction of movement suggested by contemplative practice: "[T]he very vector of this contemplation is opposite to that of his rival's teaching...." Where and how does the sought-after mystical unity with the divine take place, and what is the role of contemplative meditation? A non-knowing, found in the pursuit of union. Garb, in his comparative broad range, expresses this in the words of Walt Whitman, with whom he concludes.

Shaul Magid also uses the classical humanities trope of textual controversy to contrast the texts of Kelm (Salanter and Musar) and Karelitz, or Hazon Ish (Ultra-Orthodoxy), in an effort to sort out the interplay between the importance of Jewish law, Halacha, and the emergence of what he calls the "autonomous self," following Charles Taylor. Magid's is an attempt to explore the relation to the larger question of morality and selfhood, in the historic opposing between the Musar movement and Ultra-Orthodoxy, between an autonomous self and a self that is anchored in morality in Halacha. Here Magid works through the texts and turns not on Habad Hasidism, but on the Musar movement, an entirely reasonable selection given his emphasis on morality. His interest in the paper is less akin to Garb's "cross Hasidic comparisons" and more to a historical question of continuities and discontinuities between the early Musar movement and a contemporary form of neo-Musar. What happens to morality in the contemporary search for selfhood? Is there a "secular Torah" in the work of the current movement that preserves and transforms the pietistic teaching of Halachically oriented Musar? Or is the religious dimension lost in the effort to attain spirituality now? These are some of the questions that arise as Magid aims to trace what he refers to as the "Musar tradition and its Discontents." In the end, however, despite his differences with the scholars of Habad Hasidism, he sees them—in contemporary neo-Musar and neo-Hasidism—as similar, as "new forms of Jewish piety," and "...sharing more perhaps with forms of Jewish heresy than conventional forms of Jewish religious practice." Is there a new "secular Torah"?

In his search for contemporary manifestations, whether subversions or realizations of historical traditions, Magid is, I think, unexpectedly similar to both Sadovnik and Werczberger, who, in very different ways, trace out the tortuous paths from strong traditions and events, some favorable and some horrific.

Introduction

Alan Sadovnik takes us to the horrific "discontents" of the past, the way forward, if it is possible, as Theodor Adorno put it, "after Auschwitz." On the surface, Sadovnik's paper is a valuable autobiographical account of his career as a prominent sociologist of education and researcher in social policy, social inequality, and social reform. He does not put it this way, but we might say that his commitment to the pursuit of social justice in research practice can be seen as a "tikkun": a repair, indeed a reparation, of the historical antecedent that is the dark side of Sadovnik's text.

This is the history of his parents, which both precedes and accompanies his professional narrative. It is a history of the embodied, lived, human historical continuity of the Holocaust. In his parents' lives, though they were survivors, such a past did not end. It transmuted, in the best moments, into resilience and hopefulness, but more often into despair and depression—a depression that Sadovnik candidly and bravely shares as the underside of his professional focus and commitments.

If the Holocaust is one path from modernity, perhaps it signaled the end of modernity: its closing chapter, when the "dialectic of enlightenment" was no dialectic at all, but simply the historical, evolutionary end of societal rationalization and the instrumentalization of the individual. The capstones of the modern are a preface to what comes after—whether into the eternal time of youth, as Benjamin would have it, or toward the more commonplace faces of mystical union that appear so often in the scholarly narratives of the papers in this volume; in the messianism that becomes a sublimated utopianism; indeed, to the revitalization of a pre-modern mystical spirituality that is so present in these papers. The question is what the recovery looks like.

Is real life revision/revitalization possible? Or does the horrific repressed always return, even in altered form, to continue to wreak havoc? Or, more Brechtian than Scholemian, in Benjamin's "controversy," do revolutions in the forces of production give birth to new social forms, overturning the evil and suffering of the past, though by harsh means? Perhaps this is the meaning of the digital revolution, which these papers barely touch on, yet all are produced and streamlined through it. But the social implications of intensifying digitalization are less evident. I have only half-seriously alluded to the interplanetary, which may, however, be the crystallized societal representation of a new social form, or that may be a truly material mysticism, an incalculable cosmic unity.

Rachel Werczberger's concluding paper—on the transitory, fluid Israeli post–New Ageism—offers one answer to some of these questions. Her descriptions of a "lived religion" that has clear continuities with a traditional, belief-oriented past, but dwells in the transitoriness of still-eclectic, but recognizably ritual practices, is what she reports on from her anthropological field research. It is not that after religion there is spirituality. Rather, Werczberger describes an evolution from traditional religion that continues the historic Jewish emphasis on practice, but where the new Israeli generation "autonomously rewrote their everyday religious practices outside formal religious institutions and with disregard to religious authorities." Her examples from the women's movement's "new" religious practice, the revisiting of North African Jewish traditions of pilgrimages to saints, the blurred borders and transitory, communal non-traditionally religious venues for now-lived religion, and the warmth and informality of practical innovations—all this is evocative, but different, and beyond a new age: neo-Hasidism, as Werczberger presents it.

It is this worldly new communalism, ironically sprouting on the graves of the kibbutz movement and being "lived" in the shadow of a new Israeli hegemony of a fundamentalist religious nationalism, that in its everyday manifestation works to erode the institutional bulwarks of an informal, Jewish communalism.

Werczberger sketches what is perhaps a new Jewish hopefulness—not necessarily a secularization of religious tradition, but an ongoing improvisation; not neo-Musar, but a different "halacha" or a law of impermanent creativity. This is not the non-knowable autonomous selfhood of post-modernity, nor the permanent revolution of a past utopia, nor even the materialization of a cosmic unity beyond time and the earth. Werczberger, as a social scientist, calls instead for "more research that focuses on the everyday spiritual experiences of Jews…and across institutionally and denominationally based groups."

This is the movement outward, but still within, a new inner-worldly materialist mysticism, one that goes by the misleading name of "spirituality and society."

References

Wexler, P. (1996). *Holy sparks: Social theory, education and religion.* New York: St. Martin's Press.
Wexler, P. (2000). *The mystical society: An emerging social vision.* Boulder, CO: Westview Press.
Wexler, P. (2007). *Mystical interactions: Sociology, Jewish mysticism and education.* Los Angeles: Cherub Press.
Wexler, P. (2013). *Mystical sociology: Toward cosmic social theory.* New York: Peter Lang.
Wexler, P., & Garb, J. (2012). *After spirituality: Studies in mystical traditions.* New York: Peter Lang.

Section I

HASIDISM, SOCIETY, AND SOCIAL SCIENCE

Chapter 1

THE INSTITUTE OF JEWISH SPIRITUALITY AND SOCIETY

Philip Wexler, Hebrew University of Jerusalem (Professor Emeritus)

The work of this Institute reflects a meeting—an intersection—of at least three movements in society.

First Movement—Hasidism: The Outward Movement

While the empirical validation remains sparse, the consensus, as represented in the research reports of the Jewish People Planning Institute (2015), is that Habad is the most dynamic element in contemporary Judaism. It is hoped that we will hear more about research on the history and social dynamics of Habad, now and in the future. What I can say, after a year and a half of collaboration—firsthand "observation," as it were—is that while there is a customary sectarian movement "inward," there is also a movement "outward" to increase the visibility of Habad, in addition to the movement's stated goal of disseminating religious practice and belief.

What is especially relevant to this Institute is the commitment to gaining recognition and legitimacy for their ideas, most notably their social ideas. Among the middle generation of Habad leadership, there is a tangible, increasingly actualized drive to bring the ideas of the Lubavitcher Rebbe, and the longer lineage to which he belongs, into the public space of intellectual discourse and interchange. They want to be "taken seriously," to play on a larger playing field, to be seen on a wider screen.

This was incontrovertibly exemplified by the meeting in the summer of 2016 in the main room of the New York Public Library, in the heart of New York City. That meeting addressed a broad range of contemporary social projects, with special attention devoted to the Habad movement's role in and affinity for spiritually driven social activism. Like his predecessors, Rabbi Menachem Mendel Schneerson was a religious leader and theorist, but also an engineer of social change, engagement, and societal participation—indeed, a brilliant tactician who re-created and mobilized a transformative social movement. Habad carries on its leader's commitment to social action.

The intellectual face of this movement is no less central and is equally committed to outreach activity. Chabad on Campus is arguably the largest and certainly the most dynamic Jewish educational organization on American college and university campuses, with more than 250 "branches." It is almost inevitable, given Habad's historic intellectualism, and the fact of working in the academic milieu, that it would want to extend its outreach to the chief purveyors of ideas in these settings: the faculty. Facilitating this meeting of ideas and different discourses, particularly in the human or social sciences, has been part of the initial work of this Institute. Surprisingly, intellectually and socially different participants are exchanging ideas and, in the best cases, creating new syntheses and perhaps even new communities.

The Second Movement—Mass Culture, the Academy, and the Turn to Religion

Where there is receptivity to such emergent partnerships in theory, research, and practice, it comes in part from the movement within the social sciences to expand its horizons of discourse and to mine unsuspected stores of conceptual treasures. Part of this is normal academic imperialism, and part of it comes from a perceived need for revitalization. Alvin Gouldner (1970) announced the "coming crisis in sociology" almost fifty years ago. It is now nearly one-quarter of a century since Charles Lemert (1995) noted that we were working "after the crisis [in sociology]." The pluralization of social science theory and research follows the long-developing movements for diversity and respect for cultural and intellectual differences on university campuses. Some of this student-driven press for increased cultural openness spills over to faculty, who argue for discursive parity of the rationalized representations of these differences, as broadly termed, "indigenous knowledge."

One particular face of the pluralization of modern disciplinary knowledge is the return of marginal signs of the academic legitimacy—and even value—of religious, sacred knowledge, not as objective data but as intellectually agentic subject, with discursive parity. The "religious turn," as Bryan Turner (2010) has called it, as well as Jürgen Habermas (2015) and Charles Taylor's (2007) acknowledgment of a "post-secular society," occurs, as we have seen in the research reviewed by Grace Davie (2010) and the studies of "spiritual" expressions of religion advanced by Paul Heelas (2008), in a variety of contexts, toward an ever-wider horizon of what Thomas Csordas (2009) calls a new "globalization of religion." According to Csordas, the "sleeping giant of religion" has awakened.

On a temporally larger screen, Pitirim Sorokin (1957) argued, in his massive empirical and theoretical work, that we are at the beginning of the end of one of the organizing assumptions of culture, that is, its "basic cultural premise." A deep cultural shift is occurring, an end of the "sensate," which is to say a materialist and naturalist age. We see its death throes in myriad social crises and suffering, which are signs of the "end of the sensate culture."

It may not be so surprising to a sociologist of knowledge that wider cultural changes would be at least refracted in academic discourses, despite the internal dynamics of paradigmatic loyalty that Thomas Kuhn (1962) iconically described. Kuhn's paradigm shifts came from within disciplinary knowledge and not from broader currents of social and cultural change. Whichever the determinative variable, my own work (2013) argues for a "Mystical Sociology."

I have tried to show how a series of contemporary social issues, characteristic of a contemporary society of "excess," could be better addressed by ideas drawn from the history of Habad Hasidism. On the scales of explanatory value, the secular/sacred divide does not hold. Social practices typical of the Habad tradition can be seen as responses to contemporary social issues, as alternatives in both theory and practice. This willingness to jump the walls not only of disciplinary divides, beyond a Geertzian "blurring of boundaries," but to look toward religion as increasingly relevant to the creation and accumulation of secular knowledge is not unique to me, to Hasidism, or to Judaism more generally. Though clearly not mainstream, there are nonetheless increasingly salient instances.

In her commentary on the William James centenary, Eleanor Rosch (2002) asserted the relevance of Buddhism to cognitive psychology and cognitive science. Her call is to "take religion seriously," which means as a source of paradigmatically relevant ideas. John Millbank (1990) has worked consistently over the past twenty years to show how social theory changes, or is nudged, by Christian theology. My colleague in India, Ananta Giri, recently published his *Beyond Sociology: Trans-Civilizational Dialogues and Planetary Conversations* (2017), which, among other sources, draws on Hinduism in building alternatives. There are longstanding examples in Islam that Jewish studies scholars have built upon—for example, in the work of Henri Corbin (1970), which goes beyond religious studies to the human sciences more generally.

A Jewish Example

Nor is Hasidism the only way to approach the contemporary warranting of Jewish knowledge as an equal discursive partner in the disciplinary pantheon of academic organizations. Shortly after

I came to Jerusalem in 2000 to study Jewish sources, the well-known Princeton political theorist Michael Walzer, along with the Lorberbaum cousins, Menachem and Yair, and Noam Zohar, published *The Jewish Political Tradition* (2003), which is an intertextual dialogue between political theory in the Jewish tradition and in modern political science. Walzer's statement of purpose is instructive, I think:

> First, retrieval: we want to make its [the Jewish tradition's] central texts and arguments available to new generations of students and potential participants....
>
> Second, integration: we want to take this body of Jewish thought out of its intellectual ghetto and to begin an examination of the ways in which it follows, parallels and strains against Greek, Arabic, Christian and secular modes of thought. "Begin" is the relevant word here....
>
> Third, criticism: we want to join the arguments that have characterized the tradition, and to carry them forward...about which of them can usefully be carried forward under the modern conditions of emancipation.... (p. xxiii)

As if to complement Walzer's intellectual, academic, and even disciplinary interest in his introduction, David Hartman (my host and Walzer's in Jerusalem), took pains to underline the socially transformative aspects of the Jewish tradition, generally as we did and are doing, particularly with Hasidism. While Hartman, in his Foreword to Walzer's book, refers especially to Israel, the application goes beyond that:

> There is no escaping to the privacy of the inner soul or to some spiritual sanctuary separated from the mundane issues of everyday life: poverty, social welfare, unemployment, relations with strangers, tolerance, pluralism, security, and justice. (p. xiv)

Alongside the contemporary cultural and academic mainstream, there is an emergent religious, spiritual, and Jewish spiritual alternative, in theory and in practice. It is this mainstream that I want to now address, which is the context "behind the curtains" of the emergent alternative. This is the third movement: the relationship between religion and society.

Third Movement—Religion and Society: A Weberian Excursus

The immediate actors in the movement of an active meeting are Habad Hasidim and university academics. They are both playing on a historical and sociocultural stage. We have talked about a mass and academic cultural reassertion of religion, but we have not yet tried to explain what is propelling our "meeting" at a deeper, macro-structural level. What defines the "mainstream," what does it have to do with religion and society, and why and how do we belong to a still-wider movement in historical society?

I want to talk first about Max Weber's analysis as an answer to these questions, and then to dissent from his conclusions. The borrowing of religious and Jewish studies from the conceptual armory of social science has long been approached with appropriate caution by these scholars, accompanied by a justifiable fear of reductionism that eradicates the phenomenon and replaces it with an alien vocabulary. Yet classical sociology, especially Durkheimian sociology, which remains the deep foundation of contemporary positivist research that is social science, is borrowed as a resource in understanding religion. Now, Weberian concepts, notably charisma and authority, are imported to religious and Jewish studies—but without the wider system of meaning that generates those specific categories. This is relevant particularly because Weber's wider system of analytic meaning speaks to our times and our current interest in the role of religion in society.

Weber's theory is not part of the disciplinary mainstream, but it addresses the backbone of the society in which our action takes place. The materialism of social science and its derivative placement of religion as a secondary social phenomenon are challenged by Weber's more-than-significant "qualifications" of Marx. According to Gerth and Mills (1946): "'world images' that have been created by 'ideas' have, like switchmen, determined the tracks along which action has been pushed by the dynamic of interest" (pp. 63–64). It is religion that significantly, though not alone, sets the terms of social conduct, in its historically changing forms, and both by design and unintentionally becomes a primary causal force in history.

"Modern European civilization," as Weber (1958) calls it, is the unintended result of ascetic Protestantism, in which a cultural translation and transformation occur between transcendental beliefs that stabilize the transient magico-religious states that group the sacred into continuous social institutions. The motor of the modern economy is an internalized personal character structure of vocationalism; of a culture of specialization, of expertise, of methodical precision and calculation, of bureaucracy, and, above all, of rationalization that displaces an earlier world of direct personal relations with the instrumentalism that we take for granted. Ascetic Protestantism is its unintended progenitor, in the search for signs of elective grace from the transcendentally unreachable divinity, whose favor becomes evidenced by worldly success—success in a "calling."

Weber, himself the heir of the nascent, modern German bourgeoisie, child of a lawyer/politician father, but heir also of Calvinism and the deep religiosity of a mother carrying the commitments of her established Protestant heritage, embodies the tortuous path of Puritanism as it becomes modernity. Following is the excerpt from Weber's *The Protestant Ethic* (1958) that one of Weber's most daring and insightful biographers, Arthur Mitzman (1969), uses to summarize the famous thesis:

Christian asceticism, at first fleeing from the world into solitude, had already ruled the world which it had renounced from the monastery and the Church. But it had, on the whole, left the naturally spontaneous character of daily life in the world untouched. Now it strode into the marketplace of life, slammed the door of the monastery behind it, and undertook to penetrate just that daily routine of life with its methodicalness, to fashion it into a life in the world, but neither of nor for that world.

Weber's analysis of religion in society is ironic. Despite all the scientific methodological cautions, he moves economics aside to make room for religion, to see in religion, in spirituality, the determinant of the "conduct of life," and in the market and bureaucracy, its principal social organizational forms of expression. Rationalized, intellectualized, secularized inner-worldly Protestant asceticism conquers and displaces all other social and cultural forms and becomes modern civilization. Despite its efficiencies and virtues of calculation, what originates spiritually, in the soul, as it were, in "pneuma," is transformed into the vehicle of the destruction of the spirit.

This is how Weber concludes *The Protestant Ethic*:

> For when asceticism was carried out of monastic cells into everyday life, and began to dominate worldly morality, it did its part in building the tremendous cosmos of the modern economic order...which today determine the lives of all the individuals who are born into this mechanism.... (1958, p. 181)

He goes on to quote the Puritan divines on how external material concerns should be worn like a light cloak that "can be thrown aside at any moment." And then he adds, in a not very scientific lexicon: "But fate decreed that the cloak should become an iron cage."

> No one knows who will live in this cage in the future, or whether at the end of this tremendous development, entirely new prophets will arise, or there will be a great rebirth of old ideas and ideals, or neither, mechanized petrification, embellished with a sort of convulsive self-importance. For the last stage of this cultural development, it might well be truly said: "Specialists without spirit, sensualists without heart; this nullity imagines that it has attained a level of civilization never before achieved." (Weber, 1958, p. 182)

Asceticism is only one path to salvation. There is also the pattern of mysticism. For the most part, mysticism flees from the world, but there is a particular type, a mysticism in the world, an "inner-worldly mysticism."

> The transformation of a mysticism remote from the world into one characterized by chiliastic and revolutionary tendencies took place frequently, most impressively in the revolutionary mysticism of the sixteenth-century Baptists....Wherever genuine mysticism did give rise to communal action, such action was characterized by the acosmism of the mystical feeling of love. Mysticism may exert this kind of psychological effect, thus tending—despite the apparent demands of logic—to favor the creation of communities. (Weber, 1963, pp. 175–176)

In a world with an "absence of love" and lacking overall meaning, mysticism seems to provide a way out of the iron cage. Yet in his address in Munich in 1918—two years before a right-wing coup attempt and before Hitler was known as the "King of Munich"— in "Science as a Vocation," Weber surprisingly raised the issue of prophecy and the creation of an alternative way of life. Put baldly, his conclusion on the possibility of a spiritually inspired sociocultural alternative to the "petrification" of a rationalized, secularized

Protestantism is this: perhaps in the sixteenth century, but not in the early twentieth. The acosmism of love, the mystical basis of communities, does not overcome what he called, following Schiller, the "disenchantment of the world"—the death of the spirit.

> The fate of our times is characterized by rationalization and intellectualization, and above all, by the "disenchantment of the world." Precisely the ultimate and most sublime values have retreated from public life... today only within the smallest and most intimate circles, in personal human situations, pianissimo, that something is pulsating that corresponds to the prophetic pneuma, which in former times swept through the great communities like a firebrand, welding them together. (Weber, as cited in Gerth & Mills, 1946, p. 155)

A student of the Hebrew prophets, Weber quotes Isaiah thus: "The morning cometh, and also the night: if ye will enquire, enquire, ye: return, come."

Conclusion

Comparing his own situation to the above, Weber adds: "The people to whom this was said has enquired and tarried for more than two millennia, and we are shaken when we realize its fate" (Weber, as cited in Gerth & Mills, 1946, p. 156). And then, finally: "...we shall act differently. We shall set to work and meet the 'demands of the day,' in human relations as well as in our vocation" (p. 156).

Weber saw the possibility of a mystically inspired building of communities driven by the "ethic of brotherliness," the charisma that stands against the "absence of love," the spiritlessness and heartlessness of the current dominant "nullity." These were, however, historical examples, in ancient Christianity, the Eastern Church, the Slavophile conceptions of community, "Muhammad's belief," Buddhism, and among the "Indian intellectuals"—which he favored as an "extraordinary metaphysical achievement." For the rest—the secularized Protestant mainstream and the historical prophetic salvation religion of ancient Judaism, of the "pariah people"—he saw only the possibility of a spirituality in personal small circles, "pianissimo." He did not see the "risorgimento," the renaissance, of an inner-worldly mysticism in Jewish Hasidism, to which Buber, Scholem, and Idel all refer as a "Kabbalah become ethos."

Yet it is these social, public forces or emergent communities that are propelling the Institute forward, between religious movements, boundary shifts in the social sciences, and the dialectic of a disenchantment of the world. The basic premises and behaviors, the "life orders" of the so-called mainstream that Weber identified with impersonality and an absence of love, of the "world dominion of unbrotherliness," stand now again in tension with the possibilities of an "ethic of brotherliness." As Weber himself observed: "The religion of brotherliness has always clashed with the orders and values of this world..." (Weber, cited in Gerth & Mills, 1946, p. 330). "Meeting the demands of the day," and our vocation, means pursuing both the social and intellectual-spiritual aims of the Institute.

How this has begun and how it may develop—in the intellectual collaborations, our "science as a vocation," and in the "everyday workaday world," on subjects like education, aging, and tolerance—is what this institutionalized meeting is about and which expresses wider movements in knowledge, religion, and society.

References

Corbin, H. (1970). *Creative imagination in the Sufism of Ibn 'Arabi* (R. Mannheim, Trans.). London: Routledge and Kegan Paul.
Csordas, T.J. (2009). *Transnational transcendence: Essays on religion and globalization*. Berkeley: University of California Press.
Davie, G. (2010). Resacralization. In B.S. Turner (Ed.), *The new Blackwell companion to the sociology of religion* (pp. 160–178). Oxford: Blackwell.

Gerth, H.H., & Mills, C.W. (1946). *From Max Weber: Essays in sociology.* New York: Oxford University Press.

Giri, A. (Ed). (2017). *Beyond sociology: Trans-civilizational dialogues and planetary conversations.* New York: Springer.

Gouldner, A. (1970). *The coming crisis of Western sociology.* New York: Basic Books.

Habermas, J. (2015). Notes on post-secular society. In P. Wexler & H. Yotam (Eds.), *New social foundations of education: Education in "post-secular" society* (pp. 19–33). New York: Peter Lang.

Heelas, P. (2008). *Spiritualities of life: New Age romanticism and consumptive capitalism.* Malden, MA, and Oxford, UK: Blackwell.

Jewish People Planning Institute. (2015). *Chabad: A new format of Jewish identity and interaction.* Jerusalem: The Jewish People Planning Institute.

Kuhn, T. (1962). *The structure of scientific revolutions.* Chicago: University of Chicago Press.

Lemert, C.C. (1995). *Sociology after the crisis.* Boulder, CO: Westview Press.

Millbank, J. (1990). *Theology and social theory: Beyond secular reason.* Cambridge, MA: Blackwell.

Mitzman, A. (1969). *The iron cage: An historical interpretation of Max Weber.* New York: Grosset & Dunlap.

Rosch, E. (2002). How to catch James's mystic germ: Religious experience, Buddhist meditation, and psychology. *Journal of Consciousness Studies, 9*(9/10), 37–56.

Sorokin, P.A. (1957). *Social and cultural dynamics: A study of change in major systems of art, truth, ethics, law, and social relationships.* Boston: P. Sargent.

Taylor, C. (2007). *A secular age.* Cambridge, MA: Belknap Press of Harvard University Press.

Turner, B.S. (2010). Religion in a post-secular society. In B.S. Turner (Ed.), *The new Blackwell companion to the sociology of religion* (pp. 650–667). Oxford: Blackwell.

Walzer, M., Lorberbaum, M., Zohar, N.J., & Lorberbaum, Y. (2003). *The Jewish political tradition*, vol. 1. *Authority.* New Haven and London: Yale University Press.

Weber, M. (1946). Science as a vocation. In H.H. Gerth & C.W. Mills (Eds.), *From Max Weber: Essays in sociology* (pp. 129–159). New York: Oxford University Press.

Weber, M. (1958). *The Protestant Ethic and the spirit of capitalism*. New York: Scribner.

Weber, M. (1963). *The sociology of religion* (T. Parsons & A. Swidler, Eds.; E. Fischoff, Trans.). Boston: Beacon Press.

Wexler, P. (2013). *Mystical sociology: Toward cosmic social theory*. New York: Peter Lang.

Chapter 2

ON MYSTICAL SOCIOLOGY AND TURNING JUDAISM OUTWARD

Don Seeman, Emory University

> Insofar as life's essence goes, transcendence is immanent to it (it is not something that might be added to its being, but instead is constituent of its being).
> —GEORG SIMMEL

> For better or worse, my self-understanding is not exhausted by the fact that I am a sociologist.
> —PETER BERGER

In his *Mystical Sociology* (2013), Philip Wexler challenges us to reverse the polarity of sociological thinking: to treat Jewish mystical materials not merely as data or objects of analysis but also as conceptual reservoirs for rethinking the realm of the social. In an anthropological context, I too have argued that "theological" materials, quite broadly construed, be treated as largely untapped resources for critical research into the nature and forms of human experience under the banner of a renewed "phenomenological" or "existential" anthropology (Seeman, 2018). But the power of Wexler's analysis lies precisely in the broad height of his analytic scope, which still tends to distinguish our two sister disciplines. "Mystical sociology" is not framed merely as a new methodological arrow in our quiver but as a self-standing analysis of the broad sweep of the social and historical moment we inhabit. For Wexler, the emergence of "spirituality" as a major but diffuse social force, the flourishing of traditional mystical communities, and even the efflorescence of academic scholarship on Hasidism and Jewish mysticism all point to a set of vital reconfigurations confirming the exhaustion of classical sociological models. "Individualism, informationalism, powerlessness, and the exhaustion and routinization of ecstasy are grounds for the onset of the return of a revised and revitalized, decentered assemblage of mystical practices: an unexpected form of the return of the core of the sacred, and its integrative social functioning" (Wexler, 2013, p. 31). The current moment represents a crisis no less profound in Wexler's analysis than the one faced by the founders of modernist sociology a century ago, and calls for an equally new sociological paradigm in response. Chabad Hasidism is one of the primary resources to which Wexler turns. My goal in this short essay is to offer a friendly methodological rejoinder to Wexler's approach and to juxtapose his "mystical sociology" with recent observations by Chaim Miller (2014) and others about contemporary Chabad's "outward" turn that may help to situate these claims.

I

Wexler's understanding of the social and epistemological crisis we face seems plausible enough, but my instinct as an anthropologist is to adopt a much closer horizon of analysis, so I'd like to temporarily bracket his broad epochal argument in order to focus on some more local methodological observations. Mystical sociology is a powerful construct, but it runs the risk of collapsing into a reified binary—the mystical against the rational, modern against postmodern, the free-flowing liberation of spirituality versus the iron cage of Weberian roles and categories. This has, in fact, been a major analytic dilemma posed by the growing popular and scholarly discourses on "Buddhist modernism" in the West and in Asia (McMahan, 2008), the gravitational pull of charismatic "gifts of the spirit" in contemporary Christianity (particularly of the global south) (Robbins, 2004), the "spiritual but not religious" movement in the United States and Europe (Bender, 2010; Forman, 2004; Seeman et al., 2016), and the rise of "mystical psychologies" like those identified with Hasidism in both classical and contemporary forms (Scholem, 1961; Seeman and Karlin, forthcoming). Taken together, these phenomena seem to offer support for Wexler's claims about the shifting nature of late modern social life but they can sometimes be misconstrued—indeed, frequently misconstrue themselves—as analytically neutral depictions of "things as they are" rather than the result of complex cultural and historical choices that have been made over time. We are witness to a period of convergence between several distinctive and, in some cases, overlapping examples of social and religious reconfiguration along the lines that Wexler describes, including the increasingly global Chabad movement to which his own research has been drawn, but I think he would agree that this only points to the need for more detailed intellectual genealogies alongside qualitative studies of the ways in which these reconfigurations are lived, invoked, and contested in particular local moral worlds. This means attending, among other things, to the contingency of categories like mysticism or spirituality and to the complications of Hasidic life on which Wexler's particular account of mystical sociology rests.

Two related methodological claims ought to be made explicit in this context. The first is that I believe social scientific approaches to the study of Hasidism must engage much more directly than they have done with the texts, practices, and theologies that animate these communities; many sociological and anthropological accounts proceed as if the religious and intellectual *content* of Hasidic teaching and its associated practices were merely epiphenomenal to more properly sociological concerns (cf. Seeman, 2018). It is worth noting that many anthropologists of Christianity and Islam have developed useful and productive paradigms for bringing textual and theological traditions to bear on the analysis of social experience and culture, while the anthropology of Jews and Judaism still lags in this regard (Seeman & Stern, forthcoming). Yet the reverse is also true: outside of recent promising trends in social history, the bulk of research on Hasidism in Jewish studies, for example, has focused almost exclusively on what can be gleaned from analysis of elite texts without doing much to situate these culturally or with respect to the themes and concerns of everyday life. I agree with Elliot Wolfson (cited in Chapter 4 of this volume by Rubin) that social scientific paradigms are "hardly adequate to comprehend the contours of [Hasidic] soteriology," but neither, I have argued (Seeman, 2008), are intellectual history and philosophical paradigms alone adequate. We need to be more creative and interdisciplinary in our approach.

Anthropologists of religion have labored to demonstrate the analytic benefits that may accrue when our gaze is displaced to at least some degree from the formalized rituals and sacred texts that are often said to constitute religious traditions so that we may also focus on the ambiguities, resistances, and complex commitments of everyday life (Wikan, 1990; Schielke, 2015; Seeman, 2015; Seeman & Stern, forthcoming). Wexler himself cites the sociologist Robert Wuthnow (1998), who writes that the "elementary forms of religious practice, such as prayer, sacrifice, meditation and contemplation, prophecy, trance, ecstasy, union and absorption in the divine…come to have a more general, everyday, existential meaning in daily life" (Wexler, 2013, p. 29). The way I would frame it is that these everyday existential meanings or contexts are in nowise separable from the contours of more formally ramified soteriologies to which Wolfson points; they inform one another in such innumerable ways that it makes sense to read them in light of one another, as Hasidim themselves frequently do. Is *bittul* ("self-nullification") in the Hasidic context primarily a mystical hermeneutic, for example, a Hasidic "doctrine" about the nature of reality, or a set of everyday ethical and soteriological practices that inform everything from social organization to political judgments? I will have more to say about this in the next section, but the short answer is that these each seem to be a different register in which the same basic set of themes plays itself out in Hasidic life. The phenomenology of Hasidism is not, I am arguing, exhausted by the writings and inspiration of its most important expositors, the Rebbes and *tsaddikim*, but needs *also* to be viewed from the perspective of how these teachings enter social life. I am arguing, in other words, that alongside sociological breadth of analysis and close attention to the textual-intellectual history of religious movements, Wexler's mystical sociology also requires an ethnographic perspective in order to reach its ambitious goal of understanding.

Though he does not explicitly use this language, "mystical sociology" is inherently an existential project, similar to the existential anthropology (Seeman, 2015; Premawardhana, 2018; Willen & Seeman, 2012; Jackson, 2005) with which I have come to identify. That is because Wexler's argument stresses implicitly that the locus of analysis for sociology—or at least *one* important locus of analysis—ought to be the human problems to which Hasidism or other forms of religious life provide an answer in some particular social and cultural matrix. He calls us back repeatedly to the problems of "individualism, informationalism, powerlessness and the exhaustion and routinization of ecstasy," which he identifies as necessary precursors of the mystical turn. But this means that mystical sociology has a human shape as it responds to human needs that may be contoured by current circumstances as well as more perduring elements of the human condition, like the need to modulate centrifugal and centripetal forces in social life, and the need for autonomy as well as solidarity (Seeman, 2018). One topic that Wexler crucially refrains from exploring in this context, but which a clear-eyed ethnographic approach might underline, is what human problems mystical sociology might also exacerbate or throw up in its wake, assuming that every form of social life brings its own unique susceptibilities to bear (see my comments on "terror as a mystical technique" [Seeman, 2005] in this context).

One important benefit of an existential approach is that it offers a way out of the persistent constructivism-perennialism debates that have characterized and sometimes paralyzed studies of mysticism over the past several decades. Perennialists assert that they can identify a common core of mystical experience or spirituality that occurs with regularity across religious and cultural traditions (Forman, 1990, 2004); constructivists argue just as vociferously that mystical and religious expressions are unique historical and linguistic constructs, necessarily recalcitrant to understanding or comparison across those divides (Katz, 1978). In some cases, constructivists go so far as to argue that there really is nothing to examine but distinctive cultural and linguistic categories, such that any appeal to religious or mystical experience in the abstract can only be considered a result of some categorical confusion or intellectual bad faith.

It is worth noting that studies of Jewish mysticism were crucial to some of the most influential accounts of the constructivist position, which quite rightly resisted the tendency to subsume Jewish materials within implicitly Christian intellectual frameworks. Among the most important statements of the constructivist position have been those identified with Steven T. Katz, a scholar of modern Judaism who acknowledges his indebtedness on this score to the doyen of Jewish mysticism studies, Gershom Scholem. At the other extreme are scholars like Jordan Paper (2004), who argues that concepts like *bittul* in Hasidism are exemplars of a universal "zero experience" that is available across religious traditions as well as what he calls "secular mysticism," an experience that may sometimes even come upon people unawares or without preparation. Tellingly, Paper invokes the experience of *unio mystica* that Scholem (1961) denied but that Moshe Idel has affirmed in Jewish mystical contexts as evidence for his perennialist views. But this may be an unfair reduction of Idel's contribution. More to the point from my own perspective is Idel's insistence on the validity of phenomenological comparison across schools or traditions and his ongoing critique of Scholem's linear historicism (Idel, 1990, 1995)—the notion that a phenomenon like Hasidism must be viewed primarily as an unfolding of its immediate historical antecedents (i.e., Lurianic kabbalah) rather than allowing for the dynamic influence of textual traditions from earlier periods (Cordovero, Abulafia, etc.). Both elements of Idel's critique are important to our concern: his validation of phenomenological comparison does indeed return lived experience to a place of central concern beyond the endless documentation of historical and philological specificity; his nuanced historical and textual genealogies, on the other hand, also push against the typically perennialist impatience with anything that is culturally specific or historically contingent in human affairs. It is in the productive tension between these two analytic poles that real progress can be made.

The conflict between perennialists and constructivists in religious studies has been at least analogous to that between human universalists and devoted cultural constructivists within anthropology. The role of culture in anthropological theory throughout much of the twentieth century was, after all, to oppose nearly any assumption of shared human characteristics or values (other than the cultural-making faculty itself) through the endless appeal, as Geertz (1973, p. 23) once said, to "yet another country heard from." In some forms of American anthropology, critics have maintained, culture became a kind of self-contained semiotic system that left vanishingly little room for the indeterminacies of lived experience, suffering, or ethics (Seeman 2004). My favored solution to that conundrum involves a principled and methodological admission that cultural categories and constructs can only emerge and attain whatever significance they may hold through the social realities and lived experience of real people, whose lives are always only underdetermined by culture. We are not called upon merely to "interpret cultures," in other words, but to become interpreters of human tribulation and of the ways in which cultural patterns intersect in complicated ways with other features of the human condition, including but not limited to power dynamics, individual aims of social actors, institutional forces, and social suffering (Wikan, 1990; Seeman, 2005, 2008). The point of such critique is not merely to shift the object of study so that we now privilege social context or everyday life over ideas, texts, and semiotic systems, but rather to establish more adequately how these different registers of human life may be related or mutually constitutive.

This is where a broadly existential approach might help to deconflict the perennialist-constructivist debate. My contention, which must remain preliminary here, is that one way out of the perennialist-constructivist box that currently constrains scholarly discourse requires a reconfiguration of research around the culturally and historically contingent responses to shared sorts of human problems—problems like the ones that Philip Wexler (2013) outlines in *Mystical Sociology*. Through ethnography I have learned that Chabad *bittul* is not, for example, just a metaphysical doctrine grounded in the inexorable unfolding of a closed textual corpus, but also a set of nested social practices through which Hasidim modulate everyday social boundaries and exclusions, make moral claims on one another, and strive to transform the phenomenal world into a fitting home for divinity. It may also, in our current reality, be invoked against problems like powerlessness and hyper-individualism mentioned by Wexler as the ground in which mystical sociology takes root, but this doesn't really settle the perennialist-constructivist debate. What it does suggest is that a complex social and religious construct like *bittul*, for all its distinctiveness, may at least be thought of as commensurable with other theologically or culturally distinctive responses to similar dilemmas. The principled submission of some Christian and Muslim women (Griffith, 2000; Mahmood, 2011), the mindful selflessness that characterizes some forms of modern Buddhism (McMahan, 2008; Seeman & Karlin, forthcoming), Sufi *fana* (Schimmel, 2011), and Chabad *bittul* need not be assimilated to some avowedly universal human experience in order to appreciate their phenomenological family resemblance or to explore what common human problems might call forth such similar kinds of human responses.

I have found Hasidic participants in my ethnography to be themselves very astute in identifying the kinds of sociological pressures that help to shape their community and its teaching. Recently I asked a sophisticated young *shaliah* (emissary) why he thought Chabad had not done more to disavow violent or extremist teachings from an individual identified with the movement in

Israel. He agreed with me that the lack of official disavowal was a problem but suggested that I needed to understand the complex but imperfect overlap between "two different Chabads...Chabad as a social community and Chabad as a network of official institutions," which makes formal disavowal of *anyone* difficult to achieve. Furthermore, he wrote to me that "Chabad communities and institutions *both* function more by the dictate of local pragmatic needs and opportunities than by the dictate of a centralized and authoritative leadership body," which conforms to my own observations and also contributes to Chabad's ethos of stubborn inclusiveness. "It is very hard," another rabbi told me in a different context, "to kick anybody out. If I tell someone they are not Chabad, they'll just tell me I'm not Chabad." These are subtle sociological observations levied by Chabad insiders puzzling over their own movement's sometimes uncomfortably permeable boundaries and the tensions that arise for them over what constitutes authentic Chabad teaching or interpretation. And this points toward the kinds of cultural and sociological underpinnings of theological—*hasidic*—discourse, even though my interlocutor did not initially frame it that way.

Interpretive give-and-take isn't always represented in published records, but it is almost always part of the ethnographic process. "In terms of your characterization of the two Chabads," I suggested by return email, "I would only add that there is of course a third, which is the Chabad of the *Rebbeim* as embodied in their writings and teachings. I suspect most insiders would say that the latter is the 'true Chabad' though of course the other two you mention are the ones we have sociological access to." His response was gratifying: "The *Chassidut* of the *Rebbeim*! You really put me in my place there. It's important to put the sociological cap on if we want to get a clear picture of what's going on, but you're reminding me to keep my *chossid* cap on all the time...." Not all Chabad Hasidim value academic perspectives to this degree, but I have found a surprising number who do, and it has been my experience that this represents not just a perfectly natural curiosity about different ways of understanding a subject dear to their hearts but also speaks to the critical empathy of entrepreneur-practitioners who want to make their own practice a little bit *better* or more thoughtful than it would be if they lacked this curiosity. It is an existential stance to which many academic scholars might also aspire.

It isn't only the intellectually serious Hasid, after all, who has to remember to don both hats from time to time, but also the ethnographer, inasmuch as *hasidus*—the discursive *content* of the sacred tradition—animates and permeates the social network in ways that are central to any adequate depiction of Hasidic life. This is particularly true in a community like Chabad, where ongoing study and deep engagement with Hasidic texts and oral teachings in a range of different settings have become increasingly central and widespread for expanding circles of participants, including not just adult men to whom the classical obligation of study or *talmud torah* would have been applied in classical Orthodox and Hasidic circles (Seeman & Kobrin, 1999), but also women, children, and, increasingly (as I will discuss below), some non-Jews as well. The Chabad ideal of *hafatzat maayanot chutzah* ("spreading the wellsprings [of Hasidic teaching] outward") explicitly links the theoretical matrix of *hasidus* with quotidian praxis and emergent forms of everyday life. This is a space where ideology meets the immediate needs of persons and communities—not just Chabad Hasidim, for example, but also their fellow travelers, followers, critics, and antagonists. This is a space that ethnography can help to illuminate, and it is arguably where "mystical sociology" begins.

II

Chaim Miller's recent (2014) biography of the Lubavitcher Rebbe makes the eminently plausible argument that R. Menachem Mendel Schneerson's half-century of leadership should be viewed as an attempt to "turn Judaism" (and Chabad Hasidism) "outward" on a whole variety of different fronts. It wasn't only his massive efforts at outreach toward non-observant Jews, for which Chabad is primarily known today in the public eye, his "mitzvah tanks" and "mitzvah campaigns" that make the case for Miller, but also the way in which R. Schneerson shifted the *internal* mechanisms of Chabad Hasidism toward greater inclusivism. Miller notes, for example, that while the previous Rebbe presided over an organization known as *nishei uvnot hasidei Chabad*—wives and daughters of Chabad Hasidim—the organization founded by R. Menachem Mendel was titled simply *nishei Chabad*—"Chabad women." This was more than a merely stylistic change, and it presages the revolutionary role played by Chabad *shluchot* (female emissaries), which has already been described elsewhere. While R. Schneerson is famous for being one of the two most prominent twentieth-century Orthodox Jewish religious authorities who encouraged or permitted high-level women's Talmud study (the other being R. Joseph B. Soloveitchik), the far more dramatic change *within* Chabad circles has been the training and empowerment of women in *hasidus* and Hasidic outreach praxis, breaking quite openly with the nearly universal ultraorthodox consensus that the "glory of the king's daughter is [only] within."

Other features of modern Chabad to which Miller can point in defense of his thesis include the extraordinary enlistment of children in mitzvah campaigns and in *tzivos Hashem*, the Rebbe's explicit concern for opening *hasidus* to the blind or physically disabled, his practical advocacy of projects such as U.S. government food aid to Africa, and his exhortations for spiritual outreach (but not conversionary efforts) toward non-Jews, including the teaching of some *hasidus* and appropriate topics in Jewish law as well as political advocacy for (non-Jewish) school prayer. On virtually every front, the Rebbe sought the influence of *hasidus* to expand beyond its traditional boundaries, irrespective of whether this would lead in any discernible way to the generation of new Hasidic followers. I have argued elsewhere that the willingness to teach *hasidus* without insisting on the creation of *hasidim* has been one of the great keys to Chabad success on American college campuses and elsewhere. It was accompanied during the Rebbe's lifetime and increasingly since his death by a broad decentralization of the Chabad movement as a whole, empowering the *shluchim* to act as relatively autonomous (but fiercely loyal) spiritual entrepreneurs on their rebbe's behalf. The nature of an emissary, R. Schneerson once wrote, is to identify totally with the *mission* of the sender and, simultaneously, to exercise all of his or her creativity in the exercise of the sender's mandate. "In Chabad unlike other forms of Hasidism," one campus emissary told me, "everyone is a *shtickle* [a little bit of a] *rebbe*."

Miller deals only briefly with the theological backdrop to all this inclusivity in the Rebbe's acute messianic passion or, to use more evocative and locally significant terms, his radical understanding of *dirah ba-tachtonim* [revealing the phenomenal world as a fitting habitation for divinity] as a kind of radical *bittul* to the divine essence that always suffuses the world without displacing it. I experienced an indication of what this might mean in sociological terms at the Chabad house in Toulouse, France, where I was attending an academic conference on the Jewish thought of Emmanuel Levinas. It must have been providential, but I found an old *sicha* (a pamphlet of one of the Rebbe's talks) sitting on the table in front of me when I came for Shabbat services that week. The theme of the discourse, which had been given many years prior, was a refutation of Moses Mendelssohn's oft-cited motto that emancipation would require Jews to bifurcate their existence or "Be a Jew at home and a man [i.e., a religiously and ethnically unmarked citizen] in the street!" Whether or not Mendelssohn ever actually used those words, the shape of that bargain has clearly been key to the form of Western Jewish modernity. It led to the emergence of "Judaism" as a privatized religion of doctrines and rituals, the splitting off of Jewish national or collective sentiment, and the emergence of an avowedly neutral or secular public square in which Jews could in theory participate equally with the dominant (and Christian) national groups of Europe. While these promises have been inconsistently fulfilled over the past two centuries, they have also become central to the way that many Jewish groups view their own destinies and have contributed to their fierce defense of the avowedly neutral public sphere. So the Rebbe's laconic retort cuts to the quick of American Jewish sensibilities: "a person who agrees to be 'a Jew at home and a man in the street' will soon not even be a Jew at home anymore." Rather than try (like some more insular Hasidic and ultraorthodox groups) to avoid the price of modernity by ceding the "street," as it were, entirely to the secular sphere, Chabad took the opposite tack of bringing Judaism (or as they would be more likely to say, "godliness") out into the streets. Public menorah lightings, opening hundreds of campus "Chabad houses," advocacy for school prayer, and public recognition of the seven Noahide laws all represent attempts to sanctify the non-Jewish public sphere. But this is also one of the reasons that these campaigns have sometimes proven so controversial among American Jews. Opponents may not always be aware of the ritual efficacy claimed by Hasidim, but they could not help but note the transgression of deeply rooted taboos regarding the separation of sacred and profane in American Jewish life.

This is worth belaboring here because the world of modernist sociology that Philip Wexler wants to remake, the world of Durkheim and Mauss, Freud, Marx, and Lévi-Strauss, was also in many ways a world specifically defined by Mendelssohn's bargain, not just because these scholars were Jews who each occupied a tenuous and sometimes vulnerable position in European civilization (Seeman & Stern, forthcoming), but also because the very terms of Durkheimian sociology and its successors were secularizing, objectivizing, and compartmentalizing. It is no surprise, given this background, that Wexler's quest for a new sociological model should draw him to Chabad, which has done so much to promote a kind of resacralization and "re-enchantment" of late modernity. Rather than simply trying to rebuild the traditionalist piety of Eastern Europe, Chabad under R. Schneerson participated in a programmatic attempt to suffuse the whole of contemporary society, with its political and bureaucratic apparatus and its overwhelmingly non-Jewish population, with a new register of spiritual consciousness. Embedded in a reading of Chabad's traditional acosmism is the claim repeatedly emphasized in the teachings of R. Schneerson that the immanence of the phenomenal world and the transcendence of *atzmut*—the divine itself—must come to be viewed as one and inseparable.

There are complications to this model that ought at least to be mentioned here, though I cannot explore them in any detail. The Rebbe himself frequently chided his followers for being slow to take up the more radical aspects of his message, including the now eminently successful emissaries' campaign and the still-nascent campaign of non-conversionary outreach to non-Jews. It is worth trying to understand what these fits and starts teach us about what is at stake in these developments for all three of the Chabads mentioned above—the Chabad of informal social networks, institutional Chabad, and the Chabad of the Rebbe's teaching and charisma. On the one hand, one detects a certain reluctance by social and institutional Chabad toward the increasing inclusivism of the Rebbe's message; at the same time, one notes how the Rebbe seems, despite his inclusivism, to have resisted the distillation of *Hasidut* into the kind of generalized spiritual "technique" (see Seeman & Karlin, forthcoming) that Wexler's mystical sociology should lead us to expect.

III

Canadian sociologist Véronique Altglas's study *From Yoga to Kabbalah* (2014) confirms some of the features of contemporary resacralization (though this is not her terminology). Alongside *Vedanta Yoga*, one of her primary case studies involves the *Kabbalah Center*, a movement that shares some similarities with modern Chabad. One contrast I want to focus on here, however, is that while both Chabad and the Kabbalah Center have systematically opened themselves much more than previous Jewish mystical schools to non-observant Jews and indeed to non-Jews, the Kabbalah Center has accomplished this to a large extent by decoupling its mystical techniques and literature from traditional linkages between mystical practice, *halakha*, and Jewish peoplehood. This has by and large not been the case with Chabad, where apparent exceptions tend mostly to prove the rule.

Chaim Miller (2014) describes an intriguing episode in which the previous Rebbe tasked his young son-in-law Menachem Mendel with developing a meditative system appropriate for use by non-Jews in response to a query from an eccentric Russian scientist with ties to the KGB, but nothing much seems to have come of this. Years later, at the beginning of his third decade as Rebbe in his own right, R. Schneerson made several urgent attempts to launch the development of what he called "kosher meditation," which was to take the place of popular Eastern-derived practices like transcendental meditation that were widely decried by contemporary rabbinic authorities, including R. Schneerson himself, for the taint of idolatry. But what is crucial about this call from my point of view is that R. Schneerson specifically did *not* favor the replacement or adaptation of traditional Chabad contemplative practice for this purpose. Against what he took to be a thinly veiled attempt to promote some form of Hinduism in therapeutic guise, he seems to have been adamant (though there is some dispute about this among contemporary followers) that therapeutic and Hasidic meditation should be treated as essentially distinct and unrelated (Seeman & Karlin, forthcoming). The therapeutic, in this way of thinking, should never be confused with the mystical. To one psychiatrist who answered his call to try to create a new therapeutic modality, the Rebbe gave specific instructions that this should not be combined with the simultaneous attempt by non-Chabad rabbi Aryeh Kaplan to develop and popularize Kabbalistic meditation techniques for modern Jews.

Given these tensions, "turning Judaism outward" was neither easy nor always successful. "During the first decade of his reign," one elder Hasid and scholar remarked to me, "the Rebbe was busy trying to teach us how to be Hasidim." In the aftermath of President Kennedy's speech launching the Peace Corps in 1961, R. Schneerson (at the ten-year mark of his leadership) expressed somewhat acerbically that *now that it had been stated in English by the president*, Hasidim might begin taking to heart his own message that they must begin to levy their own "peace corps" to spread Hasidic life and teaching beyond its traditional enclave. Despite fits and starts, it is often suggested that this program of *shluchim* now represents the heart of contemporary Chabad and was the seventh Rebbe's most transformative contribution. In some cases *shluchim* themselves have returned after many years to themes that the Rebbe raised with only limited success during his lifetime.

While the Rebbe's 1970 call for therapeutic meditation went mostly unanswered, for example, some Chabad writers and teachers have more recently engaged, invoked, or adapted secularized therapeutic models developed under Buddhist influence, such as Mindfulness-Based Stress Reduction (MBSR) and other mindfulness-related practices, as well as positive psychology. However, the question as to how much these therapeutic modalities resemble or ought to be combined with—or even just invoked to generate interest in—more traditional Chabad disciplines remains fraught (Seeman & Karlin, forthcoming; Karlin, 2014). Such tensions can turn into fault lines along which contemporary initiatives falter. Michael Karlin's (2014) ethnographic study of an attempt by one group of North American emissaries to launch their own training program in life coaching shows how the program ran aground in part over conflict about the limits of life coaching's non-judgmental and therapeutic/self-help ethos. While one emissary described her setting aside her own beliefs when necessary to help her clients, as a form of *bittul*, or self-nullification, other members of the group expressed real discomfort with the idea that the life coaching model might force them to prioritize the goals of their clients even when these might conflict with fundamental precepts of Jewish or Hasidic life. The hypothetical case of a client who might seek help in thinking through the best way to pursue a marital relationship outside of his or her religion underscored for several participants that they could not reconcile life coaching (no matter how efficacious) with their mission as emissaries. Nor were many of them willing, when push came to shove, to separate therapeutic technique from the whole moral cosmology to which they were committed as Hasidim.

Which brings us to the Institute of Jewish Spirituality and Society, under whose auspices this volume has been produced. The Institute, which is led by Philip Wexler, and whose goals include the promotion of research on the application of Jewish "spirituality" (particularly Hasidic spirituality) to human problems such as aging or education, represents in my view a fascinating confluence of "mystical sociology" and modern Chabad's outward turn. It is, moreover, not unique in this regard. The Tag Institute for Jewish Social Values in Britain and the Aspen Center for Social Values in the United States are each moving simultaneously in similar directions. Each was founded with the implicit or explicit support of Chabad intellectual and institutional leaders—but without, as far as I know, the imprimatur of "official" Chabad—and all three have sought partnership with non-Chabad (though sometimes Orthodox) Jewish academics or intellectuals, such as myself. All, moreover, have set their sights in slightly different ways on the application of Jewish or Hasidic wisdom to what are framed as enduring and universal human problems that were not previously at the forefront of Chabad's public activism. Will this turn out to be a more sustainable model than Chabad-affiliated life coaching or "kosher meditation"? Time will tell.

Collaboration may be too dualistic a term to adequately describe this development. It speaks to a context in which some Hasidim increasingly consume or even produce academic scholarship (Chabad is the first Hasidic group, I am sure, to employ an "academic liaison"), while some non-Chabad scholars have come to view the Hasidic group not just as objects of analysis but as potential research partners, consumers of public scholarship, or fellow travelers in the attempt to deploy scholarship for useful human ends. The extent to which both parties to this exchange may evolve as a result remains to be seen, but it implies at the very least a reformulation of the tense binary between Hasidism as a subject of academic research or academic researchers as objects alternately of suspicion and of religious "outreach" by Hasidim. Volumes like the present one need to be understood reflexively as themselves evidence of a dynamic new social field whose contours have not yet been fixed or meaningfully analyzed. For some participants this field may constitute evidence (for better or worse) of Chabad's inexorable outward turn; for others it may participate in what they experience as an epochal shift toward mystical sociology, but contestation is in any case inevitable. It is in the scope of those contestations that some understanding of ongoing social process may emerge.

References

Altglas, V. (2014). *From Yoga to Kabbalah: Religious exoticism and the logics of bricolage.* Oxford: Oxford University Press.

Bender, C. (2010). *The new metaphysicals: Spirituality and the American religious imagination.* Chicago: University of Chicago Press.

Forman, R.K.C. (Ed.). (1990). *The problem of pure consciousness.* Oxford: Oxford University Press.

Forman, R.K.C. (2004). *Grassroots spirituality.* Charlottesville, VA: Imprint Academic.

Geertz, C. (1973). *The interpretation of cultures.* Boston: Basic Books.

Griffith, R.M. (2000). *God's daughters: Evangelical women and the power of submission.* Berkeley: University of California Press.

Idel, I. (1990). *Kabbalah: New perspectives.* New Haven, CT: Yale University Press.

Idel, I. (1995). *Hasidism: Between ecstasy and magic.* Albany: State University of New York Press.

Jackson, M. (2005). *Existential anthropology: Events, exigencies and effects.* New York: Berghahn Books.

Karlin, M. (2014). *To create a dwelling place for God: Life coaching and the Chabad-Lubavitch Hasidic movement in contemporary America.* Unpublished doctoral dissertation, Emory University.

Katz, S.T. (1978). Language, epistemology and mysticism. In S.T. Katz (Ed.), *Mysticism and philosophical analysis* (pp. 22–74). Oxford: Oxford University Press.

Mahmood, S. (2011). *The politics of piety*. Princeton, NJ: Princeton University Press.

McMahan, D. (2008). *The making of Buddhist modernism*. Oxford: Oxford University Press.

Miller, C. (2014). *Turning Judaism outward: A biography of the Rebbe*. New York: Kol Menachem.

Paper, J. (2004). *The mystic experience: A descriptive and comparative analysis*. Albany: State University of New York Press.

Premawardhana, D. (2018). *Faith in flux: Pentecostalism and mobility in rural Mozambique*. Philadelphia: University of Pennsylvania Press.

Robbins, J. (2004). The globalization of Pentecostal and charismatic Christianity. *Annual Review of Anthropology, 33*, 117–143.

Schielke, S. (2015). *Egypt in the future tense*. Bloomington: Indiana University Press.

Schimmel, A.M. (2011). *The mystical dimensions of Islam*. Chapel Hill: University of North Carolina Press.

Scholem, G. (1961). *Major Trends in Jewish Mysticism*. New York: Schocken Books.

Seeman, D. (2004). Otherwise than meaning: On the generosity of ritual. *Social Analysis, 48*(2), 51–71.

Seeman, D. (2005). Violence, ethics and divine honor in modern Jewish thought. *Journal of the American Academy of Religion, 73*(4), 1015–1048.

Seeman, D. (2008). Ritual efficacy, Hasidic mysticism and "useless suffering" in the Warsaw ghetto. *Harvard Theological Review, 101*(3–4): 465–505.

Seeman, D. (2015). Coffee and the moral order: Ethiopian Jews and Pentecostals against culture. *American Ethnologist, 42*(4), 734–748.

Seeman, D. (2018). Divinity inhabits the social: Ethnography in a phenomenological key. In D. Lemons (Ed.), *Theologically engaged anthropology*. Oxford: Oxford University Press.

Seeman, D., & Karlin, M. (forthcoming). *Mindfulness and Hasidic modernism: Towards a contemplative ethnography*. Under submission.

Seeman, D., & Kobrin, R. (1999). Like one of the whole men: Learning, gender and autobiography in R. Barukh Epstein's *Mekor Barukh*. *Nashim, 2*, 52–94.

Seeman, D., Roushdy-Hammady, I., Hardison-Moody, A., Thompson, W.W., Gaydos, L.M., & Rowland Hogue, C.J. (2016). Blessing unintended pregnancy: Religion and the discourse of agency in public health. *Medicine Anthropology Theory, 3*, 29–54.

Seeman, D., & Stern, N.A. (forthcoming). Anthropology, Judaism and Jews: The anthropology of Jewish Life. In J. Robbins & S. Coleman (Eds.), *Blackwell companion to the anthropology of religion*. London: Blackwell.

Wexler, P. (2013). *Mystical sociology: Toward cosmic social theory*. London: Peter Lang.

Wikan, U. (1990). *Managing turbulent hearts: A Balinese formula for living*. Chicago: University of Chicago Press.

Willen, S., & Seeman, D. (2012). Introduction: Experience and inquietude. *Ethos, 1*, 1–23.

Wuthnow, R. (1998). *After heaven: Spirituality in America since the 1950s*. Berkeley: University of California Press.

Chapter 3

MYSTICISM AND THE QUEST FOR UNIVERSAL SINGULARITY— POST-SUBJECTIVE SUBJECTIVITY AND THE CONTEMPLATIVE IDEAL IN HABAD

Elliot R. Wolfson, University of California, Santa Barbara

I will commence my reflections with Jean-Luc Nancy's observation that

> difference is not the opposite of identity; for difference is what makes identity possible, and by inscribing this possibility at the heart of identity, it exposes it to this: that its meaning cannot be identical to it. We are our identity, and *we* designate—once again, in the simultaneous and undecidable reference to our "singularities" and our "community"—an identity that is necessarily shared out, in us and between us. Difference takes place in this sharing out, at once a distribution of meaning into all significations and a withdrawal of meaning from all significations—a withdrawal that each signification indicates, at the limit.[1]

Nancy succinctly expresses a commonsensical point too often obscured by the cloud of political correctness: not only is difference not

---

1. Jean-Luc Nancy, *The Gravity of Thought*, translated by François Raffoul and Gregory Recco (Amherst, NY: Humanity Books, 1998), p. 64.

in opposition to identity; the former is precisely what makes the latter possible in the formation of the singularities shared in the constitution of the community, a sharing that is at once a distribution and a withdrawal of meaning into all significations, a bestowal and a retraction that are simultaneous and not consecutive. Based on this hermeneutical hypothesis—supported by the neuroscientific assumption that the cerebral coding of information precludes positioning the homogenous and the heterogeneous in binary opposition[2]—I would argue that it is still theoretically warranted and heuristically viable to ponder the variant expressions of the mystical in different settings by identifying recurring patterns of thought cohering in multidimensional systems of meaning. These patterns, I hasten to add, can be compared to DNA, which generates new molecular constellations in an apparently endless cycle of succession—the *infinite genetic variation*—while the systems provide the relatively stable frameworks through and in which those changing patterns evolve, dissolve, and revolve. We are justified, then, in postulating that sameness is precisely what engenders difference. Ideationally, the presumption that the universal must be determined continually by the constraints and possibilities imposed by the particular validates the cross-cultural study of mysticism.

Community and the Infinite Multiple Variation of the Individual

One of the more pressing questions to emerge from delineating mysticism in this way is the socio-political and ethical relevance

---

2. Jacques M. Chevalier, *Scorpions and the Anatomy of Time* (Montreal: McGill-Queen's University Press, 2002), p. 4, previously cited and discussed in Elliot R. Wolfson, *Language, Eros, Being: Kabbalistic Hermeneutics and Poetic Imagination* (New York: Fordham University Press, 2005), pp. 89–90. See also William J. Clancey, *Conceptual Coordination: How the Mind Orders Experience in Time* (London: Routledge, 1999), p. 68; Georg Northoff, *Minding the Brain: A Guide to Philosophy and Neuroscience* (New York: Palgrave Macmillan, 2014), p. 85.

of mystical experience. I am particularly interested in exploring this matter from the perspective of the relationship of the individual and the community. We may approach this problem by assuming, as various thinkers have done in the past, that true individuality is expressive of community, that the latter can only grow out of the sense of originary aloneness, that the solitude of the contemplative is precisely the womb that bears the possibility of genuine relationality.³ If we adopt the model briefly noted

---

3. For discussion of this theme and citation of some of the relevant sources, see Elliot R. Wolfson, "Theolatry and the Making-Present of the Nonrepresentable: Undoing (A)Theism in Eckhart and Buber," *Journal of Jewish Thought and Philosophy* 25 (2017): 8–12. Particularly relevant is the view on Zionism affirmed by Scholem in the essay "Abschied," published in *Jerubbaal, Eine Zeitschrift der jüdischen Jugend* 1 (1918–1919): 125–130, and translated in Gershom Scholem, *On Jews and Judaism in Crisis: Selected Essays*, edited by Werner J. Dannhauser (New York: Schocken, 1976), pp. 54–60. The relevant passage appears on pp. 55–57: "The great demand of Zionism, which is eternally one, to be a holy people, has a presupposition the misunderstanding of which is in a real sense the chimerical basis for that objective mendacity against which witness is to be given here. Community demands solitude: not the possibility of together desiring the same, but only that of common solitude establishes community. Zion, the source of our nationhood, is the common, indeed in an uncanny sense, the identical solitude of all Jews, and the religious assertion of Zionism is nothing other than this: the midst of solitude happens at the same time to be where all gather together, and there can be no other place for such a gathering together.... There is only one place from which Zion can be reached and youth restituted: solitude. And there is only one medium, brought to radiance by labor, that will be the source of renewal: the existence that must be the argument against a youth that has desecrated words." Scholem's essay was a critique of what he referred to as the "pseudo-Zionist lie of community" (p. 55) promulgated by the German Zionist youth movement, but his view is related to an idea proffered by a number of thinkers in the early part of the twentieth century, including Landauer and Buber, to the effect that true individuality is expressive of community, that the latter can only proceed from an originary aloneness, that the solitude of the contemplative is precisely what engenders the possibility of genuine sociality. A similar perspective was affirmed as well by Heidegger. See, for instance, Martin Heidegger, *Ponderings II–VI: Black Notebooks 1931–1938*, translated by Richard Rojcewicz (Bloomington: Indiana University Press, 2016), p. 45: "Only if and only as long as this originary

above, whereby the whole is configured by the ever-evolving manifold of the components, we can reformulate the relationship of the self and the other by speaking of the identity of the individual as inherently communal; the latter, however, is itself construed most authentically by the solitude of the individual. The dynamic of which I speak is not to be envisioned in Hegelian terms as the dialectical sublation of the antinomical relation between the universal and the particular, but rather in Heideggerian terms as the belonging-together of opposites in the sameness of their difference. In this chapter I will utilize Habad-Lubavitch sources to explore this larger philosophical question. More specifically, I will examine this theme from the perspective of a distinction first made by Shneur Zalman of Liadi and expounded by his son, Dov Baer, between two types of contemplation: *hitbonenut kelalit* and *hitbonenut peratit*, contemplation of the universal and contemplation of the particular.

It has been well argued that the distinctiveness of Hasidism within the history of Jewish religiosity and spirituality relates to the fact that the mystical assumes a socio-political dimension and becomes the foundation for a community. With all of Scholem's differences with Buber, he built on the latter's contention that Hasidism represents "Kabbalism turned Ethos."[4] Scholem amplified the Buberian perspective by arguing that the originality of Hasidism lies in the fact that the mystics who had attained their

---

  aloneness of Dasein is experienced can true community grow indigenously; only thus is to be overcome all publicness of those who have come together and are driven together" (emphasis in original).
4. Gershom Scholem, *Major Trends in Jewish Mysticism* (New York: Schocken, 1956), p. 342. See Martin Buber, *The Tales of Rabbi Nachman*, translated by Maurice Friedman (New York: Horizon Press, 1956), p. 10: "Hasidism is the Kabbala become Ethos." Many scholars have cited and analyzed Buber's statement. See, most recently, the chapter on "Ethos" in David Biale, David Assaf, Benjamin Brown, Uriel Gellman, Samuel Heilman, Moshe Rosman, Gadi Sagiv, and Marcin Wodziński, *Hasidism: A New History*, with an afterword by Arthur Green (Princeton: Princeton University Press, 2018), pp. 159–182, esp. 160.

spiritual aim—in kabbalistic parlance, the contemplative ideal of conjunction (*devequt*)—undertook to perpetuate the personal and solitary experience in the life of a community. The Eastern European pietism was thus a mystical movement that took the shape of a social phenomenon.[5] The dissemination of the mystical knowledge and practice occasioned a break with the code of esotericism and thereby overcame the divide between sacred and profane—or, to cite Scholem again, "Hasidism is practical mysticism at its highest. Almost all the Kabbalistic ideas are now placed in relation to values peculiar to the individual life, and those which are not remain empty and ineffective."[6] Emphasis is placed on the individual's personal relationship to God, but as we have already noted, Scholem was acutely aware of the fact that Hasidism as a historical phenomenon is oriented toward the social formation of community.

This approach has been enhanced by Philip Wexler's attempt to understand Hasidism from the perspective of a more nuanced conjecture regarding the dynamics of everyday life and the resacralization and remystification of the religious turn in critical social theory. He even goes so far as to identify Hasidism as

> an example of collective prophecy, where anticipation and prefiguration are expressed as much by socially embodied forms of life as by individual, prophetic articulations.... Hasidism is interesting as a prefigurative revitalization movement or collective prophecy because it brings the vitalizing power of mysticism into the world...and because, at the same time, it creates, at least as an aspiration, the communal ideal of "brotherly love."... Hasidism thus offers a model of the fusion of elements which Weber expressed as an ideal, but did not develop, and which Troeltsch vehemently denied: a

---

5. Scholem, *Major Trends*, p. 342.
6. Ibid., p. 341.

mystical sociality which melds the seemingly disparate roads to modernity's prophetic supersession.[7]

From Wexler's vantage point, relying in some measure on the shared belief of Scholem and Idel that Hasidism represents the attempt to bring "the vitalizing power of mysticism into the social world,"[8] Wexler surmises that Hasidism embodies a mystical sociality that resolves the tension between mystical sanctification of the individual and community solidarity.[9] In slightly different terminology, Wexler writes elsewhere that "Hasidism is additionally important beyond giving a more social face to mysticism because it proclaims, analyzes, and embodies a model of social processes that is alternative to the ideology of modernity.... Hasidism offers us also a theoretical alternative to modern social theory, and, indeed, also to critical theory."[10] What I find most intriguing in Wexler's analysis is the sense that the mysticism surfaces as a reconfiguration of the social that entails a cosmicization beyond the polarization of individual eccentricities and cultural conventionalities.[11]

In the remainder of this chapter, I will probe this assumption by inquiring if the contemplative ideal promulgated in the Habad-Lubavitch dynasty can be used as evidence for a new mechanism of social life in Hasidism, as Wexler suggests, a model that would mediate between individual and community not by internalizing the socialization process of the former but by extending the latter into a cosmic interactionism that fosters the "everyday dialectics of

---

7. Philip Wexler, *Mystical Interactions: Sociology, Jewish Mysticism and Education* (Los Angeles: Cherub Press, 2007), pp. 32–34.
8. Ibid., p. 34.
9. Ibid., p. 38.
10. Philip Wexler, *Mystical Sociology: Toward Cosmic Social Theory* (New York: Peter Lang, 2013), pp. 53–54. Compare Philip Wexler, *Mystical Society: An Emerging Social Vision* (Boulder, CO: Westview Press, 2000), p. 129.
11. Philip Wexler, "Society and Mysticism," in *After Spirituality: Studies in Mystical Traditions*, edited by Philip Wexler and Jonathan Garb (New York: Peter Lang, 2012), pp. 107–125, esp. 123.

mysticization."[12] Can we find in the mystical discernment of what is called in Habad thought the essence of the infinite (*atsmut ein sof*) that infuses all reality a path of political restoration analogous to contemporary notions of sociality and interconnectivity? I will elicit from Habad sources—chosen selectively due to limitations of space—support for the idea of universal singularity as opposed to singular universality, that is, the assumption that the universal is constructed continually in light of the singular rather than the universal instantiated comprehensively in the singular. Habad thought does yield the notion of a social horizon of the mystical informed by the premise that the inexorability of the general (*kelal*) is calibrated on the basis of the contingency of the particular (*perat*). The ideal of wholeness, on this account, is to be sought in the disjointedness of the essence, or in the Habad lexicon, the supernal unity (*yihud ila'ah*) concealing and manifesting itself in the lower unity (*yihud tata'ah*).[13] Typically, the former denotes the integration (*hitkallelut*) of everything in the light of infinity (*or ein sof*) and the latter the diffusion (*hitpashshetut*) of that light in the miscellaneous forms of existence.[14] What I will argue, however, is that the deeper, or more esoteric, intent of Habad teaching is that the incomposite oneness of the inessential being of the essential nonbeing is comprehended through the multifaceted compossibility of becoming. The one is ascertained, therefore, not by the dissolution of difference in the boundlessness of indifference, but by the unlimited differentiation of that indifference in the world of plurality. Infinity is a one that

---

12. Wexler, *Mystical Sociology*, p. 184. See ibid., pp. 169, 175; and Wexler, *Mystical Society*, pp. 136–137.

13. Regarding this terminological and conceptual distinction, see Naftali Loewenthal, *Communicating the Infinite: The Emergence of the Habad School* (Chicago: University of Chicago Press, 1990), pp. 50, 137, 147, 153, 168, 175, 184 n. 144 , 275 n. 39.

14. See Moshe Idel, "Universalization and Integration: Two Concepts of Mystical Union in Jewish Mysticism," in *Mystical Union and Monotheistic Faith: An Ecumenical Dialogue*, edited by Moshe Idel and Bernard McGinn (New York: Macmillan, 1989), pp. 27–57, esp. 41–45.

is not one, the void-multiple,[15] the multiple of multiples,[16] wherein every part can be read as a metonymy for the whole as long as it is understood that the whole is a metonymy for the part.[17]

Two Types of Hitbonenut: Universal and Particular

A crucial dimension of the comment of Menahem Mendel Schneerson from a talk delivered on the second day of Pentecost, 1960, can serve as a prelude to our discussion of the two types of contemplation:

> The Besht wrote to R. Adam, the master of the name, the reason why he did not want to be revealed because he did not want any conflict and nothing was lacking for him when he was in solitude studying the Torah with his teacher who is known. R. Adam wrote him that this is the will of the creator, and in any event, what does he care. Thus from this letter, R. Adam portrayed for the Besht the matter of equanimity [*inyan ha-hishtawwut*], that everything should be equaniminous for him and nothing should concern him except to complete the supernal intention.[18]

Schneerson goes on to say that the letter proves that the revelation to the Besht did not transpire through compulsion and coercion (*be-derekh qabbalat ol u-khefiyyah*) but rather through the per-

---

15. Alain Badiou, *Being and Event*, translated by Oliver Feltham (London: Continuum, 2005), p. 126.
16. Ibid., pp. 56, 59, 81, 265.
17. Ibid., p. 27.
18. Menahem Mendel Schneerson, *Torat Menahem: Hitwwa'aduyyot 5720*, vol. 2 (Brooklyn, NY: Vaad Hanochos Blahak, 2004), p. 120.

suasion of some of his colleagues, the righteous ones who were concealed, that he should want to be revealed. He eventually agreed, even though he attained a high level of solitude and realized that disclosure would invariably bring discord. In the end, the impulse to do the will of God was greater than these concerns, and the state of equanimity was achieved with desire and pleasure, for his will acted in accord with the supernal will. The moral to be derived from the story is as follows: "The actualization of the quality of equanimity is applied to the matter of the spreading forth of the wellsprings of the inwardness of the Torah, which must be done without any calculation, even the calculation with respect to the matter of peace, but only because it is the will of the creator."[19] Right after this statement, Schneerson mentioned the distinction made by Dov Baer, in his *Sha'ar ha-Yihud*, between the contemplation of the particular and the contemplation of the universal.[20]

The source for this distinction can be traced to Shneur Zalman. Thus, for example, in a brief excursus on the nature of *hitbonenut*, after establishing that contemplation is not merely a cognitive matter (*behinat mahashavah*) but is a probing (*ha'amaqah*) to attain a clear knowledge (*yedi'ah berurah*) that leads one to the fear and love of the divine, he notes: "The essence of contemplation is to be discerned from how he renews each day the creation from nothing to something... and if the overflow would be removed even for a second it would be as if it were not [*hayah ke-lo hayah*]... in each and every moment he brings forth and sustains all the worlds

---

19. Ibid. For discussion of the role of solitude in the Maggid's teaching about contemplation, see Joseph Weiss, *Studies in Eastern European Jewish Mysticism*, edited by David Goldstein (Oxford: Littman Library, 1985), pp. 131–141.
20. Dov Baer Schneersohn, *Ner Mitswah we-Torah Or* (Brooklyn, NY: Kehot, 1995), pp. 222–223. After completing this study, I came across a discussion of the two types of contemplation in Dov Baer's thought in the *Ma'amar ha-Kelal we-ha-Perat* by Shmuel Arenfeld, *Ke-Tse't ha-Shemesh: Be'urim we-Iyyunim al Haqdamat Rehovot ha-Nahar*, 3 vols. (Jerusalem: Makhon Yam ha-Hokhmah, 2018), 3:620–626. Arenfeld's discussion bears affinity to my own analysis.

and all created beings from nothing to something."²¹ What are we to make of the juxtaposition of contemplation and *creatio ex nihilo*? What does the latter tell us about the nature of the former? Contemplation is to be discerned from the transition from nothing to something, but the Habad perspective, which I have labelled acosmic naturalism and apophatic panentheism,²² entails that we understand the traditional theological-cosmological belief as the drawing out of something from nothing only to the extent that we comprehend that the something amounts to and is integrated in this nothing, that is, the immaterial essence of no-essence manifest as the presence of absence in the phenomenal mesh of material forms. Contemplation, therefore, is a way of seeing that alters our perception of reality, a specularity that divests the universe of its gross physicality, restoring the multiplicity of all beings to the indistinct and indifferent being that comprehends the beingness of every being in the nothingness of its being every nothing. When one appreciates that it is the perpetual influx of the divine overflow that prevents the something turning back into nothing, that if the light were removed even for a nanosecond, every existent would be as if it did not exist, then one comprehends the essential nothingness that everything in fact is, *ayin wa-efes mammash*.²³

The contemplative task is to reverse the process of *yesh me-ayin*, to turn the something back to nothing, *me-yesh le-ayin*, which is to say, to perceive the being of all beings as nonbeing. This is not a nihilistic or even an acosmic denial of nature, but rather the discernment that the substance of what exists is to be sought in the interrelatedness rather than the ontic autonomy of discrete entities. To know that everything is nothing—in the zoharic formulation

---

21. Shneur Zalman of Liadi, *Ma'amerei Admor ha-Zaqen: Al Inyanim*, vol. 1, revised edition (Brooklyn, NY: Kehot, 2007), pp. 150–151.
22. Elliot R. Wolfson, *Open Secret: Postmessianic Messianism and the Mystical Revision of Menahem Mendel Schneerson* (New York: Columbia University Press, 2009), pp. 87–103.
23. Shneur Zalman of Liadi, *Ma'amerei Admor ha-Zaqen: Al Inyanim*, p. 151.

cited repeatedly by Habad masters, "everything before him is considered as naught" (*kolla qameih ke-lo hashivin*)[24]—is not to repudiate the existence of divergent beings, but rather to perceive the nonbeing that is at the core of their being, the actual nothing that is nothing actually, the void that is the essence, the concealment (*he'lem*) that is the world (*ha-olam*).[25] Even the messianic promise of seeing the king without his garment means seeing that there is no seeing the infinite essence but through the garment of the world of finitude. Enlightenment is not the discarding of the veil, but the unveiling of the veil that no longer veils itself as the veil.[26]

Interpreting Habad material through this postmodern lens, I would contend that the essence of the infinite marks the plurivocity of the origin rather than a unitary principle that can be reified metaphysically. To be sure, when Dov Baer writes that the main objective in the contemplation of each and every particular (*ha-hitbonenut be-khol perat u-ferat*) is to discern that everything is contained in the incomposite unity of the divine (*lihyot nikhlal ha-kol be-ahdut ha-peshutah*), which is the aspect of the essence of the light of the infinite, this strikes the ear as an ontotheological way to speak of the unspeakable.[27] In my opinion, however, the Habad

---

24. *Zohar* 1:11b. See Wolfson, *Open Secret*, pp. 135, 344 n. 218.
25. Wolfson, *Open Secret*, pp. 26, 52, 93, 103–114, 128, 132, 215. The wordplay related to the word *ha-olam* in Ecclesiastes 3:11, which is written without the *waw* and thus can be read as *he'lem*, is found in *Midrash Tanhuma* (Jerusalem: Eshkol, 1972), Qedoshim, 8, p. 589. See also Daniel Abrams, *The Book Bahir: An Edition Based on the Earliest Manuscripts* (Los Angeles: Cherub Press, 1994), sec. 8, p. 121 (Hebrew).
26. Wolfson, *Open Secret*, pp. 114–129.
27. Schneersohn, *Ner Mitswah*, p. 291. For the more predictable interpretation of this passage, see Loewenthal, *Communicating*, p. 153, and see p. 168, where the upper unity is described as a state "where all is One, a perspective from which existence has no ultimate reality whatsoever." And ibid., p. 175. Loewenthal admits that there must be a turning back to the lower unity of the world from the higher unity, but he still characterizes the latter as world-denying. Other scholars have taken a similar approach. For instance, see Rachel Elior, *The Paradoxical Ascent to God: The Kabbalistic Theosophy of*

ideal of contemplation can be read as a critique of ontotheology even if the language leaves a different impression. The nullification of something into nothing (*bittul ha-yesh le-ayin*)[28] bespeaks the playfulness of the divine in dissembling a world that appears to be independent of God,[29] since it is precisely the nullification of something into nothing that triggers the drawing down of nothing into something.[30] *Ein Sof*, on this score, does not name a transcendental being that is unthinkable because it is beyond thinking but rather the fecundity of the essence that is the eradication of essence, the plenitudinal void that is the absolute determinacy of the indeterminate absolute, the namelessness that is insufficiently thought and therefore subject continuously to endless naming, the radically immanent differential foreclosed to thought except as the unthought yet to be thought. That words are inadequate signifies that the one, which is the real, is infinitely effable and not that it is irretrievably ineffable—there is always more to say concerning the nothing about which there is always less to say.[31] The unification of the infinite, accordingly, implies generic fluctuation as opposed to systematic totalization;[32] that is to say, the assimilability of the

---

Habad Hasidism, translated by Jeffrey M. Green (Albany: State University of New York Press, 1993), p. 231. See also Dov Schwartz, *Habad's Thought: From Beginning to End* (Ramat-Gan: Bar-Ilan University Press, 2010), pp. 243–244 (Hebrew).

28. Schneersohn, *Ner Mitswah*, p. 292. See Wolfson, *Open Secret*, pp. 80–81, 93–94.
29. Wolfson, *Open Secret*, p. 95.
30. See the passage from Shneur Zalman cited in Wolfson, *Open Secret*, p. 145.
31. My thinking betrays the influence of the One or the Real as delineated in the non-philosophy of François Laruelle. See Anthony Paul Smith, "Thinking from the One: Science and the Ancient Philosophical Figure of the One," in *Laruelle and Non-Philosophy*, edited by John Mullarkey and Anthony Paul Smith (Edinburgh: Edinburgh University Press, 2012), pp. 19–41.
32. François Laruelle, *Philosophies of Difference: A Critical Introduction to Non-Philosophy*, translated by Rocco Gangle (London: Continuum, 2010), pp. 70–71: "As affected by non-being, Being will remain undetermined in opposition to any 'metaphysical' type of determination. This latter concerns

general (*kelal*) is rooted in and must always be tested against the unassimilability of the particular (*perat*). Translated mathematically, the whole does not compromise the fragmentariness of the fragment, since the essence can be discerned only from the indiscernible nonessence. Instead of ascribing to *Ein Sof* a structure of being impervious to the instability of becoming, the oneness of infinity is better apprehended as a multifarious event that is continually in the process of emerging as what it is not in the cancellation of what it is. In the words of Shalom Dovber Schneersohn, the perfection (*sheleimut*) of the essence does not imply effacement of difference but is related rather to the fact that it is one subject that bears the opposites (*nose ha-hafakhim*), and hence everything is verily in the aspect of the one (*we-ha-kol bi-vehinat yahid mammash*).[33]

---

itself with the particularity of beings. The transcendental or unifying (-unified) All will thus be 'ontically' indeterminable, that is, more rigorously, indeterminable in the mode of ontic multiplicity. This indetermination...is not decided in relation to beings in general, but only in relation to beings inasmuch as in general they are multiple and particular: to think the intrinsic variety of Being itself is thus not to wish to break its (necessary) relation to beings.... Difference in general is a chiasmus and, in its superior or transcendental phase, we know that the chiasmus conserves itself, that it remains an invariant in the passage from ontic diversity to transcendental unity, that the One appears and affirms itself, certainly not in 'itself' but in the form of unifying Difference, of the indivision of Nothingness and Being, in the transcendental and no longer metaphysical sense of these words.... Being remains in every way determined, that is, relative to beings and 'beings' themselves in turn (this is the reversibility of ontological Difference)." See also François Laruelle, "The Generic as Predicate and Constant: Non-Philosophy and Materialism," in *The Speculative Turn: Continental Materialism and Realism*, edited by Levi Bryant, Nick Srnicek, and Graham Harman (Melbourne: Re.press, 2011), pp. 237–260. On the contrast between the systematic necessity of philosophy and the concept of the uni-verse embraced by non-philosophy, see François Laruelle, *Principles of Non-Philosophy*, translated by Nicola Rubczak and Anthony Paul Smith (London: Bloomsbury, 2013), p. 196.

33. Shalom Dovber Schneersohn, *Quntres ha-Tefillah* (Brooklyn, NY: Kehot, 1956), p. 12. On the distinction between *yahid* and *ehad* in the Habad lexicon, see Wolfson, *Open Secret*, pp. 79, 88–89, and sources cited on p. 334 n. 80.

With this in mind, we can go back to Shneur Zalman's distinction between two kinds of contemplation. The first type is named universal contemplation (*hitbonenut bi-khelal*), for the goal is to plumb the depth of the general matter (*inyan kelali*), which is enacted as the negation of the content of the thing whence it comes forth (*ha-yotse min tokhen ha-davar eikh she-hu batel*). This form of contemplation is described further as the constriction of consciousness (*tsimtsum ha-moah*) rather than its expansion; that is, consciousness is divested of all form until one is in a state of mind, or mindlessness, that is purely spiritual, a disfiguration of all figures that brings one to the limit of the imagination, the maximal imaginality revealed in the image concealing its character as image—"until he comes to the perimeter of the imagination... in order to divest the matter of corporeality until he is verily in the spiritual aspect, that is to say, verily a matter of the spirit" (*ad she-yavo likhlal dimyon... kedei lehafshit ha-inyan min ha-hagshamah ad she-yihyeh bi-vehinat ruhanit mammash kelomar divrei ruah mammash*).[34]

By contrast, the second type of contemplation is related to the particular (*hitbonenut bi-ferat*), the penetrating of knowledge into truth (*ha'amaqat ha-da'at ba-emet*) that entails the expansion of consciousness (*hitrahavut ha-moah*). Interestingly, this form of contemplation is compared to the quest to ascertain the literal sense (*peshat*) of the biblical text, which always involves a multivalency of meaning: "The manner of this probing is verily like searching for the literal sense with respect to the exoteric, that is, precisely the toil of thought [*tirdat ha-mahashavah*], for this is naught but the expansion of many matters and particulars [*harhavat inyanim rabbim u-feratim*] and not one general matter [*we-lo be-inyan ehad kelal*]... and in each and every word

---

34. Shneur Zalman of Liadi, *Ma'amerei Admor ha-Zaqen: Al Inyanim*, p. 159. The text was published as *Darkhei ha-Hitbonenut bi-Qetsarah* at the end of Dov Baer Schneersohn, *Quntres ha-Hitpa'alut* (Warsaw, 1876), 25a–b.

there is a particular and distinctive intention."[35] The realization or self-actualization (*hitpaʿalut*) varies in accord with the two types of contemplation: in the case of the former, the realization comes about as a combination of focus on one's own essence and on the divine matter, whereas in the case of the latter, the realization ensues solely from the divine. Inverting what we might expect, since the universal contemplation entails emptying the mind of all particulars, it can lead to the pursuit of one's own spiritual state of conjunction and to a keen sense of realization (*ha-hitpaʿalut murgeshet meʾod*), and, as a consequence, the nothingness gives way to an immense somethingness that is remote from and in opposition to divinity (*we-az naʿaseh yesh gadol we-rahoq mammash hippukh elohim*).[36] Although this form of contemplation is ostensibly about being conjoined to the divine nothing, it has the capacity to end in a state of haughtiness and arrogance.

Elaborating on his father's teaching in *Quntres ha-Hitpaʿalut*, Dov Baer notes that contemplation of the universal (*hitbonenut derekh kelal*) runs the risk of being a false or vain form of conjunction (*devequt shav*), the very opposite of genuine conjunction (*devequt amitti*), which is the divine ecstasy (*hitpaʿalut eloha*), insofar as the former is a worshipping of oneself (*oved et atsmo*) and not worshipping God (*oved ha-shem*).[37] By contrast, the contemplation of the particular (*hitbonenut derekh perat*) inculcates what Dov Baer refers to in another treatise as the humility (*shiflut*) and modesty (*anawah*) necessary to attain the essential annihilation (*bittul atsmi*)

---

35. Shneur Zalman of Liadi, *Maʾamerei Admor ha-Zaqen: Al Inyanim*, p. 160.
36. Ibid. On the roots of Shneur Zalman's alleged fear of mystical intoxication in the school of the Maggid, see Rivkah Schatz Uffenheimer, *Hasidism as Mysticism: Quietistic Elements in Eighteenth-Century Hasidic Thought*, translated by Jonathan Chipman (Princeton: Princeton University Press, 1993), p. 285.
37. Dov Baer Schneersohn, *Maʾamerei Admor ha-Emtsaʿi: Quntresim* (Brooklyn, NY: Kehot, 1991), pp. 61–62.

that results in one becoming an actual nothing (*ayin mammash*).³⁸ In attaining this nonattainment, there is no fear of egotism parading in the guise of spiritual egolessness; the magnanimity of truly being nothing—as desolate as the dust—is commensurate to the fixation on the incalculable details enfolded in the unfolding of the multiplicities present in the nonpresent of the infinite. The contemplation of particulars is thus a "realization that comes about exclusively from the side of divinity because one does not exert oneself to be conjoined, but rather one is engaged only with the contemplation, and, as a consequence, one is actualized in one's brain and comprehension [*mitpaʿel be-moḥo we-hassagato*], not because of proximity, and one does not feel this ecstasy [*hitpaʿalut*] at all since one's self has no part in it at all [*she-ein le-atsmo ḥeleq bah*

---

38. Dov Baer Schneersohn, *Shaʿarei Orah* (Brooklyn, NY: Kehot, 1979), 39a. See Wolfson, *Open Secret*, pp. 75–76. An alternate way of expressing this idea is that through contemplation in prayer one discerns and sustains the light and life of divinity in all material things and thereby transposes the sensual pleasure into a spiritual delight. See Shalom Dovber Schneersohn, *Be-Shaʿah she-Hiqdimu 5672*, 3 vols. (Brooklyn, NY: Kehot, 2011), 1:223. And compare ibid., p. 294: "Thus, even though there is no particular attribute [*middah peratit*] in this contemplation, there does arise from it the proximity to divinity in general [*ha-qeiruv le-elohut bi-khelal*], and this is the matter of the engraving from without; that is, by means of the contemplation and feeling in his soul for the divine nothing that sustains the something, and particularly in the comportment of the divine nothing [*be-eikhut ha-ayin ha-elohi*] and the particularities of the generation [*u-vi-feratei hithawwut*] that come to be from it, ones draws very close to divinity and is removed from all the material matters. . . . In order for there to be the engraving from within, this is by means of the contemplation in the aspect of the disclosure in the worlds, that is, in the aspect of the divine light and vitality that is garbed in them to sustain them . . . for every created being has within itself the divine vitality that sustains it. . . . The essence of this contemplation is that each created being has within it the divine light and vitality that sustains it . . . and by means of the contemplation and depth of knowledge one feels the matter in one's soul, and one is aroused and actualized in the love with which one loves God and desires to be conjoined to him so that the conjunction of one's soul will only be in the divine light." Compare Shalom Dovber Schneersohn, *Yom Tov shel Rosh Hashanah 5666* (Brooklyn, NY: Kehot, 2010), pp. 20–21, 519–520.

kelal]."³⁹ The supreme realization ensues, we might say, when one is not preoccupied with achieving realization.

The intent of Shneur Zalman is elucidated by Dov Baer in the passage from *Sha'ar ha-Yihud* to which I alluded above. The discussion of the two modes of contemplation, *inyan hitbonenut im derekh kelal o derekh perat*, is framed by the following overarching telos: the knowledge of the particulars of the chain of concatenation (*ha-yedi'ah bi-feratut kol ha-hishtalshelut*) is for the sake of conjoining the particular to the universal (*hibbur ha-perat im ha-kelal*).⁴⁰ The task, then, is to unite the two forms of contemplation, a directive, as Dov Baer notifies the reader, that he received from his father, who received it from the Maggid of Mezeritch.⁴¹ Commenting on this Habad teaching, Louis Jacobs wrote: "Of the two the detailed method is to be preferred, provided always that the details are connected in thought with the general idea of God's unity.... The fullest comprehension of every detail should only serve to fortify the general idea that all is in God."⁴² A similar approach is taken by Naftali Loewenthal, who speaks of the merging of the two methods until "all is subsumed in the Essence of the Divine."⁴³ I have proffered a different interpretation, indeed, one that reverses the priority of the universal and the particular. The first method of contemplation is described by Dov Baer as the effort to attain the aspect of the depth of the universal (*behinat ha-omeq bi-khelal*), which is further characterized as the aspect of the essence of the divine light (*behinat atsmut or ha-elohi*) in the aspect of the universal (*bi-vehinat ha-kelal*), a sense of containment that extends to both the supernal unity and the lower unity, which is the final goal of the disclosure of divinity in the soul (*ha-takhlit be-gilluy elohut ba-nefesh*). Reiterating the warning of his father, the Mitteler Rebbe

---

39. Shneur Zalman of Liadi, *Ma'amerei Admor ha-Zaqen: Al Inyanim*, p. 160.
40. Schneersohn, *Ner Mitswah*, p. 227.
41. Ibid., p. 223.
42. Louis Jacobs, *Hasidic Prayer* (New York: Schocken Books, 1973), p. 87.
43. Loewenthal, *Communicating*, p. 152.

says that this form of contemplation can result in great distance from the divine even though—or precisely because—one thinks one has acquired maximum closeness. However, the contemplation by way of particularity occasions a greater proximity due to an amplified disclosure of the divine light in the soul (*otsem ha-qeiruv gilluy or ha-elohi be-nafsho yoter*) because one is entangled in the indiscriminate manifold that constitutes the world of discrimination.[44] Only by scrutinizing each detail (*ha'amaqat ha-da'at be-khol perat*)[45] can the mind comprehend the divinity in its universality (*inyan elohut bi-khelalut*). The contemplation of particularity facilitates the discernment of the universality of the universal (*kelal ha-hassagah bi-khelaliyyot*).[46]

No single particular in and of itself constitutes the totality of the divine along the lines of the Leibnizian monad, but the aggregation of all the particulars is indexical of the universal. In Dov Baer's formulation, "When the meditation joins all the particulars to the universal, then the aspect of the universal is fixed more in the soul" (*ka'asher yithabber kol ha-iyyun mi-kol ha-peratim el ha-kelal az yuqba yoter ba-nefesh behinat ha-kelal*). The containment of all the particulars in the essence of the infinite signals the sustained enactment of the finite world rather than its eradication. By grasping that all differentiated being is considered as naught vis-à-vis the nondifferentiated essence of the divine light, one is awakened to the truth that the emptiness of being is the suchness of nonbeing, that the concealment of withdrawal (*histallequt*) is the disclosure of expansion (*hitpashshetut*), that existence is procured through the nullification of existence.[47] Only through contemplating that the somethingness of being emanates from and returns to the absolute

---

44. Schneersohn, *Ner Mitswah*, p. 222.
45. Ibid., p. 223. On the deepening of knowledge (*ha'amaqat ha-da'at*) and the contemplation of divinity (*hitbonenut elohut*), see Schneersohn, *Ma'amerei Admor ha-Emtsa'i: Quntresim*, p. 70.
46. Schneersohn, *Ner Mitswah*, p. 222.
47. Wolfson, *Open Secret*, pp. 109–114.

nothing (*ayin wa-efes muhlat*), one apprehends the nothingness at the core of one's being, which leads first to self-annihilation (*bittul ha-yesh*) and then to annihilation of existence (*bittul bi-metsi'ut*), which is the annihilation of the annihilation that heralds the transfiguration of the spatiotemporal reality such that it no longer conceals the essence beyond space and time.[48]

Conclusion

Our close textual analysis indicates that the idea of contemplation developed in Habad literature does provide a paradigm that is useful in addressing the question with which we began concerning the viability of the ideal of mystical ecstasy serving as a model for social perfection. From the Habad perspective, the attainment of this ideal is predicated on the need to uphold meticulously the particularity of the particulars, for the oneness of the universal being can be discerned only from the multiplicity of beings "all united and bound together in their thoroughgoing specificity in the essentiality of the infinite light" (*kullam meyuhadim u-mequsharim kol perateihem be-atsmiyyut or ein sof*). The specificity is not dissolved in the singularity of the essence; on the contrary, the differentiation is hidden in and constitutive of the universal unity (*yihud kelali*). Indeed, the union of the particular to the universal, which is the purpose of the contemplative practice, is realized by one attuned to the fact that every individual is contained in its irreducible individuality in the universal source (*maqor ha-kelali*).[49] The mystical task is to expand one's consciousness from the disintegrated unity of the particular to the integrated unity of the universal, the essentiality of the light of the infinite (*yimshokh nafsho le-yihud ha-perat el ha-yihud bi-khelal ad*

---

48. Ibid., pp. 75–76, 96, 112–113, 122–123, 139, 319 n. 50, 332 n. 58.
49. Schneersohn, *Ner Mitswah*, p. 230.

atsmiyyut or ein sof mammash),⁵⁰ but within that essence the universal is itself constituted by the particular, and hence the path of meditation that leads one to the universal is designated *hitbonenut she-marhiv bi-ferat*, contemplation that expands the particular.⁵¹ It is worth remembering that in his comments on the Maggid's tradition received from his father, Dov Baer emphasizes that immersion in and focus on the specific words of the prayers, when understood kabbalistically, enhances contemplation of the general.⁵² Consciousness can know the universal only through the particular, because universality is confabulated by particularity.

This theme, enunciated often by the seventh Rebbe, was linked especially to the idea that the ultimate purpose of the Torah is to reveal the simple unity of the infinite in the world, to provide a habitation for the divine below (*dirah ba-tahtonim*). This undertaking is allocated uniquely to the Jews, who through ritual purification become vessels for godliness in the material world. To become this vessel, however, it is not sufficient to focus only on the general; the worshipper must contemplate the proliferation of the details embodied in the labyrinth of the commandments.⁵³ An indissoluble nexus is thus forged between "the root of the matter of the incomposite unity above and the manner of the propagation of the plurality below."⁵⁴ Even though the essence is the simple unity (*ahdut ha-peshutah*) to which neither multi-

---

50. Ibid.
51. Ibid.
52. Ibid., p. 223.
53. Menahem Mendel Schneerson, *Torat Menahem: Hitwwaʿaduyyot 5724*, vol. 2 (Brooklyn, NY: Lahak Hanochos, 2008), p. 387. On the connection between self-annihilation and the performance of the commandments in Habad, see Elior, *The Paradoxical Ascent*, pp. 131–138; Moshe Idel, *Hasidism: Between Ecstasy and Magic* (Albany: State University of New York Press, 1995), pp. 123–124.
54. Schneerson, *Torat Menahem: Hitwwaʿaduyyot 5724*, vol. 2, p. 408. Compare Menahem Mendel Schneerson, *Liqqutei Sihot*, vol. 17 (Brooklyn, NY: Kehot, 2000), pp. 409–418, esp. 412.

plicity nor its opposite applies, the light of the infinite is a root for the division into diversity (*hithallequt ha-ribbuy*), and therefore the purification of Israel through ritual observance requires a plethora of acts to achieve the unity; the unity is facilitated and not obliterated by fragmentation.[55]

It behooves me to conclude by saying that the social-political usefulness of this paradigm depends very much on the possibility of transforming the ideal of ethnic particularity—the notion of chosenness or election—that is exceptionally inclusive to an ideal of exemplarity that is inclusively exceptional. The inclusion of the excluded in the traditional claim to exclusivity—and this extends even to the campaign of the seven Noahide laws—only renders the inclusivity even more exclusive.[56] One would be hard-pressed to rationalize or justify such a claim to exceptionality masked under the pretense of universality. But there is a surplus of meaning to be elicited from the Habad insight that the particularity is nullified and thereby affirmed through the particular. The path of the mystical experience voiced by the Habad masters leads out of its own specificity, but it does so in a manner that compels one to walk the path repeatedly to find the way out. If one envisions the possibility of abandoning the path definitively, then one is decidedly off the path and will never venture beyond the path.[57] In accord with the gnosis that has enlightened mystics in many religions and spiritual disciplines through the ages, we can say that to appreciate what is the same in the diverse traditions, one must be attentive to what is different, not because difference is a repetition of the same but because the same is a replication of difference. In my judgment, this wisdom can be elicited in its idiosyncratic way from the Habad understanding of contemplation. The question that is truly vital for the future is to figure out the strategy by which Habad can become

---

55. Schneerson, *Liqqutei Sihot*, vol. 17, pp. 413–414.
56. For a more extensive discussion, see Wolfson, *Open Secret*, pp. 224–264.
57. Elliot R. Wolfson, *Venturing Beyond: Law and Morality in Kabbalistic Mysticism* (Oxford: Oxford University Press, 2006), pp. 262–263.

the path that leads away from the path, that is, a path that is both paved and subverted by the very traversing of the path. I do not know how this will be accomplished, but I am quite sure that there can be no overcoming except by undergoing.

Chapter 4

HABAD HASIDISM AND THE MYSTICAL RECONSTRUCTION OF SOCIETY

Eli Rubin, University College London, Chabad.org

A New Theoretical Paradigm: The Socio-Mystical Constitution of Hasidic Phenomenology

Mystical experience is usually understood to belong intrinsically to the realm of the individual, to the private realm of consciousness and contemplation. Almost all studies of Jewish mysticism take this assumption as an unquestioned axiom and assume, accordingly, that it constitutes an inherent counterpoint to the realm of social interaction and real-world practice. It is partly for this reason that the modern movement of Hasidism has been such an object of fascination, both in scholarly literature and in popular culture. Hasidism—which took root in Eastern Europe in the latter part of the eighteenth century and is today especially vibrant in Israel and the United States—is enchanting to some and disturbing to others, precisely because it is simultaneously characterized by mystical spirituality and this-worldly exuberance; by elitist esoterism and exoteric populism; by the individualistic figure of the tzadik and the ideal of communal egalitarianism in collective life.

At the outset of Gershom Scholem's discussion of Hasidism in his *Major Trends in Jewish Mysticism*, he emphasizes the need "to consider...the social function of mystical ideas." Returning to this theme several pages later, he takes note of the "paradox" according to which the Hasidic leader, the tzadik, "felt the urge to perpetuate his mystical and solitary experience in the life of a community."¹ Both of these formulations harbor the axiomatic assumption that the coincidence of the mystical and the social is an anomaly, even an intriguing mystery. That subsequent generations of scholars found Scholem's phraseology compelling can be seen in the title of a pivotal conference held at University College London in 1988, "The Social Function of Mystical Ideals in Judaism: Hasidism Reappraised."²

In his recent book *Mystical Sociology: Toward Cosmic Social Theory*, Philip Wexler offers a substantive critique of Scholem's approach as set out in the latter's 1967 paper "Mysticism and Society."³ According to Wexler's reading, Scholem's analysis provides an account of five social dialectics, each of which describes the social context, the "conditions and influences," that provide a frame for mystical attainment. Scholem does not arrive at an understanding of the mystical constitution of mysticism, but preserves the original assumption that the gap between mysticism and the social is insurmountable and can only be understood in dialectical terms. As Wexler puts it, Scholem's account actually provides an unwitting "de-socialization" of mysticism that "obviates understanding mysticism as a *socially constituted process*, as *internally* social."⁴

---

1. Gershom Scholem, *Major Trends in Jewish Mysticism* (New York: Schocken, 1946), p. 327.
2. The proceedings were later published as Ada Rapoport-Albert (ed.), *Hasidism Reappraised* (Oxford: Littman Library of Jewish Civilization, 1996). See also Joseph Weiss, "Contemplation as Solitude," in *Studies in Eastern Jewish Mysticism and Hasidism* (Oxford: Littman Library of Jewish Civilization, 1997), paper ed., 132, on the novelty and "paradoxical nature" of "R. Israel Baalshem's...claim that *devekuth* was possible *precisely* among the trivialities of social intercourse." Though Weiss italicized the word "precisely," he did not unpack the intimation that social intercourse might indeed be conducive to mystical attainment.
3. *Diogenes* 15 (1967): 1–24.
4. Philip Wexler, *Mystical Sociology: Toward Cosmic Social Theory* (New York: Peter Lang, 2013), p. 92.

Against the prevailing approach, Wexler argues for a deeper exploration of "the social constitution of mystical phenomena," and further that we should look to Jewish mystical texts as an indigenous source of such sociological explanation. Hasidic teachings and practices, including those that are ostensibly mystical in orientation, "embody ideas about the social dynamics of everyday life" and "also a *theoretical* alternative to modern social theory."[5]

Wexler contextualizes his argument with Randall Collins' theorization of interaction ritual, which originates in the Durkheimian theory of religion. Collins argues that "we should not project the modern concept of the individualist" onto pre-modern "religious mystics [who] engaged in meditation or inward prayer," and asserts that "moments of inwardness...were not interpreted as being concerned with the self but with collective representations in the form of religious emblems."[6] In Wexler's language, this means that mystical experiences were socially constituted. To view the relationship between mysticism and society as antithetical or dialectical is therefore to wrongly impose on religious mysticism the distinctly modern conception of inwardness as anti-social individualism, as an introversion that one might describe as selfish in orientation. The inwardness that characterizes religious mysticism in its pre-modern form—which has arguably been sustained in modern Hasidism—should better be conceptualized as unselfish in orientation.

Taking this line of thinking even further, Wexler argues that Hasidism should no longer be reduced to the subject of the sociological gaze, and that Hasidism should instead be seen as a new resource for the human sciences, as a socio-mystical reservoir of antidotes to contemporary social challenges. In the classical sociological assessment, Wexler notes, "the failure to control...excessive individualism...is one of the major pathologies of modern society." Hasidism may offer a cure for these pathologies since it "proclaims,

---

5. *Ibid.*, pp. 53–69, 87–108.
6. Randall Collins, *Interaction Ritual Chains* (Princeton, NJ: Princeton University Press, 2004), pp. 356–357, 365–366.

analyzes, and embodies a model of social processes that is alternative to the ideology of modernity."[7]

Collins explicitly preserves the axiomatic divide between secular sociology and religious mysticism.[8] Wexler, in contrast, critiques that binary, advocating a "mystical sociology...disprivileging academic sociology and making mysticism into a...generative source of sociological explanation." Sociologists, he concludes, should be "taking mysticism seriously" as "indigenous" sociological knowledge. The "collective representations" described by the mystics should, according to Wexler, be seen as a legitimate source of sociological explanation, and one that has been almost entirely ignored by sociologists.[9]

When we heed Wexler's call and look to Hasidic texts for sociological content, the Durkheimian paradigm is turned on its head. Durkheim's reductionist "apotheosis" of society, according to which the deity and the society "are one and the same," might be described theologically as pantheistic in orientation, a materialization of the deity.[10] In Hasidism, by contrast, we find an *apophatic* apotheosis of society, according to which G-d is affirmed in society to the degree that society is transparent to, and thus effaced within, the divine source of social integrity. Theologically, this follows a model of "apophatic panentheism," a term coined by Catherine Keller and applied to Habad Hasidism by Elliot Wolfson, according to which "the One is affirmed in everything to the extent that everything is negated in relation to the One, but the

---

7. Wexler, *Mystical Sociology*, pp. 32–37, 56–57, 67–69. See also Naftali Loewenthal, "The Hasidic Ethos and the Schisms of Jewish Society," *Jewish History* 23 (2013): 377–398.

8. Collins, *Interaction Ritual Chains*, p. 33.

9. Wexler, *Mystical Sociology*, p. 102.

10. See Émile Durkheim, *The Elementary Forms of Religious Life*, trans. Karen E. Fields (New York: The Free Press, 1995), p. 208. Cf. Elliot R. Wolfson, *Open Secret: Postmessianic Messianism and the Mystical Revision of Menahem Mendel Schneerson* (New York: Columbia University Press, 2009), 150.

One is negated in relation to everything to the extent that everything is affirmed in the One."[11]

Wexler's general critique of previous scholarship on the social aspects of Hasidism can be fruitfully compared with Elliot Wolfson's sharper critique of the application of sociological and anthropological methodologies to the study of Habad Hasidism, and Habad messianism especially. Though Wolfson admits that such methodologies are "necessary to evaluate... the social evolution and changes to the sect," he insists that "they are hardly adequate to comprehend the phenomenological contours of the soteriology." In a statement that is crucial to much of his work on Habad, he concludes that "with respect to this movement... the phenomenological explains the historical, not the other way round."[12]

Unlike Wolfson, Wexler is first and foremost a sociologist. Yet he argues that taking Hasidic phenomenology seriously will yield new sociological insights. Taking the different methodological trajectories of Wexler and Wolfson together, we might suggest that the phenomenological contours of Hasidism, and especially of Habad Hasidism, are at once mystical and sociological in their constitution.

Foundational Teachings, Part 1: Mystical Union as the Deconstruction of Social Difference

Within the theoretical framework outlined above, we can cast a fresh eye on one of the best-known passages in the foundational text of

---

11. Wolfson, *Open Secret*, pp. 87–103; Catherine Keller, *The Face of the Deep: A Theology of Becoming* (New York: Routledge, 2003), p. 219. Cf. Eli Rubin, "'The Pen Shall Be Your Friend': Intertextuality, Intersociality, and the Cosmos—Examples of the Tzemach Tzedek's Way in the Development of Chabad Chassidic Thought" <chabad.org/3286179>, n. 49.
12. Elliot R. Wolfson, "Achronic Time, Messianic Expectation, and the Secret of the Leap in Habad," in Jonatan Meir and Gadi Sagiv (eds.), *Habad Hasidism: History, Thought, Image* (Jerusalem: The Zalman Shazar Center, 2016), p. 46*.

Habad Hasidism: Chapter 32 in Rabbi Schneur Zalman of Liadi's *Liqutei Amarim—Tanya*, published in 1796. In contemporary Habad it is often noted that the Hebrew representation of 32, **lamed-bet**, spells the word *lev*, meaning heart. Not only is this an apt association for a chapter dealing with love of one's fellow; it is also understood as signifying that this chapter embodies the very heart of *Liqutei Amarim* and, by extension, the very heart of all Habad teachings. The Seventh Rebbe of Habad, Rabbi Menachem M. Schneerson (1902–1994), linked this to the statement of Hillel: "What is hateful to you do not do to your fellow, this is the entirety of the Torah, and the rest is commentary."[13] From the Habad perspective, accordingly, Rabbi Schneur Zalman's teaching on interpersonal love in Chapter 32 of *Liqutei Amarim* constitutes the heart of the entire Torah.[14]

Wexler has already noted the relevance of this text to the general question of interpersonal love and its constitution.[15] It is my contention, however, that this chapter contains a full explication of how the mystical is constituted by the social, and of how the social is constituted by the mystical. Perhaps even more counterintuitive than this coincidence of the social and the mystical is its dependence on a contemplative practice that is explicitly ascetic in its theoretical orientation, if not necessarily in its practical implications. This contemplative practice, designed as a means to overcome bitterness and depression arising from personal failures, is more fully described in Chapter 31:

> This you shall settle in your heart... saying to your heart: "Yes, it is correct, without doubt, that I am ultimately very far from G-d, and despised and despicable. Yet, all this is on the part of myself alone, that is to say, the body with the vivifying soul that is in it. Nevertheless, there is within

---

13. Talmud Bavli, Shabbat, 31a.
14. Rabbi Menachem M. Schneerson, *Torat Menachem—Hitvaduyot 5747*, Vol. 2 (New York: Lahak Hanochos, 1998), p. 75.
15. Wexler, *Mystical Sociology*, pp. 67–69.

> me a literal part of G-d that is even present in a *qal she-be-qalim* [a representative of society at its most vacuous and frivolous], which is a divine soul, with a literal spark of G-d vested in it to give it life, only that it is in a state of exile.... Therefore, I shall direct all my aim and desire to extricate her and raise her up from this exile... [that] she shall be encompassed and united with G-d, blessed-be-He when I direct all my aim into Torah and the commandments...." This shall be your work all your days with great joy, that is to say, the joy of the soul in its exodus from the despicable body, and in its return to her father's house as in her youth... in action, speech and thought of Torah....[16]

While acknowledging the truth of one's bodily failures, one can nevertheless achieve joy through a conscious bifurcation of the G-dly soul from the body. In Chapter 32, Rabbi Schneur Zalman continues to explain that this forms the basis for

> a direct and easy way to approach and fulfill the commandment to love your fellow as yourself.... Since your body is contemptible on your part, and the soul and spirit who knows their greatness and loftiness in their root and source in the living G-d, and moreover, they are all alike, and there is one father to all of them.... Only that their bodies are divided, and therefore those who make their bodies primary and their souls secondary cannot possibly have true love and comradeship between them, but only [love] that is contingent on something else.[17]

The mystical sense of the soul's liberation from bodily constraint brings the individual to overlook the bodily shortcomings of the

---

16. Rabbi Schneur Zalman of Liadi, *Tanya* (Vilna: The Widow and Brothers Romm, 1900), 40a–40b.
17. *Ibid.*, p. 41a.

other and to consider the shared root of self and other in the one G-d. This leads the individual to the realization that all divisions among people result from bodily incarnation, which gives rise to a set of external constructs that obscure the true reality of our collective identity. To see the body as a facade is to see that the incarnate souls are in truth united in their singular root, the living G-d.

In direct continuation to this passage, Rabbi Schneur Zalman cites the aforementioned saying of Hillel, explaining that the reason why love of one's fellow is the entirety of the Torah is that "the foundation and root of the entire Torah" is directed toward two ends: first, "to raise the soul over the body... to the trunk and root of all worlds" wherein they are encompassed alike, and second, "to draw the infinite revelation of G-d (*ohr ain sof barukh hu*) into collective Israel (*kenesset yisrael*)... that is to say, into the source of the souls of all Israel, making one in one, which cannot occur when there is divisiveness among them." The one G-d, in other words, only dwells within a people who are one.

The foundation and root of the entire Torah, it emerges, is the synonymous attainment of mystical union and social harmony. In the theoretical terms outlined above: The phenomenological contours of mystical union are socially constituted as the collective union of all souls within their divine root.

Here it is worth noting Collins's distinction between the social construction of mystical experience, on the one hand, and the stripping away of "meanings already constructed," on the other.[18] The locus of spiritual work described by Rabbi Schneur Zalman, it can be argued, does not lie in constructing an internal experience of mystical ascent, but rather in stripping away the false impression accrued through bodily incarnation and experience, thereby rediscovering the soul's axiomatic state of union.

Earlier, in Chapter 30, Rabbi Schneur Zalman prescribes a contemplative strategy that cultivates a stance of humility even in relation to a *qal she-be-qalim*, the most vacuous and frivolous of

---

18. Collins, *Interaction Ritual Chains*, p. 378.

individuals. This is another example of this sort of stripping away, or deconstruction, not only of *bodily* perceptions, but also of accrued *social* constructions:

> This is in accord with the saying of the sages, "don't judge your fellow until you reach his place," for it is his place that causes him to sin, that his livelihood is earned by going to the marketplace each day, to be one of those who sit on the street corners, where his eyes behold all temptations, and the eye sees, and the heart desires, and his inclination burns like a fanned fiery furnace... which is not the case with one who goes to the marketplace infrequently.

It is social circumstance, in other words, that is often the key factor in constructing both our worldly interactions and our inner experiences. It is these external social constructions that create a facade of difference between one individual and another, and thereby we are led into the trap of judgmentalism and self-righteousness. When these external constructs are stripped away, a more egalitarian view of moral status can emerge. Rather than judge the other by their behavior, Rabbi Schneur Zalman instructs us to meditate on the

> great and awesome battle to shatter the [bad] inclination that burns like flaming fire, through fear of G-d.... Each person, according to his own place and station in the service of G-d, must weigh and test himself, whether he is in service of G-d according to the measure and aspect of such an awesome battle as this....

One who is in a position to know what service of G-d demands, and possesses the knowledge and capacity to overcome other inclinations, yet does not invest comparable effort to "battle and overcome... according to the measure and aspect of the aforementioned awesome battle" must realize that "his sin is greater, doubled and redoubled... in comparison to that of the *qal she-be-qalim*... who is far from G-d."[19]

Foundational Teachings, Part 2: Deconstructing the Boundaries of Love

The centrality of Rabbi Schneur Zalman's teachings on interpersonal love and unity was especially underscored by the Seventh Rebbe, who devoted countless talks to elaborations on this theme and its practical applications. The following is an extract from a talk he gave in 1951, the self-described "statement" that he offered when he publicly accepted the leadership of Habad-Lubavitch:

> The first thing people want to hear is a statement, and the procedure is that it must contain something innovative, something provocative. I don't know if this is provocative, but if you want to hear a statement, the Rebbe said that there are three things: There is love of G-d, and there is love of Torah, and there is love of the Jewish people, and these three things are all one. This means that it is impossible to distinguish between one and the other, for they are all one, as a single essence... [and] when one grasps hold of something that is a part of the essence one grasps the essence in its entirety.... Accordingly, everyone must know that when you grasp hold of love of G-d, one cannot make do with that, and one cannot grasp hold of that if you don't also grasp hold of love of the Torah and love of the Jewish people. But, on the other hand... if we begin with love of the Jewish people, which is ostensibly a logical commandment, one will eventually achieve love of Torah and love of G-d.... One must also see to it that one's love of the Jewish people should not only be constituted in giving

---

19. Rabbi Schneur Zalman of Liadi, *Tanya*, 38a–39a.

food to the hungry and water to the thirsty, but also...in bringing Jews to love of Torah and love of G-d.[20]

Later in the same evening, he explicated the activist implications of this triadic vision:

> This is demanded of every one of us...to know that one's entire purpose is...in emulation of Abraham, our forefather, who when arriving in a place where they didn't know of G-dliness, didn't know of Judaism...put himself aside.... One must see to it that such people shall shout "G-d world" (*el olam*)...that G-dliness and the world are one.[21]

Love of G-d alone, it is implied, may actually be a mask for selfish and unholy spiritualism or religiosity. Love of the Jewish people, on the other hand, provides an unselfish basis upon which an all-encompassing union with G-d can eventually be built.

The locution "love of the Jewish people," *ahavat yisrael*, follows the traditional *halakhic* position that the commandment to "love your fellow as yourself" applies only to "your fellow in Torah and the commandments."[22] But this should not lead us to the default position that its principles apply, from the Habad perspective, only to the Jewish people. We should first note that the exclusionary implication of "your fellow" is specifically extended by the *halakhah* to disqualify a Jewish sinner, who is rather to be hated.[23] Yet Rabbi Schneur Zalman sharply qualifies this mandate of hatred, concluding that "even those who are far from G-d and His service, and are therefore

---

20. See *Sihot Qodesh 5711* (New York, 1985), p. 123.
21. Rabbi Menachem M. Schneerson, *Torat Menachem—Sefer Ha-mamarim Meluket*, Vol. 2 (New York: Lahak Hanachos, 2002), p. 270, following the Talmudic gloss to Genesis, 21:33, in Tractate Sotah, folio 10.
22. Maimonides, Mishneh Torah, Hilchot Aval, 14:1; Hilchot Deot, 6:34.
23. Maimonides, Mishneh Torah, Hilchot Rotse'ah, 13:14.

called by the designation 'creatures' alone, we must draw with strong cords of love, and thereby one might be able to bring them close to Torah and service of G-d, and if not, you have not thrown away the reward for the commandment to love your fellow...."[24]

Elliot Wolfson has already devoted an extensive and important study to Habad's discourse of exclusion and inclusion, of difference and the overcoming of difference, between Jew and non-Jew, focusing especially on the teachings of the Seventh Rebbe. Despite the complexities, and indeed the problems, that Wolfson unearths, he concludes that from a "relatively early date, the Seventh Rebbe was pondering the manner in which non-Jews can participate in the holiness attributed to Jews" and that "this vision only intensified in the years of his leadership."[25] Accordingly, the Seventh Rebbe often affirmed that non-Jews, too, have a spark of G-d within their souls, even while maintaining that the spark that is within the Jewish soul is of a more transcendent quality.[26]

This principle also has strong precedent in a well-known text by Rabbi Schneur Zalman in which he defends a teaching attributed

---

24. Rabbi Schneur Zalman of Liadi, *Tanya*, 41a–b.
25. Wolfson, *Open Secret*, pp. 224–264.
26. For some examples, see Rabbi Menachem M. Schneerson, *Torat Menachem—Hitvaduyot 5720* (New York: Lahak Hanachos, 2004), p. 401; Idem., *Torat Menachem—Hitvaduyot 5744*, Vol. 4 (New York: Lahak Hanachos, 1990), p. 2308; Idem., *Liqutei Sihot*, Vol. 21 (New York: Kehot Publication Society, 1983), p. 107. Especially relevant to the present discussion is the formulation in the last of these sources: "The giving of the Torah effectuated...also on the part of noahides [i.e., non-Jews], that they too shall awaken to the divine power that is vested within them—and thereby...a certain element of unity will also be effectuated in them, *analogous* to the unity of the Jewish people (but not literally so...)" (emphasis in original). In this source it is also emphasized that non-Jews, too, can "awaken to an element of divinity that entirely transcends the realms...[and] intellect...," thereby attaining "the true unity 'as one man.'" This references Rashi's comment to Exodus, 19:2, which describes the Jewish people's encampment "as one man with one heart" at the foot of Mt. Sinai. In expanding this formulation to include non-Jews, the Seventh Rebbe implies that the unity of the Jewish people is expanded to include all people.

to the Baal Shem Tov to the effect that there is a spark of the supernal word of G-d vested even in the words of an idol worshipper who is attempting to disturb the prayer of a Jew. As Rabbi Schneur Zalman continues to say, we cannot evade the simple meaning of the verse, "the heavens and the earth I fill, says the Lord."[27] There is nothing that is not filled with the indwelling of G-d, nothing that is not encompassed in our shared and singular root. The differences are constructs of corporeal division, and they depend on the exile of the *shekhinah* herself within the unfolding of creation.[28]

The Seventh Rebbe, in a 1986 talk, made the case that "all aspects of Torah" that are relevant to the settlement of the earth and the civilization of society apply to non-Jews as well as to Jews. The benchmark for this category, he argues, is that the precept be "understandable and mandated by human intellect." This, he emphasizes, applies even to commandments that are not explicitly included in *halakhic* discussions of the seven noahide laws that apply to humanity universally.[29] This offers a *halakhic* opening, and not merely a spiritual one, for the universal expansion of the commandment to love your fellow as yourself, since it is one that can logically be understood to advance the social good. In the words of the popular medieval code of the commandments, *Sefer Ha-hinukh*: "The root of this commandment is known, for as one does to his fellow so his fellow will do to him, and thereby there shall be peace among creatures."[30]

The Habad texts cited above endow this commandment with far greater spiritual and theoretical import, but the *Sefer Ha-hinukh*'s formulation remains foundational. We are all creatures of G-d,

---

27. Jeremiah, 23:24.
28. Rabbi Schneur Zalman of Liadi, *Tanya—Igeret Ha-qodesh*, Epistle 25, 138a–142a.
29. Rabbi Menachem M. Schneerson, *Torat Menachem—Hitvaduyot 5746*, Vol. 4 (New York: Lahak Hanochos, 1990), p. 254. See also Idem., *Liqutei Sihot*, Vol. 38 (New York: Kehot Publication Society, 1999), p. 28.
30. *Sefer Ha-hinukh*, Commandment #243.

and it is only via that recognition that we can attain the universal union foreseen by the prophet, and often cited in Hasidic literature: "Then I will transform the peoples to a pure language, that all of them shall call on the name of the Lord, to worship Him of one accord."[31]

Life and Practice, Part 1: Prayer, Charity, and the Reconstruction of Society

In its first generation, Habad's socio-mystical ethos was principally given expression through prayer and charity, which are often linked together via the Talmudic adage that "Man gives a coin to a pauper and merits to receive the revealed indwelling of G-d (*pnei ha-shekhinah*).... Rabbi Eliezer would give a coin to a pauper and afterward would pray."[32]

A prayer technique described in a teaching by Rabbi Schneur Zalman expands on this theme and relies on the bifurcation of the G-dly soul from the body and the resulting emergence of a collective consciousness, strongly echoing our earlier discussion of Chapters 31 and 32 of *Liqutei Amarim—Tanya*:

> When you have separated yourself from your fellow via any separation, that is, you have disconnected your heart and will from him, from one of his issues, concerns, and emotions, or from his intellect and service in matters of heaven, in Torah and prayer...you are missing an organ in the intention of your own heart.... Therefore, when you pray you shall resolve in your heart that it is not the body or the animal soul that prays. Rather, it is "the

---

31. Tsfanyah, 3:9. See also Shaul Magid, *Hasidism Incarnate* (Stanford, CA: Stanford University Press, 2015), pp. 62–66; Eli Rubin, "The Pen Shall Be Your Friend," n. 69.
32. Talmud Bavli, Bava Batra, 10a.

part of G-d above" that prays, speaking within you the words of prayer.... When you resolve so and actualize this form of worship it is called receiving the revealed indwelling of G-d, meaning that the service of collective Israel (*kenesset yisrael*), which pleads and throws herself before G-d, is called the revealed indwelling of G-d....[33]

In prayer, one must raise the soul above the body, thereby becoming transparent to the collective song of all souls as they are encompassed in their divine root. Mystical attainment in prayer depends upon the attainment of an inclusive collective identity and an intellectual and affective state of social harmony.

To read this as a replacement of real social action with an internal contemplative practice that is merely orientated to the social would be to tear prayer from its broader context in the life and practice of Habad. Jonathan Garb has observed that the climax of prayer in Habad is the somatic prostration of the body in the *nefilat apayim* prayer, when "both body and soul are 'totally included in union with G-d.'"[34] Moreover, prayer is consistently framed as the spiritual foundation that inspires divine service throughout the day. Witness *Liqutei Amarim—Tanya*, Chapter 42:

> When you contemplate this for a great while each day, how G-d literally fills the upper and lower realms, and the heavens and the earth literally... the awe shall be fixed in your heart for the entire day completely when you return to think of this even in momentary contemplation, [and] at every time and every instant you will avoid evil and do good in thought, speech and action,

---

33. Rabbi Schneur Zalman of Liadi, *Liqutei Torah, Shir Ha-shirim*, 45c–d.
34. Jonathan Garb, *Shamanic Trance in Modern Kabbalah* (Chicago and London: University of Chicago Press, 2011), pp. 80–81, citing Rabbi Schneur Zalman of Liadi, *Commentary on the Prayerbook* (New York: Kehot Publication Society, 1986), 26a.

so as not to rebel, G-d forbid, in the sight of His glory, which fills the entirety of the earth.[35]

Habad's path may accordingly be described as an "innerworldly mysticism" that reconstructs the social transactions of daily life—in thought, speech, and action—as the mystical task of maintaining cosmic union.[36]

The centrality of social practice in early Habad is further evidenced by the public letters issued by Rabbi Schneur Zalman of Liadi on a roughly annual basis, reminding the diaspora Hasidim of their charitable obligation to their brethren in the Holy Land. In one example, Rabbi Schneur Zalman begins by describing a contemplative technique designed to inspire the individual to have compassion "on the spark of the divine in his soul, which is distant from the luminosity of G-d's countenance when it journeys in the darkness and vanities of the world." The purpose of cultivating this sense of compassion is that the individual will thereby be inspired with love and awe before G-d, who shields the divine spark of the soul. Crucially, however, Rabbi Schneur Zalman also emphasizes the inadequacy of love and awe generated through such contemplation, and contrasts it with the superior love and awe that "comes from above as a gift":

> Certainly there is no comparison at all between the former, which are the product of the intellect of a creation, and the latter, which are from the Creator, blessed be His name. Therefore, it is specifically the latter that are described as "true," for the seal of G-d is truth, for He is the perfect truth (*emet ha-amiti*), and all the truth of

---

35. Rabbi Schneur Zalman of Liadi, *Tanya*, 60b.
36. Cf. Idem., *Torah Ohr*, 9c–10b: "Every action that one executes throughout the day, whether in eating or even in Torah study, is raised up in prayer...." On the Weberian concept of "innerworldly mysticism" and its manifestation in Hasidism, see Wexler, *Mystical Sociology*, pp. 157–158.

> the creations is as nothing in comparison. But what then is the path that a person shall merit the truth of G-d? This is achieved through arousing great compassion before G-d on the spark of G-d in his soul.... However, the arousal of great compassion before G-d must also be through truth. But even if it is his personal truth, how can his personal truth arouse supernal compassion from G-d's truth? The solution to this is the quality of charity, which is the quality of compassion for one who has nothing of their own, to rejuvenate the spirit of the abject etc. And the arousal from below elicits an arousal from above... to bring great compassion and supernal kindness from concealment to revelation... to illuminate with the light of life, the truth of G-d....[37]

Charitable social practice, it transpires, is the only path to the attainment of perfect, G-dly truth. The contemplative process stamps one's charitable actions with integrity. At the same time, "personal truth" can only be stamped with the seal of divine truth when it spills over into real charitable activity in the concrete social realm.

Life and Practice, Part 2: Physicality, Kindness, and the Realization of Essential Truth

Turning again to the Seventh Rebbe, we find further interplay among questions of truth, spirituality, and the realities of social life. In one characteristic example, he offers a novel reading of an abrupt and cryptic passage said to have been penned by Rabbi Schneur Zalman shortly before his passing. Here is the relevant excerpt:

> The vocation of the soul that is, in its root, lowly in perfect truth, is physical Torah, whether for herself or (to

---

37. *Tanya—Igeret Ha-qodesh*, Epistle 6, 110b–111a.

> provide understanding) for others, and whether in doing physical kindness through bringing minds closer (*qiruv ha-daat*) and [offering] solutions from afar in all household affairs. Though most of them are falsehoods it is impossible that it be otherwise, that you should do true kindness, for there is no truth other than Torah, and truth said do not create (for it is full of falsehoods) etc., and kindness said create for it is full of kindnesses, and truth was sent to the ground and the world was built with kindness that is not of truth....[38]

Here the truth of Torah is set in opposition to the physical kindnesses that are so necessary for the peaceful negotiation of life's mundanities. Perhaps surprisingly, it is the latter that Rabbi Schneur Zalman champions, even at the apparent expense of the former.

The Seventh Rebbe, however, deconstructs this binary opposition altogether. He does so by distinguishing between *the circumscribed measure of divine truth*, on the one hand, and *the infinite truth of G-d's essence*, on the other:

> The measure of truth... reaches only the place where its (divine) truth is recognizable; and because this world is a world of falsehood, where the truth of G-d is not recognizable, therefore "truth said do not create." But the infinite truth of G-d's essence has no constraint. This truth is not circumscribed by the need for G-d's truth to be recognizable. For even in a place of hiding and concealment, even including such a concealment that

---

[38]. This passage is known by its opening words, "*Nefesh Ha-shefeilah*." For details of its text, publication history, its context within the history of Rabbi Schneur Zalman's life and ideas, and its reception in later Habad literature, see Yehoshua Mondshine, *Hamasa Ha-aharon* (Jerusalem: Knizhniki Publishing Houses, 2012), pp. 158–165, 236–246.

appears to be a falsehood... in truth and its interiority its entire existence... is the truth of the essence.[39]

Here the Seventh Rebbe cites Maimonides' statement that "all the beings... do not exist *except* by virtue of G-d's true being."[40] The being of physical creation, he emphasizes, is nothing more and nothing less than a manifestation of the true being of G-d's essential self. The requirement to immerse oneself in kindness, in household transactions and worldly negotiations, is accordingly not an abrogation of Torah's truth. It is rather a call to engage in the socio-mystical reconstruction of reality, a call to realize that— in their essence—the world and G-d are one.

"Doing physical kindness through bringing minds closer (*qiruv ha-daat*) and [offering] solutions from afar in all household affairs" is a phrase authored by Rabbi Schneur Zalman of Liadi, and yet it aptly describes the work of Habad emissaries today. Habad emissaries are certainly providers of religious services, working as rabbis, teachers, kashrut supervisors, and so forth. But first and foremost they are builders of communities, pastoral carers who nourish their constituents spiritually and physically, mentally and emotionally. They enfold the households of their communities within their own households, and—especially in the case of Habad on Campus— create homes for people who are "away from home."[41]

Just as Habad's contemplative practice cannot be reduced to individual mystical activity, so Habad's communal work cannot

---

39. Rabbi Menachem M. Schneerson, *Liqutei Sihot*, Vol. 16 (New York: Kehot Publication Society, 1980), pp. 43–44.
40. Maimonides, *Mishneh Torah*, Yesodai Hatorah, 1:1.
41. See the Chabad on Campus "About" page <http://www.chabad.edu/templates/articlecco_cdo/aid/387553>: "Chabad seeks to be a 'home away from home' for Jews on Campus." See also Barry Chazan and David Bryfman, *Home Away from Home—A Research Study of the Shabbos Experience on Five University Campuses: An Informal Educational Model for Working with Young Jewish Adults*, Chabad on Campus International Foundation, August 2006 <http://www.bjpa.org/Publications/details.cfm?PublicationID=3623>.

be reduced to social activity. The communal activism of contemporary Habad is inspired and driven by the socio-mystical teachings explicated in the texts and teachings described above. Habad emissaries—and lay people, too—are schooled in these texts and life-practices from their earliest youth, and most maintain a regimen of daily *Tanya* study throughout their lives. Contemporary Habad activism is, in fact, the culmination and realization of an intellectual tradition of great depth and breadth, at the heart of which stands the fundamental axiom that the mystical and the social are one and the same.

Section II

HABAD IN THEORY AND PRACTICE

Chapter 5

CHASSIDIC PRAYER AND SOCIETY

*Naftali Loewenthal, University College
London (London University)*

In this chapter we pose the question of the possible relevance of Chassidic teachings on prayer for the contemporary Chassidic community, for wider Jewish society beyond the Chassidic community, and for society as a whole.

Chabad Contemplation

Let us outline the principal ideas about Chabad contemplation by considering a basic text that provides material for contemplation: Rabbi Shneur Zalman of Liadi's *Tanya* Part 2, entitled *Gate of Unity and Faith*. This work was first printed in 1796, although prior to that time it had been circulating in manuscript form for several years.[1] (There are certain differences between the earlier manuscript version and the printed book, which we will consider

---

1. This book was first published with the title *Likkutei Amarim* (Slavuta, 1796); the title *Tanya* was used in the second edition (Zolkiew, 1799). The standard edition is that of Vilna, 1900. Our references will be to a reprint of this (Brooklyn: Kehot Publication Society, 1984). The original manuscript version has been published by S.B. Levine, *Likkutei Amarim: Mahadura Kama (mi-kitvei yad)* (Brooklyn: Kehot Publication Society, 1982). An annotated English translation of the second section, *Shaar ha-Yihud ve-ha-Emunah* (*Gate of Unity and Faith*), by R. Nisen Mangel, was published in Brooklyn in 1965 and is included in the Soncino edition of *Likkutei-Amarim–Tanya* (London: Soncino Press, 1973).

below.) The context for the contemplative system it expresses can be understood as Maimonides' statement at the beginning of his *Mishneh Torah*: the basis of everything is the existence of G-d, and the individual should seek to feel love and awe of G-d[2]—"you should love the L-rd your G-d" (Deut. 6:5, 11:1), and "you should fear the L-rd your G-d" (Deut. 6:13, 10:20). For Maimonides, the key to feeling such love and awe is contemplation, and, as many have pointed out,[3] Rabbi Shneur Zalman's system builds on a basis of Maimonidean thought.

Introduction to Gate of Unity and Faith

Rabbi Shneur Zalman's teachings on gaining inspiration are written in the general framework of the Chassidic movement founded by Rabbi Yisrael Baal Shem Tov (1698–1760). One of Elie Wiesel's books about Chassidism is called *Souls on Fire*,[4] and this beautiful phrase describes the "naturally inspired" person, sometimes called the Tzaddik, the person who doesn't need to "contemplate" in order to feel love of the Divine. He or she feels it burning within the heart by default, as soon as they open their eyes in the morning, or even while they sleep.

But Rabbi Shneur Zalman's quest was to make the Baal Shem Tov's teachings meaningful to a person who wasn't a "soul on fire." His introduction to *Gate of Unity and Faith* makes this clear. The naturally inspired person, whom we are calling the "soul on fire," doesn't usually need a system of contemplation to arouse his or her

---

2. Laws of the Foundation of the Torah, 1:1 and 2:1.
3. See Roman A. Foxbrunner, *Chabad, the Hasidism of R. Shneur Zalman of Lyady* (Tuscaloosa and London: University of Alabama Press, 1992), p. 178. Foxbrunner cites *Mishneh Torah*, Hil. Yesodei HaTorah 2:1–2, Hil. Teshuvah ch. 10, *Guide*, I 39, III 28, 44, and especially 51; *Sefer HaMitzvot* Positive Commandments 3–5; Mishnah Commentary, Avot I:5.
4. Elie Wiesel, *Souls on Fire: Portraits and Legends of Hasidic Masters* (New York: Vintage Books, 1972).

heart, but others do, and his tract is written for those others, the non-Tzaddik. At the same time, he explains, sometimes even the Tzaddik falls to a lower level, and the inner flame is temporarily hidden. Then he or she,[5] too, could benefit from the contemplative system described in *Gate of Unity and Faith*.

The first chapter quotes a scriptural verse that speaks of meditating in one's heart that the L-rd is G-d in the heavens above and the earth beneath; "there is nothing else" (Deut. 4:39).[6] What is there to *meditate* on, asks the author. One believes in one G-d; isn't that a straightforward concept? This question opens the door to outlining a step-by-step process of thought in which one comes to realize not only that there is only one G-d, but that there is *only* G-d; that "there is nothing else," *eyn od,* means simply that: G-d is all.

The first stage in this process is the idea that the Divine Creation of the universe was not a single event, but rather an ongoing process in the present. Citing the Baal Shem Tov's reiteration of a concept in the Midrash,[7] Rabbi Shneur Zalman explains that G-d's words "let there be a firmament" (Gen. 1:6) not only created the firmaments (which we can understand as levels of "heaven," the basic framework of the universe) at the beginning of creation, but also continue to maintain their existence into the present. Conceiving Divine creative energy as a stream of Hebrew letters, the words "let there be a firmament" continue to flow from the Divine and keep the firmaments in existence at this moment. If this stream of Divine energy were to cease, then the firmaments (and the universe as we conceive it) would disappear. We could imagine this as the force of

---

5. In historical terms, there is no indication that Rabbi Shneur Zalman expected his tract to be utilized by women for contemplation, although there is a tradition that he taught Chassidic teachings to his daughter Freida. However, in the contemporary context, many women and girls study *Tanya* and are able to use its teachings on contemplation to heighten their own sense of inspired contact with the Divine. Hence I feel it appropriate to employ gender-inclusive phrasing.
6. This verse is included in the *Aleinu* Prayer.
7. *Midrash Tehilim* to Psalm 119:89.

an electric current that initiates and maintains a complex system of lighting. If the electricity stops, the lights go out.

Rabbi Shneur Zalman elaborates that this idea includes not only the mystical firmaments, but everything in existence, from the highest of the kabbalistic "worlds" to our low physical world, in all its details, down to an inanimate stone. Every object—large or small, the sun in the sky or a pebble in the garden—is kept in existence by a stream of Divine energy, which is expressed in the Hebrew letters of the words that give them being. Rabbi Shneur Zalman presents a conceptual system based on the early mystical work *Book of Creation*,[8] whereby the relatively brief text of the Ten Divine Utterances in Genesis 1 that initially created the universe[9] becomes the source for the continued being of all existence, through a process of substitution and "transformation" whereby one letter is substituted for another. Thus, the entire dictionary of the sacred tongue, Hebrew, can be generated from the Ten Utterances. The highest level of energy is in the Ten Utterances themselves, which give existence to grand phenomena such as the sea and the dry land, the sun, the moon, and the stars. The transposed letters, and even lower—*gematriot*—words with numerical affinity are sources of milder forms of energy, giving life to the smaller details of the world. Rabbi Shneur Zalman tells us, citing Rabbi Isaac Luria, that because of this flow of Divine energy, everything, even an inanimate object such as a stone, has a "soul," and this is none other than the spiritual energy expressed in the Hebrew name for that object.

This is an interesting way of understanding the significance of the Hebrew language. We could compare it to the chemical formula for a substance. Common salt is called, variously, salt, du sel, Saltz, and so on. But the chemical formula NaCl is the true chemical "identity" of salt. In the same way, the Hebrew word for salt, מלח, is the spiritual identity of salt.

---

8. For an English version, see Aryeh Kaplan, *Sefer Yetzirah, the Book of Creation, in Theory and Practice* (York Beach, ME: S. Weiser, 1997).
9. Ethics 5:1. There are actually only nine, but "In the beginning" is also to be counted as an Utterance (TB Rosh Hashanah 32a).

This first chapter of *Gate of Unity and Faith* thus presents us with a way of looking at the world in which we are in a continuum of spiritual energy, expressed as the sacred Hebrew letters and words, emanating through myriad graded transpositions from the Ten Utterances of Creation.

The second chapter builds on this by making us aware that, since every particle of existence is continuously kept in existence by a Divine flow of energy, there is nothing surprising about miracles. At any moment the flow of energy can change, altering the reality around us. A further image in this chapter links the stream of Divine energy, packaged as "letters," creating existence, with the stream of energy entering the mind of a prophet, which he or she expresses as Divine teaching. The effect of this image is to draw the various texts of the Torah into the continuum of streams of sacred Hebrew letters. Bearing in mind that we are reading this tract in relation to contemplation in prayer, we see the individual seeing himself or herself as surrounded by Divine energy, whether in the form of the tree seen through the window, the furniture in the room (whether the kitchen at home, or the sanctum of a synagogue), and also the texts in the Prayer Book in one's hand.

A further contemplative step is presented in Chapter Three. If all reality is created, activated, and kept in existence by Divine energy, asks the author, what in effect is really there? The bookcase, or G-d? The tree, or G-d? The house, or G-d? Rabbi Shneur Zalman leads the reader through a beautiful mental exercise involving the nullification of a sunbeam in the body of the sun, whereby he or she discovers that the only reality is G-d.[10] In fact, the chapter ends with the puzzle of why we see the world as existing and, even more,

---

10. The sunbeam, visible to us on a summer afternoon, represents existence. The body of the sun represents the Divine energy that is the source of that existence. If we consider the sunbeam in its source, it is nullified. There is no sunbeam, only the sun. Now, we see the sunbeam, because the sun itself is at a great distance from the earth. But when we consider the relationship between existence and its Divine source, we see that unlike the case of the sunbeam and the distant sun, existence is totally immersed in its Divine

the age-old kabbalistic puzzle of how anything *can* in any way exist, in the face of the Infinite radiance of the Divine.[11] At this point, for the reader—אין עוד מלבדו—there is nothing apart from Him: the radiant oneness of G-d is all and everything.

We can suggest that these opening chapters of *Gate of Unity and Faith* provide a simple contemplative system that can easily be used in prayer, or in going for a walk, whether through a quiet and lonely forest or in the hubbub of a crowded city center. Does it need adaptation to make it more useful to people of our time? It is interesting that the other-worldly focus I have presented was the theme of the manuscript version of *Gate of Unity and Faith*, possibly written around 1793. When the author prepared this for publication in 1796, he subtly changed the focus. The first version simply reaches beyond the world, toward the Oneness of the Divine in a great acosmic leap: there is no world, only G-d.

For the printed version, Rabbi Shneur Zalman added a second stage to the contemplative process, in which one recognizes that there is a world, but it is (or can be) imbued with G-dliness. He called the first stage the Upper Unity, expressed in the first line of the Shema, said with one's hand covering one's eyes: "Hear o Israel, the L-rd is G-d, the L-rd is One." There is *only* G-d, nothing else, אין עוד. But the second line of the Shema ("blessed be the Name of the Glory of His Kingship for ever") expresses the Lower Unity: the idea that there is a real world with all its practicalities, challenges, and temptations, and in this world the Divine radiance is hidden just beneath the surface, waiting to be revealed.[12]

---

    source, which is omnipresent. How, then, do we perceive a universe at all? Surely, all is simply One, the oneness of the Divine.

11. The question is answered in Chapter Four by explaining the concept of *Tzimtzum*, the "veiling" of the Divine, which permits the worlds to exist.
12. An introductory paragraph at the beginning of the version printed in 1796 (and subsequently) quotes Zohar I 18b, where the terms "Higher Unity" and "Lower Unity" are employed with reference to the Shema prayer (Tanya fol. 66b). The earlier manuscript versions omit this passage and also lack a long section of chs. 6–7 in which this concept is elaborated upon. The manuscript

In the section of Chapter Seven added for the printed edition, Rabbi Shneur Zalman presents the two stages of this contemplative process in terms of the confluence of the Sefirot, the Divine attributes, and also in terms of the interleaving of two Divine Names. To summarize this very briefly: the physical universe exists by virtue of the Divine Attribute "Kingship." If Kingship is absorbed above, among the higher Sefirot, it and the worlds dependent on it are nullified, and one's consciousness adopts the Higher Unity perspective. But if Kingship is again considered to be in its normal "place" as the lowest Sefirah, absorbing the spiritual radiance from above and giving life to the worlds below, then one moves to the Lower Unity perspective.

As mentioned above, Rabbi Shneur Zalman also presents this in terms of Divine Names: The Name A-D-N-Y represents Kingship, while the Tetragrammaton expresses the higher spiritual realms. Rabbi Shneur Zalman explains that the two names can be interleaved in such a way that the Y of the Tetragrammaton is dominant as the initial letter of the interleaved Name, expressing the Higher Unity (Y-A-H-D-V-N-H-Y). Taking this acosmist perspective, there is no world, only G-d. Then, in the second mode, with the A of A-D-N-Y being dominant as the initial letter (A-Y-D-H-N-V-Y-H), the Lower Unity is expressed, with its implication that all aspects of daily life, guided by the Torah and its laws, can become a means of discovering the Divine.

The personal effect of such teachings can be seen in the first part of *Tanya*, Chapter 3, which describes the intense love and awe of the Divine that proceed from one's mental perception of G-d's immanence, and also His transcendence, as expressed in Chabad Chassidic teachings. This passage closely parallels Maimonides' Laws of the Foundation of the Torah 2:1–2, except that there the expression of

---

version of this tract therefore emphasizes chiefly the "Higher Unity" mode of contemplation, reaching toward the perception of the dissolution of all existence: there is nought but the Divine. Cf. *Mahadura Kama*, p. 457, and p. 465 n. 1. The printed text, presented to a wider public, makes more prominent the contemplative "return" to the world, described as the "Lower Unity."

G-d that is contemplated is "His wondrous and great works," which one can interpret as Nature, the tangible expression of G-d's presence and power. In the broader dissemination of Jewish teachings on contemplation, this focus might be seen as particularly relevant: the glory of the Divine as seen in a landscape, an underwater photo, or glimpsed through a microscope lens.

How relevant might this contemplative system be today to members of Chabad? To other Jews? To non-Jews?

The Chabad Community

First let us consider the members of Chabad during the leadership of Rabbi Menachem Mendel Schneerson (1902–1994), the Seventh Rebbe. In the second half of the twentieth century he developed exponentially the activism that had begun in the time of his predecessor, R. Yosef Yitzhak Schneersohn (1880–1950).

A key element was the initiation of the "Mitzvah Campaigns," which were a call to personal involvement of the entire Chassidic membership of Chabad. Their initial focus was on the male and female Chabad students, but it extended throughout the community in an attempt to spread the observance of practical Jewish laws such as the donning of Tefilin, having Mezuzot on one's doors, Kashrut of food, the lighting of candles for the Sabbath by women and girls, and similar activities.[13] This intensive activism, conducted by means of advertising, leaflets, "Mitzvah Tanks," dedicated *shluchim* running Chabad Houses, and many members of the Chabad community, both male and female, characterizes a prominent aspect of the ethos of Chabad in the second half of the twentieth century.

---

13. This activism had a messianic aspect that is highlighted in Yitzchak Kraus, *The Seventh: Messianism in the Last Generation of Chabad* (in Hebrew) (Tel Aviv: Miskal–Yedioth Ahronoth, 2007). Kraus successfully describes the development of the successive stages of the "outreach" dimension of Lubavitch, pp. 56–91.

One may well ask whether attempts to achieve the ideal of contemplative prayer continued in this atmosphere. Let us examine some of the sources indicating that, while the practice of contemplation may have become more infrequent in the second half of the twentieth century, it still existed (and continues to exist) in some form.

Contemplative Prayer in the Seventh Generation

During the 1960s in Kfar Chabad (formerly Safaria) in Israel, there was an interesting confrontation between the old world of Russian Chassidism and the new generation of western newcomers to the Chabad movement, who had come there to study in the Yeshivah. The Yeshivah and the community around it had become a haven for Chabad refugees from Russia, who came in 1949.[14] Even today, this is one of the main locations where the ideal of contemplative prayer is practiced. The *mashpia* (spiritual guide) there, R. Shlomoh Chaim Kesselman (d. 1971), was famous for his contemplative approach to prayer, which he endeavored to impart to many of his students. However, he was critical of the potential of those who came from western countries to aspire to the contemplative path. One individual from England who inquired about it was told that "the first step is to gain total control over thought, speech and action." When he achieved this, he was told, he should come back for further guidance.[15] The effect of this was to deter the youth from asking again. Another English student was told by R. Shlomoh Chaim, when he asked about contemplation, *du bist nit shayakh far dem* (meaning, in effect, "it is totally beyond you!").[16]

---

14. See Levine, *Toledot Chabad be-Eretz ha-Kodesh 5537–5710* (Brooklyn, NY: Kehot, 1988), p. 242.
15. Oral communication from the individual concerned.
16. Oral communication from that student, who later became an active Rabbinic figure in Anglo-Jewry.

A more accommodating approach is seen in a letter from the Seventh Rebbe, Rabbi Menachem Mendel, written in 1952 to the non-hasidic head of the Yeshivah in Manchester, England, Rabbi Yehudah Zev Segal (c. 1911–1993). The Rebbe expressed his belief that the attempt to achieve spirituality in prayer, even if not matched by other aspects of a young person's life, would help ensure his remaining in the camp of traditionalist orthodoxy. There were some boys from Lubavitch families in the Yeshivah who were clearly trying to follow the contemplative style. In other respects, however, they were perhaps not atypical youth of the 1950s, at least in the eyes of their austere Rosh Yeshivah. The Rebbe writes as follows:

> As for what you write concerning the conduct of certain of the students... that you are not pleased about their lengthy prayer since this does not match their behaviour in other matters.... Perhaps your claims are justified. However, it is clearly apparent to anyone considering the nature of the youth of this generation that for them in particular it is a time of crisis. One therefore has to be very careful not to weaken their power to reject the "winds" which are blowing through the world.[17]

The "winds" refers to everything other than dedication to Torah, and especially the available forms of secularism. The inner experience in contemplative prayer was a resource that would strengthen a teenager's affirmation of traditional values in a period of change.

A number of letters by Rabbi Menachem Mendel Schneerson give guidance to individuals regarding contemplative prayer, as a kind of general *mashpia*, giving counsel on what to do if you get headaches in the middle of contemplation,[18] how to deal with

---

17. Rabbi Menachem Mendel Schneerson, *Iggrot Kodesh, Admur R. Menahem Mendel*, ed. S.B. Levin, 32 vols. (Brooklyn, NY: Kehot Publication Society, 1987–2015), vol. 5, p. 325.
18. *Iggrot Kodesh, Admur R. Menahem Mendel*, vol. 10, p. 396.

the conflicting demands of lengthy, solitary contemplation, and the halachic imperative of "prayer with the community,"[19] and the question of the clash between work—possibly rabbinic communal work—and the ideal of lengthy contemplative prayer.[20] There is also advice to earnest enquirers such as how to go about the process of contemplation,[21] including warnings against extreme behavior such as beginning to recite the morning service at 2 o'clock in the afternoon![22]

Rabbi Mendel Futerfas (c. 1908–1995) was a major *mashpia* in the post-war period. Imprisoned for nine years in the Soviet Union for his efforts to strengthen Judaism and to assist Jews in escaping to the West, Futerfas, with the help of the British politician Harold Wilson (later prime minister), succeeded in leaving the USSR in 1963. For eight years he lived in London, but later moved away to become the *mashpia* in the Yeshivah in Kfar Chabad. He was famous for his lengthy and melodious prayer, and adults and youths alike would come together at a *farbrengen* that he would lead after several hours of solitary prayer on a Sabbath afternoon. "One should weep in prayer," he said. "And if you cannot weep—then weep about that!"[23]

Another contemporary *mashpia* is Rabbi Shneur Zalman Gafni (b. circa 1940) who, for many years, headed the *baal teshuvah* sec-

---

19. *Iggrot Kodesh, Admur R. Menahem Mendel*, vol. 4, pp. 478–479; vol. 18, p. 81.
20. *Iggrot Kodesh, Admur R. Menahem Mendel*, vol. 18, p. 126; vol. 21, p. 140. A prominent Chabad emissary asked the Seventh Rebbe about this problem. He was told that if he could not pray with contemplation every day, he should do so at least once a week. (Oral communication, 1994.)
21. *Iggrot Kodesh, Admur R. Menahem Mendel*, vol. 10, pp. 234, 244–245; vol. 15, p. 239; vol. 17, p. 111; vol. 20, pp. 52–53.
22. Ibid., vol. 6, p. 354. The Rebbe states that it would be another matter if the inquirer started praying earlier, and his prayer continued until late. He advises the inquirer to discuss the matter with "*ziknei anash*," the older hasidim, and, in any case, not to begin after midday. See also ibid., vol. 5, p. 310.
23. Heard in a talk by Rabbi Futerfas in London in the summer of 1993. Later he said that he had heard from the Seventh Rebbe: "You should pray at length [i.e., with contemplation]. If you cannot do that, you should weep. And if you cannot weep, you should weep about that!"

tion of the Yeshivah in Kfar Chabad. A former student described how, day after day, he would sit almost immobile in the Yeshivah hall, wrapped in his Tallit, engaged for three hours in silent meditative prayer. He also expected attempts in this direction from his students. This is particularly interesting, for they were fully Westernized *baalei teshuvah* [repentants].[24] It is likely that the intensity of contemplation and the warmth of R. Gafni's *farbrengen* gatherings helped these students affirm their commitment to an ideal that blatantly went against the current of the secular society from which they had come. Further, contemporary young men and women who had tasted Eastern systems of meditation, when turning back to their "roots" in Judaism, may have welcomed something comparable in terms of personal spiritual intensity. In 1992 an English translation of *Tract on Prayer* was published by Kehot, the Lubavitch publishing house,[25] presumably aimed at the wider community of *baalei teshuvah*, who can more easily read such a text in English. In 2013 the central Lubavitch publishing house, Merkos, published *The Siddur Illuminated by Chassidus* by Rabbis Eliyahu Touger and Shalom Ber Weinberg, which focuses on the weekday prayers. On each page there are several brief essays in English providing inspirational insights about the text of the prayers. This was followed two years later by a second volume in the same style devoted to the Sabbath prayers.

If contemplative prayer continues to have some significance for "spiritual" *baalei teshuvah*, what is its force for the generality

---

24. On the modern phenomenon of *teshuvah*, see Janet Aviad, *Return to Judaism: Religious Renewal in Israel* (Chicago and London: University of Chicago Press, 1983); Benjamin Beit-Hallahmi (ed.), "Return to the Fold: The Return to Judaism," in Z. Sobel and B. Beit-Hallahmi (eds.), *Tradition, Innovation, Conflict, Jewishness and Judaism in Contemporary Israel* (Albany: State University of New York Press, 1991), pp. 153–172; William Shaffir, "Conversion Experiences: Newcomers to and Defectors from Orthodox Judaism (hozrim betshuvah and hozrim beshe'elah)," in ibid., pp. 173–202.

25. Rabbi Shalom Dovber, *Tract on Prayer*, translated by Rabbi Y. Eliezer Danzinger (Brooklyn, NY: Kehot, 1992).

of the Chabad leadership and wider following in the twenty-first century? Is it swallowed up in the practical thrust to gain funding for one's Chabad House or school, or the politics of erecting large Chanukah Menorot in city squares? Or is it simply forgotten in the struggle to make a living and care for one's large family?

A key figure in the history of Chabad in the post-war period was Rabbi Chaim Mordechai Aizik Hodakow (1902–1993).[26] He was the personal secretary and aide of the Seventh Rebbe throughout the period of his leadership, and headed the Merkos L'Inyonei Chinuch organization, which still functions as the central base and coordinating organization for the Lubavitch emissaries and outreach activities. In an intense and demanding way, he represented the activist ideal in terms of organizations and of practical, tangible achievement.

Rabbi Hodakow would regularly communicate by phone with various international emissaries. Sometimes, when he did so, the Rebbe would be on the line as well, and would occasionally add a comment. Rabbi Nachman Sudak (1936–2014), head of Lubavitch in the UK, would record these phone conversations with Rabbi Hodakow and make transcripts of them. A transcript of one of these talks, a phone call in 1990, urges the need for contemplative prayer and the Chassidic *farbrengen*. "There has to be the reality and the image of people praying at length with hasidic feeling, and the hasidic *farbrengen* with warmth, love between hasidim like one family."[27]

An interesting link between contemplative experience and the outreach ideal is seen in a striking passage in one of the central works of the contemporary movement, *Hayom Yom,* a "diary" with a saying for each day, compiled by R. Menachem Mendel during

---

26. For information concerning him, see Baruch Oberlander and Elkanah Shmotkin, *Early Years: The Formative Years of the Rebbe, Rabbi Menachem M. Schneerson, as Told by Documents and Archival Data, 1902–1929* (Brooklyn, NY: Kehot, 2016), pp. 263–264.

27. Unpublished text of transcript of talk from R. Hadokov to R. Nahman Sudak of London, dated Shevat 5750 (1990) (author's collection).

the lifetime of his father-in-law, R. Yosef Yitzhak Schneersohn. Arranged for the year 5703–5704 (1943), the diary consists of passages extracted from talks, discourses, and letters of Rabbi Yosef Yitzhak. Virtually every member of the movement possesses a copy of this diary, and many study daily the "thought for the day." Although the diary is over seventy years old, we can see it as representing the idealized values of the contemporary movement.

Here we read the following passage, a fragment of a letter:

> The beginning of the descent, G-d forbid, is lack of service in [contemplative] prayer. Everything becomes dry and cold...one hurries, one loses the delight in Torah, the air thickens. It is obvious that one is quite unable to have any [positive] effect on another person.[28]

In order for the Chabad hasid to be able to see another person with a sense of recognition, acceptance, and love, the attempt to take steps toward inner spirituality is required. Of course, there are many pathways toward an inkling of inner spirituality, and the specific practice of contemplation is not the only one. *Some* form of the spiritual is needed, however, in order for a member of Chabad to live up to the ideals expressed in its extensive literature.

An objective study of the current situation in Chabad communities in regard to contemplative prayer would be welcome. In each locale, one would imagine, much depends on the specific educators in schools, and in yeshivot for boys and seminaries for girls. Concerning the latter, one can suggest that these teachings on spiritual prayer are also relevant for girls and women, who nowadays often study *Tanya* daily, along with other Chabad Chassidic texts such as Sichot, inspirational talks by the Rebbe, and also discourses that have a more overtly kabbalistic style.

---

28. Entry for 23rd Iyar, based on a letter of 1932, in Rabbi Yosef Yitzhak, *Iggerot Kodesh*, ed. S.B. Levin, 17 vols. (Brooklyn, NY: Kehot Publication Society, 1982–2011), vol. 2, p. 510.

General Jewish Society

It can further be suggested that these teachings could be made more accessible to Jewish society as a whole, through courses, personal instruction, publications, and the Internet. In regard to orthodox Jews who read Hebrew fluently, and especially hasidim of various groups (as distinct from Chabad followers), there is a strong movement in this direction. The *Hasidut Mevu'eret* project, published by the Heichal Menachem bookstore based in Borough Park, Brooklyn, presents works of Chabad Chassidic teaching with Hebrew explanatory commentaries, making them accessible to those who have not had specific training in the study of Chabad texts. Five volumes in an ongoing series explaining *Tanya* have been published, as well as explanations of discourses by Rabbi Shneur Zalman about the Sabbath and the Festivals, a volume on the system of the Sefirot, and another on the spiritual service of prayer. The Heichal Menachem bookstore and library in the Geulah district in Jerusalem, set up in 1988 by Rabbi Yosef Yitzhak Havlin, similarly seeks to make Chabad Chassidic thought accessible to the Haredi community, and has undertaken a number of other educational projects. There are several networks of study circles in Israel, the United States, and Britain for Haredi participants exploring Chabad Chassidic thought. All of the above can be seen as potentially helping to broaden consciousness of the spiritual dimension of Judaism, especially of contemplative prayer. However, further research is necessary to explore how this study of Chabad Chassidic texts is understood by the participants in these projects. Do they consider Chabad Chassidic teachings as simply a further interesting area of Torah study, or as a pathway to personal spirituality, possibly including contemplative prayer?

Further, what about making such teachings more widely available in the English-speaking world? In recent years a strong interest has emerged in varieties of Jewish mysticism and spirituality. This could help pave the way for wider use of the Chabad approach to contemplation described above.

In addition, it might be felt that other Jewish contemplative techniques would be useful, such as those taught by Rabbi Kalonymos Kalman Shapira (1889–1943), the Piaseczno Rebbe. One of these was that the person should imagine during prayer that he (and today we would add "she") is entering the Temple. This is enhanced by being conversant with the details of the Temple, and their further symbolism, to help persons to feel moved as they progress through their prayer and deeper into the Temple—through the Outer Courtyard, and then the Inner Courtyard, into the sacred Temple Hall with its Golden Menorah, Golden Altar for incense, and Golden Table, and then finally into the Holy of Holies where there is the Golden Ark, surmounted by the golden Cherubs with their outspread wings, and with the Tablets of the Law within.

General Society

This essay claims that these contemplative teachings are also relevant to non-Jewish society. It is with this last point that I would like to conclude.

It is interesting that the Lubavitcher Rebbe considered the *Gate of Unity and Faith,* discussed above, as relevant to Gentiles. In 1965, Rabbi Nisen Mangel's English translation of *Gate of Unity and Faith,* the second section of Tanya, was published. A few years later the Rebbe stated in a public gathering that one of the reasons for publishing the translation of the second section of Tanya was so that it would be accessible to non-Jews, thus enabling them to attain a clearer concept of the Divine. In this talk the Rebbe claimed that if the Jew would only attempt to explain such spiritual ideas to a Gentile, he would likely be surprised that the Gentile would want to hear more, with further explanation.[29]

---

29. From a talk on the Sabbath of portion Bereishit 1968, section 6, *Torat Menachem,* vol. 54, pp. 240–241.

A closely linked issue was the campaign by Rabbi Menachem Mendel for a "moment of silence" in the public schools.[30] At the "Tenth of Shevat" gathering on January 24, 1983, the Rebbe claimed that a daily moment of silence was in the spirit of the Constitution and the American tradition of religious freedom: "There should be instituted in all public schools a 'Moment of Silence'—a moment of contemplation and prayer to the Creator and Master of the world, consistent with what the child has surely heard from his parents, concerning the existence of the Creator...."[31]

President Ronald Reagan was at the forefront of the campaign for a moment of silence or some kind of prayer in public schools, and he spoke of this in his State of the Union address in January 1984. However, in June 1985 the U.S. Supreme Court ruled against the moment of silence in public schools, declaring it to be unconstitutional.[32] Despite this, there have since been a number of attempts in various states to institute a moment of silence, many of which have been successful. In 2014 there were 34 states that permitted a moment of silence or "of quiet reflection," or prayer, to take place in their public schools.[33]

---

30. See ibid., pp. 327–329; Kraus, *The Seventh*, pp. 240–242. This was a renewed version of his endeavor in the 1960s to promote the recital of the "Regents Prayer" in the public schools. See Chaim Miller, *Turning Judaism Outward: A Biography of the Rebbe Menachem Mendel Schneerson, the Seventh Lubavitcher Rebbe* (Brooklyn, NY: Kol Menachem, Gutnick Library of Jewish Classics, 2014), pp. 249–251; and Leo Pfeffer, "The New York Regents' Prayer Case (Engel v. Vitale)," *Journal of Church and State* 4:2 (1962): 150–158 <www.jstor.org/stable/23913195> (accessed 02/05/17).

31. Rabbi Menachem Schneerson, *Hitvaaduyot* (Brooklyn, NY: Vaad Hana'hot BeLahak, 1982–1993, 41 vols.), 10 Shevat 5743, sec. 29. This Hebrew date commemorates the passing of the previous Lubavitcher Rebbe, Rabbi Joseph Isaac Schneersohn, and is therefore also the anniversary of Rabbi Menachem Mendel Schneerson succeeding to his position. Since this talk was not on the Sabbath, it was heard in many locations around the United States and internationally through a sophisticated telephone link.

32. Miller, *Turning Judaism Outward*, p. 329.

33. See <https://www.gtbe.org/uploads/images/files/States%20with%20Moment%20of%20Silence%20Feb%202014.pdf> (accessed 08/05/17).

In light of this thrust by the Lubavitcher Rebbe, it would seem reasonable to attempt to make some aspect of the contemplative teachings of the kind we have discussed available not only to the wider Jewish community, but to society as a whole. The goal would be to use the resources of Chassidic teaching, and particularly of Chabad, to help each man and woman to attain a closer personal relationship with the Divine.

For Additional Reading

A very brief selection of works in English promoting contemplation or meditation, which can be seen as evidence for a certain level of current interest in this area of thought:

Rabbi Shalom Dovber Schneersohn, *Tract on Prayer*, trans. Rabbi Y. Eliezer Danzinger (Brooklyn, NY: Kehot, 1992).

Aryeh Kaplan, *Jewish Meditation: A Practical Guide* (New York: Schocken Books, 1995).

Rabbi Avraham Katz, *A Practical Guide to Davening: Ideas and Guidance on How to Daven Based on the Teachings of Chassidus* (Brooklyn, NY: 2016).

Dov Ber Klein, *Sea Traveler, a Practical Step-by-Step Guide to Prayer and Chassidic Meditation* (Brooklyn, NY: Ezra Press, an imprint of Kehot, 2016).

Rabbis Eliyahu Touger and Shalom Ber Weinberg, *The Siddur Illuminated by Chassidus*—for the weekday prayers (Brooklyn, NY: Kehot, 2013); for the Sabbath prayers (Brooklyn, NY: Kehot, 2015).

See also an online spiritual commentary to the Prayerbook, <https://www.chabad.org/library/siddur/default_cdo/aid/1495868/jewish/Online-Siddur-with-Commentary.htm#!/aid:1618653/title:%D7%A4%D7%AA%D7%97%20%D7%93%D7%91%D7%A8%20-%20Siddur>

Chapter 6

MODEST DRESS: THE RULES, THE CONTROVERSIES, AND THE EXPERIENCES

Kate Miriam Loewenthal, Royal Holloway, University of London (Emeritus Professor)

This chapter explores issues involved in religiously based modest dress for women, the controversies surrounding issues involved in modest dressing, and the experiences of women dressing modestly. Thus, three issues will be examined:

1. **RELIGIOUS ISSUES:** Some religious rulings will be described, offering examples of their content, both in Judaism, in other religions, and in non-religious cultures. The spiritual basis for these rulings will be considered, as will the value of modesty and the question of the emphasis on women rather than men.
2. **CONTROVERSIES:** A number of questions will be raised and claims made, and some of these will be examined for validity. Claims include these:
    - Modest dressing reduces the objectification of women/ women as bodies, modesty as changing the focus from the body to inner qualities. This raises the question of whether the practice of modesty may reduce the risk of eating disorders.
    - Modest dressing has been de-territorialized since the advent of the Internet. To what extent has the successful

    selling of modest clothing on the Internet given women
    from different faith traditions a sense of commonality?
  - Modest dressing is claimed to have become more fashionable and less dowdy, a situation that appears to have given rise to controversy over whether this is desirable.
3. **EXPERIENCES:** Finally, the chapter will examine the *experiences* of women with modest dress, including the difficulties of modest dressing, identity issues, relations with men, and spirituality.

There will be a concluding discussion of whether the values underlying modesty and modest dress can be applicable to wider society.

1. Religious Rulings: Examples of Their Content in Judaism, in Other Religions, and in Non-Religious Cultures

Based on the *Code of Jewish Law* (see Ganzfried's translation of the *Brief Code of Jewish Law*, 1928) and subsequent and contemporary rabbinic rulings, the orthodox rulings—which apply to both men and women—include:

- Keeping the majority of one's body covered in respectable clothing at all times. This includes, for example, hair covering for married women (wig/*sheitel*, headscarf or *tichel*, or hat/turban).
- Avoiding the company of uncouth individuals or situations where an atmosphere of levity and depravity prevails. This includes men not listening to a woman singing (*kol isha*), and a generally quiet, composed demeanor.
- Not looking at/thinking about pictures/scenes/thoughts that are lascivious or immoral, not staring at members of the opposite gender.

- Refraining from touching a person of the opposite gender other than immediate family (shaking hands very quickly in greetings between sexes is a point of dispute) (*Shomer negiah*).
- Not hugging or kissing (or touching) one's spouse in public.

Each major religion has developed moral codes covering issues of morality, ethics, and so forth. These moral codes seek to regulate the situations that can give rise to sexual interest and to influence people's behavior and practices that could arouse such interest. These codes have an influence on people's attitudes toward issues of modesty in dress, behavior, speech, and thought (see *Wikipedia*, 2017). For example:

Islam emphasizes decency and modesty: "modesty is a part of faith." Modesty is required in the interaction between people. Dress code is part of that overall teaching. Muslim dress codes include, for example, head covering for both women and men and, as in other religious traditions, clothing that conceals much of the body and does not arouse sexual interest. *Hijab* is a veil that covers the hair and is worn by Muslim women, particularly in front of adult males who are not members of the woman's immediate family. *Hijab* also has the wider meaning of modesty, privacy, and morality (see Loewenthal & Solaim, 2016).

Other world religions (Christianity, Buddhism, Hinduism, etc.) also offer guidelines regarding dress and behavior that are applicable to both men and women. Example: In Roman Catholicism, Pope Pius XII stated that women should cover their upper arms and shoulders, that their skirts should cover at least as far as the knee, and the neckline should not reveal anything (see *Wikipedia*, 2017).

In all religious traditions, details may vary in different branches within the tradition—for example, beliefs and customs regarding head covering in Judaism, Islam, and Christianity.

Contemporary secular Western norms: Western standards of decency require people to cover their private parts in public.

The Spiritual Bases and Impact of *Tznius* (Modesty in Judaism)

Note that the Hebrew/Yiddish term *Tznius* (modesty) is spelt thus throughout this chapter, in the customary Ashkenazi manner, unless quoting from a source which uses the modern Hebrew/Sefardi spelling *Tzniut*.

In examining Jewish rulings on modesty, three points are salient:

1. Dress, including head covering, is an important feature.
2. Rulings apply to men as well as to women.
3. Modest *behavior* is important both religiously and spiritually.

It is clear that both dress and behavior can be seen to reflect back on the inner life of the individual. Claims include:

> "...many educators stress the *benefits of tzniut*...children grow to be unique in their *spiritual* sensitivity." (Sosevsky, 2001)

> "What are the *effects [of tzniut]*? *Tzniut* is a consciousness that the Torah demands both men and women to develop, because it is a prerequisite to possessing a *spiritual* worldview." (Kohn, 2017)

> "[Modesty] generates within them a renewed desire to live in the full *spirit* of Torah." (Falk, 1998)

> "The main component of *tznius* is quiet and modest behavior at home. Appropriate conduct outside the home then flows from this as a matter of course." (Schneerson, 1968)

Emphasis is on consistency in the practice of modesty, expressing concern over the manner of conduct and attire in the summer resort areas:

> "The proper manner of dress for women is clearly stated in the *Shulchan Aruch* (Code of Jewish Law)...which is valid even during the summer months. It should be remembered...that modest attire must not only be heeded by women, for the Shulchan Aruch prescribes the moral manner of dress for men as well as women.... [H]e hoped the Shulchan Aruch would go along with the vacationers as an important guide at this crucial time." (Schneerson, 1964)

> "When partially uncovering themselves to impress others, it is as if they are carrying a poster announcing that they have nothing else to show for themselves—neither intelligence nor *middos,* nor even a pleasant face.... Now, why would anyone want to proclaim such a situation publicly? But in fact that is not the true situation. In fact, every individual girl has her own innate inner qualities...." (Schneerson, 1970)

Empirical studies of these effects could be worthwhile.

Is modesty more important for women than for men?

Men are required to dress and behave modestly, but modest dressing and behavior by women is also said to protect men (from desire). *Tznius* is emphasized more in curricula of Orthodox Jewish girls' schools compared to boys' schools. Cultural pressures on women may be greater than those on men, notably as expressed in the contemporary focus in Western society on the importance of body and appearance, including pressure to dress in a revealing/

immodest manner. So it could be perceived that there is a greater need to emphasize modest dress for women.

2. *Controversies*

Turning now to controversies over the growth of modest dress marketing on the Internet, a number of questions have been raised and claims made. Are they valid? Claims and questions include:

1. Modest dressing shifts the focus from women's bodies to their inner qualities. One impact is that the risk of eating disorders may be reduced.
2. Internet selling of modest dress has de-territorialized modest dressing and given women of different faiths a sense of commonality.
3. Has modest dress become more fashionable? Are modesty and fashion compatible?

Examining each of these issues in a little more depth, and turning first to the suggestion that modest dressing shifts the focus from outward appearance to inner qualities, we can mention the feminist claim that current fashion involves objectification of the body and encourages eating disorders. A current movement in feminism attacks advertising involving women immodestly dressed, arguing that this emphasis on the attractive body objectifies the body and reduces a woman's self-image to the "attractiveness" of her body (see, e.g., Kite & Kite, 2017). Demmrich, Atmaca, and Dinc (2017) have shown that Turkish Muslim women who practice veiling (*Hijab*) are significantly less prone to anxiety about body image than are women who do not practice religious rulings on modesty. Modest dressing may reduce a tendency to eating disorders (EDs). For most ED sufferers, the focus is on the body and its slimness. The current cultural emphasis on slimness is said to have an important connection to the media attention given in the 1960s to the British model Twiggy. The contemporary media perpetuates the idea of attractiveness of anorexic girls. Examples of Internet link headers include: "Why do men want anorexic-looking women?" "A Little Anorexia is Hot." "Do you guys find Anorexic Girls Attractive?" Amanda Fortini (2008) reported that after losing weight (from illness), she was startled to find men expressing attraction with unwanted "frequency and audacity." "A little anorexia is hot" was stated semi-facetiously by one would-be admirer.

The two most common feeding and eating disorders, mainly but not entirely affecting women, are Anorexia Nervosa and Bulimia Nervosa. Anorexia is the most lethal of all psychiatric conditions, with a mortality rate of approximately 10%. It involves refusal to maintain a body weight normal for one's age and height, intense fear of gaining weight and being thought fat or overweight, and a distorted perception of body shape and size: seeing a fat body even though it is skeletal. Sometimes menstruation has ceased, but this feature is no longer essential to a diagnosis of anorexia. Bulimia Nervosa involves recurrent episodes of binge eating, such that in a fixed period of time, abnormal quantities of food are consumed, and the person is unable to stop eating. There are recurrent and inappropriate efforts to compensate that may involve compulsive forced vomiting, use of laxatives and other medications, and excessive exercise. Self-perception is excessively influenced by weight and body shape. Other eating disorders include the purging disorder, Pica (compulsive eating of non-nutritive substances), and night-eating syndrome.

What is the situation with regard to claims about modesty and (fewer) eating disorders in the Jewish community? There has been some research on the effects of religiosity on adolescent Jewish girls' eating behaviors and attitudes (see the review below). Generally, but not always, the risks of eating disorders seem to be lower among the more religious. But there has been no direct study of modest dress behavior and attitudes in relation to eating behavior and attitudes. Modest dress is suggested to deflect concern about slimness and hence might lower the prevalence of eating disorders in orthodox Jewish (OJ) girls and women keeping *tznius*. Note, however, that in the OJ community, obesity is said to make girls less marriageable—a factor that, of course, can lead to dieting and eating disorders notwithstanding modest dressing.

The following are some specific findings regarding religiosity and disordered eating in the Jewish community. Gluck & Geliebter (2002) compared 78 OJ women with 48 secular women. The latter group had more eating disorder symptoms, more fear of being fat, and more shame about appearance. The researchers conclude that membership in a strict, insulated religious group such as Orthodox Judaism may protect women, to some extent, from developing body dissatisfaction and eating pathology. Shafran and Wolowelsky (2013) state that research has indicated that women who feel loved and accepted by G-d are buffered from eating disorder risk factors. More specifically, they suggest that following *halachah* related to eating may protect OJ women from eating disorders—for example, observing *kashrut*, making blessings before and after eating, and eating only at prescribed times. However, Pinhas et al. (2008) discovered no differences by religiosity in disordered eating attitudes in a sample of 898 Canadian high school students. Jewish girls had more disordered eating attitudes than non-Jewish girls, but there were no differences between girls and boys. It is possible that these findings may have resulted from the lack of inclusion of *strictly* OJ students in the sample tested. Latzer et al. (2015) studied 102 adolescent religious Jewish girls in Israel. In their sample, negative religious coping predicted lower self-esteem, which in turn predicted disordered eating pathology (DEP). Findings also revealed relatively lower overall levels of DEP among this sample, compared to similar populations in Israel and the United States. These results suggest that a strong religious and spiritual identity may serve as a protective factor against DEP. Indeed, a systematic review involving 22 studies of religion and spirituality in relation to disordered eating and body image concerns supports this conclusion (Akrawi et al., 2015).

The evidence about religiosity and disordered eating in the Jewish community hints at the possibility of an association, but the evidence is somewhat mixed.

Turning now to issues relating to the development of the Internet, we can examine the question of whether modesty is de-territorialized, and whether this has led to improved commonality between different faiths. Lewis & Tarlo (2010) (from the London College of Fashion and Goldsmiths University of London) describe a project in which they interviewed retailers and consumers in a range of locations (worldwide) and from several faith traditions (Islam, Mormonism, and Judaism). Their findings suggest that the Internet offers international marketing for clothing meeting religious requirements of modesty more readily and inexpensively than do local shops. Women can express opinions and religious interpretations outside the male-dominated context of religious organizations. They can compare differences and similarities in modest fashion with women from other faith traditions. Further, modest fashion on the Internet enables women to maintain their piety while feeling and looking good.

As mentioned above, there have been suggestions that the retailing of modesty on the Internet has increased commonality between different faiths. The main way in which this seems to have happened is that retailers are targeting buyers outside their original faith group and adjusting their product range for other faith groups, perhaps for simple commercial reasons. This may lead to difficulty. Clothing that is modest for one faith group might seem unacceptable or unfashionable once changes have been made to achieve commonality/acceptability to other faith groups.

The Internet has enabled a closer monitoring of trends and controversies. In some media coverage, modesty has become "cool" for several reasons. Some recent headlines include: "The new modesty: A new age of fashion is dawning" (Aly, 2017); "With both designers and high street brands waking up to the power of the Muslim pound, a new age in 'modestwear' is dawning" and "What is behind the trend for modesty in fashion?"; "How could there be anything wrong with being modest? It's the truly universal virtue. As prized in the courtyards of Asian temples as it is in the pews of American churches, modesty is so woven into human society that every culture has its silent codes encouraging women to dress and behave respectably. The

Duchess of Cambridge, Kate Middleton, proves that high necklines and low hemlines are how we know a lady has class" (Saini, 2016).

"What does modest fashion mean?" (Bauck, 2016). "There's a general misconception that modest clothing is inherently oppressive," said Michelle Honig, the keynote speaker at a symposium on modest dressing, and an Orthodox Jewish fashion journalist. "But if women in so-called 'liberated countries' still choose to cover their bodies, then they have made a choice.... Interpretations of modesty differ across religious boundaries and even within them. 'Modesty' in a Muslim context may be expressed by wearing loose-fitting pants and covering one's head with a hijab, while an Orthodox Jewish woman may wear skirts or dresses only and cover her head with a wig.... Still, the shared interest in staying relatively covered up while still looking stylish is enough to connect women across religious, racial and cultural boundaries. Many of them cite devotion to God and a desire to present themselves as 'more than a collection of body parts.'"

3. Experiences of Practicing Modesty

Finally, I examine some experiences of women with modest dress. The main challenges they mention are expense, the fact that nice clothes that are modest are hard to access, discomfort, anti-semitism, lack of social approval, and frumpy styles. In a study by Loewenthal and Solaim (2016), three themes emerged as important from interviews of religious Jewish and Muslim women about head covering: identity, relations with men, and spirituality. These themes seem generally applicable to modest dressing.

IDENTITY: Head/hair covering is a key feature of identity expression and was seen as indicating one's distinct difference from the surrounding society (J = Jewish woman; M = Muslim woman). *"An important feature of her Jewish identity"* (J). *"A good example... as to how we are a different people and have different ethics and code from others in society"* (J). *"When becoming more religious (and was about to get married), I* wanted to do things properly and I saw that wearing a sheitel [wig] was one of the crucial features. It was expensive and uncomfortable and awkward but all those disadvantages were outweighed by the feeling that it was the right thing to do as a Jewish woman" (J). "In the Quran the hijab was asked of the wives of prophet Mohammed (peace upon him) to distinguish them from other women" (M). "As a part of practicing Islam—to identify themselves as Muslims" (M). "It's important in my opinion to wear hijab with faith, not because you want people to think you are a good Muslim [but] because hijab represent Islam and should be respected" (M).

RELATIONS WITH MEN: Modest dressing (in Judaism, where hair covering is done at marriage) preserves and builds closeness to her husband, and (in Islam) gives the woman a sense that she is safe from masculine attention. There is the view that caring about appearances may include being attractive to men, and modest dress including hair/head covering protects from masculine attention and strengthens the marital bond. *"Provides a sense of privacy, modesty and morality and also women wearing hijab can control how much man can see them or cannot, so that they feel protected"* (M). *"To be modest in dress. Women, more than men, are judged by their looks so they might be wearing hijab because they don't want to be judged by their looks. It's one less thing to worry about at a time when women are obsessed with looks and image, when you wear hijab you are less aware of trying to look 'right' all the time with the perfect hair and clothes"* (M). *"To create a unique intimacy and the deepest bond with one's husband"* (J). *"By keeping such a crucial aspect of a woman's whole persona for the unique benefit of her husband is a key tool in building their whole relationship, trust & bond over time"* (J). *"It helps create a kind of wall around the holiness of marriage"* (J).

SPIRITUALITY: For both Muslims and Jews, head/hair covering is understood to be a religious commandment. There are two sets of concepts and feelings here: first, that to disobey would be wrong, going against religious law, and a cause of guilt; second, head/hair covering is reported as a source of positive, sometimes mystical feelings. Some respondents felt their self-control was enhanced by this practice. *"[Wearing Hijab makes one] more aware of G-d on a daily basis and hopefully become more practicing as a Muslim in many other ways"* (M). *"She will be sinful if she wouldn't do it [wear Hijab]"* (M). *"It is a requirement in Jewish Law as set out in the Torah"* (J). *"Appreciating the mystical significance & tremendous benefits that such self-control can have"* (J). *"I really do not understand the spiritual aspects even though I accept that they are there"* (J).

Conclusion: How Might the Values Underlying Modesty and Modest Dress Be Applicable to Wider Society?

There are several relevant areas of general interest and concern:

- Concern by some feminists and others about emphasis in general society on the exposed female body as "beautiful" and attractive. Societal emphasis on the body is seen as harmful, and so in this case, a feminist argument can serve to forward religious views.
- Concern about the stress placed, in general society, on the importance of the body compared to mind and spirit. This is a potentially unfortunate prioritization of values, and thought needs to be given to reprioritization.
- Concern about eating disorders related to the emphasis on the slim female body. Eating disorders are potentially lethal, destroy health and quality of life, and cause enormous pain to families. Unfortunately, modest dressing may not guarantee total immunity to eating disorders, but it is hoped that it can be a helpful factor.
- The increasing popularity, vogueish aspect, and attractiveness of modest styles. This may be ephemeral, but it could be part of a movement to embed a greater valuing of modesty in wider society.

- Most important, people in the wider society can be very receptive to spiritual messages—in this case, the message that reserve and modesty can help to enhance spiritual sensitivity and spiritual awareness.

References

Akrawi, D., Bartrop, R., Potter, U., & Touyz, S. (2015). Religiosity, spirituality in relation to disordered eating and body image concerns: A systematic review. *Journal of Eating Disorders, 3*, 29 <https://doi.org/10.1186/s40337-015-0064-0>

Aly, R. (2017). The new modesty: A new age of fashion is dawning. *Stylist Magazine.* <https://www.stylist.co.uk/fashion/the-new-modesty-a-new-age-of-muslim-fashion-is-dawning/118304> accessed December 24, 2017.

Bauck, W. (2016, November 1). What does modest fashion mean? *The New York Times.* <https://www.nytimes.com/2016/11/03/fashion/what-does-modest-fashion-mean.html> accessed December 24, 2017.

Demmrich, S., Atmaca, S., & Dinc, C. (2017). Body image and religiosity among veiled and non-veiled Turkish women. *Journal of Empirical Theology, 30,* 127–147.

Falk, P.E. (1998). *Modesty: An adornment for life.* New York: Feldheim.

Fortini, A. (2008, March 15). The year my body shrank. *Elle.* <http://www.elle.com/beauty/health-fitness/advice/a9444/the-year-my-body-shrank-261302/> accessed December 24, 2017.

Ganzfried, S. (1928). *Kitzur Shulchan Aruch* (Brief Code of Jewish Law) (H.E. Goldin, trans.). New York: Hebrew Publishing Company.

Gluck, M.E., & Geliebter, A. (2002). Body image and eating behaviors in Orthodox and secular Jewish women. *Journal of Gender-Specific Medicine (JGSM), 5,* 19–24.

Kite, L., & Kite, L. (2017). *Beauty redefined.* <http://www.beautyredefined.org/blog/> accessed December 24, 2017.

Kohn, L. (2017). *Body and beauty in our physical world: A Jewish perspective, part III.* <https://torah.org/learning/women-class14/> accessed December 22, 2017.

Latzer, Y., Weinberger-Litman, S.L., Gerson, B., Rosch, A., et al. (2015). Negative religious coping predicts disordered eating pathology among Orthodox Jewish adolescent girls. *Journal of Religion and Health, 54*, 1760–1771. doi:10.1007/s10943-014-9927-y

Lewis, R., & Tarlo, E. (2010). *Modest dressing: Faith-based fashion and internet retail.* <http://www.arts.ac.uk/research/current-research/ual-research-projects/fashion-design/modest-dressing/> accessed December 24, 2017.

Loewenthal, K.M., & Solaim, L.S. (2016). Religious identity, challenge, and clothing: Women's head and hair covering in Islam and Judaism. *Journal of Empirical Theology, 29*, 160–170.

Pinhas, L., Heinmaa, M., Bryden, P., Bradley, S., & Toner, B. (2008). Disordered eating in Jewish adolescent girls. *Canadian Journal of Psychiatry, 53*, 601–608.

Saini, A. (2016, December 19). What is behind the trend for modesty in fashion? *New Humanist.* <https://newhumanist.org.uk/articles/5123/what-is-behind-the-trend-for-modesty-in-fashion> accessed June 20, 2017.

Schneerson, Rabbi M.M. (The Lubavitcher Rebbe). (1964). Letter dated 12 Tammuz 5724.

Schneerson, Rabbi M.M. (The Lubavitcher Rebbe). (1968). *Sichos Kodesh 5728* (Collected talks), vol. 2, p. 159. New York: Kehot.

Schneerson, Rabbi M.M. (The Lubavitcher Rebbe). (1970). *Sichos Kodesh 5728* (Collected talks), vol. 1, p. 122. New York: Kehot.

Shafran, Y., & Wolowelsky, J.B. (2013). A note on eating disorders and appetite and satiety in the Orthodox Jewish meal. *Eating and Weight Disorders, 18*, 75–78.

Sosevsky, C. (2001, Fall). A modest proposal: How Tzniut liberates and enriches. *Jewish Action* <https://jewishaction.com/opinion/a-modest-proposal-how-tzniut-liberates-and-enriches/> accessed May 7, 2018.

Wikipedia. (2017). Modesty <https://en.wikipedia.org/wiki/Modesty> accessed December 21, 2017.

Chapter 7

EDUCATION AS LIFE: REFLECTIONS FROM THE FIELD BY A CHABAD *SHLUCHA* ON A COLLEGE CAMPUS

Rivkah Slonim, Rohr Chabad Center for Jewish Student Life at Binghamton University

Sometimes the longest journey is from the periphery to the innermost core.

In late 1984, my husband, Rabbi Aaron Slonim, and I moved with our first child, then a few months old, from the Crown Heights section of Brooklyn as *shluchim*, Chabad emissaries of the Lubavitcher Rebbe, Rabbi Menachem M. Schneerson (1902–1994), to Binghamton, New York. We were young, filled with conviction, and completely unaware of how we were going to fulfill our mission. That we had a mission seemed to be the only thing that mattered.

In those days, before *shluchim* were diversified and stratified (today's emissaries typically choose to serve a specific demographic), we were simply dispatched to Binghamton. But from the beginning, it was clear that our focus would be to minister to the large—and decidedly underserved—Jewish demographic at the State University of New York at Binghamton.

A kind Jewish attorney in town incorporated us as an organization in our basement apartment, and we were officially in business. We looked to our older colleagues on other college campuses—there were about fifteen at the time—for cues, but for the most part we were on our own.

We began modestly, with perhaps five students around our Shabbat table. I used china, flatware, and a beautiful white damask tablecloth. I cooked with great care—although I never enjoyed cooking—because that seemed like a practical way to ensure the success of some part of our mission. In addition to the Shabbat dinners and lunches, we offered holiday services and celebrations, social gatherings, classes, and, most important, an address to which Jewish students could turn.

Today, Binghamton University is home to one of the most robust Jewish communities on any campus in the United States. Chabad on Campus International (established in 1998) serves as an umbrella organization to over 265 full-time Chabad centers on campuses worldwide, with hundreds more served part-time. Emissaries on campuses are supported by a network of colleagues and have access in person and online to a vast reservoir of resources.

As a rule, life as a *shliach* or *shlucha* offers little time for introspection. The Rebbe, in public addresses[1] and private communication, made clear that our job is not done until we have in some way impacted all Jews in our town/university to seek a deeper engagement with their Jewish core. There is always more to be done. For us, the term "assimilation" is not academic; we stare it in the face each hour of each day, and it suffuses our work with urgency.

In a sense, every time we meet a student for the first time, it feels like we are new to our job. We constantly seek to innovate in an effort to make more of an impact; to effectively leave a lasting mark on young Jews at a critical juncture in their lives. No matter the complexity of the infrastructure, the variety of the events, or the multiplicity of amenities we offer, over and over again, impact comes back to education; that is the heart and soul of our mission.

As such, I should emphasize something about Chabad emissaries that most people simply don't understand: Those seeking to truly understand the movement would do well to look beyond the brick-and-mortar structures, the ubiquitous presence on the Web, the high-profile campaigns, and the substantial budgets. To understand

---

1. See, for example, Kislev 19, 1960 (*Tof Shin Chof*), Sicha 10.

Chabad—who we are, what we are, and why we are—one must shift focus to the teachings, and more specifically, what those teachings have to say about education.

The huge corpus of Chassidic teachings—specifically of the seventh Lubavitcher Rebbe—but more broadly of all his predecessors[2] beginning with Rabbi Schneur Zalman of Liadi,[3] the first Chabad Rebbe—constitute our training, our playbook, and our strategy. This was true for us in 1985, and it is just as true today, even as the Chabad-Lubavitch network, comprising over 5,000 emissary couples worldwide, moves increasingly from the periphery to the mainstream of Jewish communal life. To understand Chabad's posture on education—that is, Chabad seeks to effect more than transmission; Chabad seeks transformation, *penimiut* (inwardness), and internal cohesion—one must delve into Chabad teachings on this subject. And when I speak of education, I mean both the formal teachings and the informal instruction that, of necessity, informs each interaction. It is these two approaches that I want to discuss through the lens of Chassidic teachings.

Chassidus teaches that there are two modalities when it comes to effecting transformation:

1. *Hashpaah* (communication)—consciously teaching, guiding, or counseling.
2. *Dugma Chaya* (functioning as a living model)—just being who you are.

---

2. The Chasidic Heritage Series (Kehot Publication Society), currently comprising 20 volumes, offers the English reader access to some of the most seminal *maamorim*, Chassidic discourse, taught by the Chabad Rebbes.

3. *Likutei Amaraim* [Tanya], written by Rabbi Schneur Zalman in 1796, is considered the *Torah Shebichtav*, the "written Torah" from which all other Chabad Chassidic teachings flow. It was first translated into English in 1962 by Rabbi Nissan Mindel (Brooklyn, NY: Kehot Publication Society). See Rabbi Yosef Weinberg, *Lessons in Tanya*, translated by Rabbi Levy Weinberg (Brooklyn, NY: Kehot Publication Society, 1982); Rabbi Adin Steinsaltz, *Opening the Tanya* (San Francisco: Jossey-Bass, 2003); and Rabbi Chaim Miller, *The Practical Tanya* (Brooklyn, NY: Kol Menachem, 2006).

Sovev *and* Memaleh: *The Binary within the Creator*

This binary is rooted in the paradoxical paradigms we understand to be true regarding God's relationship with creation: the way in which God is *sovev kol almin*, encompasses all worlds, and *memaleh kol almin*, fills all worlds.

From the perspective of *sovev*, God is transcendent, remote, aloof, inaccessible, and impermeable to overtures from anything other. Simultaneously, God is *memale*: immanent, accessible, up close and personal, and desirous of a relationship with humankind.

Concerning creation, scripture states that "all that God wants, He did."[4] The world was created because of, and through the agency of, God's will (*ratzon*) or desire (*cheifetz*)—in other words, God's transcendence.

On the other hand, scripture states: "Through the word of God were the heavens fashioned."[5] The world came into being specifically through God's speech, through a series of ten fiats,[6] the most famous of which is "Let there be light."[7]

It is through this second aspect, God's immanence, that the elements of the world were actually created. But the power to create *ex nihilo*—the creation of something from nothing—flows from God's transcendence and infinitude. It is this aspect of the Divine, the exalted will, that precipitated creation.[8] Only later could there follow a physical plane in which God's presence can be sensed and His/Her desire fulfilled.

---

4. Psalm 135.
5. Psalm 33.
6. Ethics of the Fathers 5:1.
7. Genesis 1:3.
8. The mystics refer to this process as *seder hishtalshelut*, the evolutionary process—or perhaps more correctly, the process of devolution—in which God condenses and compresses His energy and His light. Only in this manner can physical matter emerge. See Rabbi Jacob Immanuel Schochet, *Mystical Concepts in Chassidism* (Brooklyn, NY: Kehot Publication Society, 1979).

Stated differently: the power of creation is not about what God can do but rather about who God is. It's not about what is said (immanence); it's about who is saying it (transcendence).

Sovev *and* Memaleh: *The Binary in the Personal Realm*

This same *sovev/memaleh* binary exists within the soul and psyche of humankind.

Man is vested with cognitive abilities and emotive faculties. With the former—subdivided into *chochmah*, wisdom, *binah*, understanding, and *daat*, knowledge—man amasses information and develops intellectual grasp. Through the agency of the emotions, man relates to others and to the world around him. These two aspects of man constitute the *memaleh*, the limited and uniquely tailored energy allotted to each person. The *memaleh* aspect can be qualified and quantified both by the person himself and others around him. It is constantly in flux, reacting to stimuli from within and without.

Beyond this discernible and accessible plane, there is the *sovev*, the transcendent aspect of each person that might best be described as the suprarational, or the static, unchanging truth. This aspect has a "one size fits all" feature about it; it suffuses everything one does in equal measure, and yet we are most often unaware of this unfettered energy. For instance, the single strongest urge within man is the existential desire to live.[9] This will is essential and is not a response to anything external. It also subconsciously affects each rational decision and premeditated action taken by the person.

Emunah, faith, shares these same characteristics; it is essential and defies evaluation and analyses. And when ignited, faith propels one's every action.

---

9. The will to live is inherent in every aspect of creation. Only humankind, however, possesses the ability to choose the "why" of his/her life and therefore the "how."

There are people who are drawn to Judaism through intellectual engagement; others come to appreciate the beauty and relevance of their religion through an emotional experience. Both offer viable portals for continued investigation, and each bolsters the other.

But an individual will not likely commit to Jewish observance simply because they cannot think of a cogent argument to dispute the revelation at Sinai, or because they deeply enjoyed a Shabbat dinner. For one's faith—which Jewish tradition posits is essential to each person—to be activated toward continued and consistent commitment to Jewish observance, it must be ignited by something that surpasses both the intellect and the emotion.[10]

---

10. Beyond the educational offerings, the *hashpaah/memale* aspect, and the organic Jewish "laboratory of life," the *dugma chayah/sovev* aspect, offered by each Chabad center, there is a third—and arguably least understood—component of our work. That is the effort expended to access the *atzmut*, the very essence, sometimes referred to as the *yechida* of each Jew. This illuminates an approach unique to Chabad-Lubavitch. Chassidim of the Lubavitcher Rebbe, young and old alike—those who have dedicated their lives to serve as *shluchim* and those who have not—routinely seek every opportunity to connect another Jew with their essence by giving them the chance to perform a mitzvah, a ritual commandment. It might be encouraging candle lighting before Shabbat and holidays, donning *tefillin*, or performing a ritual connected with a certain holiday like blessing over the four kinds on Sukkot. Over the years, the Rebbe's "Mitzvah Campaigns" and "Mitzvah Tanks" have gone from a curiosity to something Jews expect to encounter.

Often these efforts take the form of a quick interaction: what might appear to be a fleeting experience. A less sympathetic observer might call it useless. The student of Chassidus, however, understands that a mitzvah connects the Jew to his/her Creator. It is the conduit through which finite man reaches across the great divide and touches the infinite Divine. By definition, a mitzvah changes the practitioner; it brings the essence of the soul to the fore, it "speaks" both to, and of, the unspeakable. The power that lies in this type of encounter is profound. At the same time it can be fleeting if it is not followed up by study and sustained Jewish experience. *Atzmut*, essence, requires expression through intellect and emotions, to affect the person and their actions. But uncovering *atzmut* is often the first step, and sometimes the only way in which a given individual might be reached.

It is not hard for people to talk about *what* they understand or what they feel. It is far more difficult for people to articulate *why* it is they feel or think a certain way. That is because the "why" resides in a place beyond cognition or emotion; it exists on the level of *sovev*, the encompassing energy. It is on that deepest level, where a person's love of self and desire to live resides, that enduring transformation can occur. It is there that they will sense that a "truth" is *their* truth. In this place, *emunah* (faith) and *daat* (reason) become inextricably bound.

Sovev *and* Memaleh: *The Binary in Education*

In his celebrated treatise on education titled *Klolei Ha-chinuch Ve'hahadracha*,[11] the Sixth Lubavitcher Rebbe, Rabbi Yosef Yitzchak Schneersohn (1880–1950), explained the difference between "teaching," transmitting information, and "*chinuch*, education," molding the character of students. A teacher's function is to impart information. If one teacher is not stellar, another instructor, it is hoped, will fill those gaps in knowledge. An educator, on the other hand, is a *dugma chaya*, a living example. In that context no overture is merely neutral; it is always either positive or negative.

A Jew is enjoined to use his/her intellect in pursuit of Godliness; to understand God's Torah to the extent that is humanly possible. We were created as rational beings, and not to exercise our cognitive ability would be to excise a most important part of the self. Jewish education is the process of transmitting this information in a way that whets the appetite for continued learning and hones the tools that make that possible.

---

11. In 1898, Rabbi Yosef Yitzchak, who would become the sixth Lubavitcher Rebbe, compiled this treatise at the behest of his father, Rabbi Shalom DovBer, for use by the counselors at the first Lubavitch yeshiva, *Tomchei Temimim*. In English, *Principles of Education and Guidance*, translated and annotated by Rabbi Y. Eliezer Danzinger (Brooklyn, NY: Kehot Publication Society, 2004).

On the other hand, we acknowledge that man cannot possibly "apprehend" the Divine. In this respect, the function and importance of learning Torah can be understood as analogous to the function of windshield wipers that serve to wipe away the grime that obscures the clear window. Faith can be defined as "what the soul knows," and study "cleans the window" of the soul. *Chinuch*, education, then, must mean something different from conventional teaching.

To truly affect someone, one needs much more than well-crafted classes and lectures. The transcendent, suprarational aspect of the teacher has to touch the suprarational plane of the student.

To access this place—the *sovev* within man—*hashpaah* (communication) is simply not enough; the teacher needs to be a *dugma chaya* (living model). What we say to our students, what we teach them, is only as affective as who we are as living examples and models of the values we espouse.

Honesty and ongoing self-scrutiny on the part of the educator is essential to this endeavor. My students always were, and continue to be, my most important teachers and deepest source of inspiration. With their questions and probing they hold up a mirror to my soul and cause me to look deep inside, painful and humbling as it often is.

As *shluchim* and *shluchos*, we are *always* modeling. It is ultimately this aspect of our work, the informal education—the ways in which our homes become classrooms and laboratories of life—that impacts our students most profoundly.[12]

---

12. The following vignette provides an example.

    Professor Velvl Greene, former chair of Epidemiology and Public Health at Ben-Gurion University and director of its Lord Jakobovits Center for Jewish Medical Ethics, was a pioneer in the field of hygiene and the development of sanitary standards used in hospitals. He also contributed to NASA's search for extraterrestrial life.

    Greene identifies the 1960s as the time when he realized there is more to life than being famous and resolved to live a more spiritual existence. At the time he lived in Minnesota, and that opportunity came knocking in

Education as Life

After teaching for over three decades, I wonder out loud: what do I and my many colleagues have to offer those who look to us for spiritual guidance and teaching? The obvious answer would be Judaism, Torah, Mitzvot. As Chassidim we are also heirs to a rigorous, intellectual system called Chabad chassidus, which we feel privileged to share. But there might be something even more important that we can bring to the table.

---

the person of Rabbi Moshe Feller, director of Chabad-Lubavitch activities in Minnesota. Greene described his first meeting with the young, newly married rabbi as "a comedy."

At the time, Feller just wanted to meet one of Minneapolis's most famous scientists and ask him to support his new center's activities. Greene originally didn't want to meet the rabbi, and only after some prodding granted Feller 10 minutes.

"What did a black hat and beard have to do with me? I was a space scientist," he once told an interviewer.

In the middle of their conversation, according to a 1972 account in *Time* magazine, Feller "suddenly looked out the window at the setting sun. [He] realized that it was time for prayer, and, asking Greene's pardon, abruptly stopped the conversation. He turned to the window to pray."

"I had never seen this before in my life," Greene recalled. "Here he came into my office, wasted my time and stood there embarrassing me.

"I didn't know what he was doing or why," he continued. "I didn't know Jews prayed outside a synagogue. I didn't know they prayed in the afternoon. I didn't know they prayed on weekdays. And I didn't know how anyone could pray without someone announcing the page!"

After finishing his prayer, Feller apologized, telling him that "if [he] hadn't prayed then and there, the opportunity would have been lost forever."

Greene told the rabbi that he was a Jewish agnostic, but Feller the rabbi told him that he was just ignorant in Jewish teachings, "just as I am ignorant in microbiology."

At the end of the meeting, Greene was "impressed by his sincerity and intrigued by his dedication."

He later recalled that the exchange was "the first time [he] heard a rabbi mention the word 'G-d' seriously."

Greene and his wife invited Feller to speak at their Jewish book club, and were similarly affected by the rabbi's authenticity and wholeheartedness. Greene and Feller began studying together, and over the years, the Greenes became religiously observant.

"We became family," said Feller.

Chabad: Judaism as Life

In the 1950s, Rabbi Herbert Weiner, a longtime Reform Rabbi and the author of *9½ Mystics*,[13] had a deeply illuminating conversation with the Rebbe, Rabbi Menachem M. Schneerson. In Rabbi Weiner's words:

> I opened my notebook and sat back in the chair, again conscious of how comfortable and relaxing it was in the Rebbe's office. Then I remembered that this was my last chance and resolved to ask even the most embarrassing questions in an effort to solve the enigma of Lubavitch. I explained to the Rebbe that more than a year had passed since I began trying to understand the movement, and that I had come to him now with a confession: I did not understand. Would he mind if I started this interview by asking him about the character of a Hasid?
>
> Rabbi Menachem Mendel smiled and told me to go ahead; as before I could speak English but he would answer in Yiddish.
>
> "Isn't the fact that Hasidim turn to the Rebbe for almost every decision in their lives—isn't this a sign of weakness, a repudiation of the very thing that makes a man human, his *b'chirah*, freedom of will?"
>
> The Rebbe's answer came without hesitation, as if he had dealt with the question before. "A weak person is usually overcome by the environment in which he finds himself. But our Hasidim can be sent into any environment, no matter how strange or hostile, and they maintain themselves within it. So how can we say that it is weakness which characterizes a Hasid?"
>
> I pressed my question from another angle and told him that I sensed a desire in chabad to oversimplify, to

---

13. *9½ Mystics: The Kabbala Today* (New York: Simon and Schuster, 1969).

strip ideas of their complexity merely for the sake of a superficial clarity. As a matter of fact, I blurted out, all his Hasidim seemed to have one thing in common: a sort of open and naive look in their eyes that a sympathetic observer might call *t'mimut* (purity) but that might less kindly be interpreted as emptiness or simple-mindedness, the absence of inner struggle.

I found myself taken aback by my own boldness, but the Rebbe showed no resentment. He leaned forward. "What you see missing from their eyes is a *kera*!"

"A what?" I asked.

"Yes, a *kera*," he repeated quietly, "a split."

I want to suggest that the most powerful type of role model we can provide is that of a person who does not suffer a *kera*, internal strife, and confusion: a splintering or fissure within one's self-identity.[14]

Among the Rebbe's chassidim there is often a joy and a confidence, an absolute seamlessness and a lack of self-consciousness. This should not be mistaken for mindless faith; neither is it achieved without considerable effort.[15] Even as we struggle with our weaknesses and

---

14. In private conversation with me and my husband, Dr. Gerald Schroeder, a noted physicist, shared with us an experience that was seminal in his journey toward Jewish observance. Then a student at MIT, Schroeder came to Crown Heights, Brooklyn, during his winter break to participate in an "encounter" weekend. He enjoyed the lectures and the home hospitality, but he was most taken, he related, with the Shabbos afternoon *Farbrengen* with the Rebbe. Being unfamiliar with the Yiddish language, he was unable to understand the Rebbe's talks that spanned many hours. Nor was he swept up in the fervor of the Chassidic melodies sung by the assembled. What made an indelible impression on him was the way in which the Rebbe and his Chassidim were so intensely focused and seemed completely oblivious to and certainly unperturbed by the fact that this was Christmas weekend and that the rest of the world was celebrating in a decidedly different manner.

15. It is the result of sustained study and practice, hashpaah/*memale*, coupled with submission to a *mashpia*, a spiritual mentor or *dugma chaya*, who can take a person beyond his/her limited understanding to the place of truth, *sovev*.

failings—and we do struggle—we understand this process to be integral to our life's work. It is this wholeness that we must model if we are to be effective educators and successful facilitators of Jewish life.

The fifth Lubavitcher Rebbe, Rabbi Sholom Dov Ber (1860–1920), stated[16] that just as a Jewish man has an obligation to don *tefillin* each day, each Jewish parent has an absolute obligation to think about the education of their children for half an hour each day. But, I wonder, if you have three children, can a half hour suffice? What if you have ten children? How then does this compute?

The Rebbe was underscoring the depth and importance of education. But I think that his injunction can be understood additionally as shining the spotlight on the educator himself.

Perhaps what this means is that for at least a half hour each day, one has to contemplate one's own moral and spiritual standing. An educator has to meditate deeply and consistently on what it is *they themselves* are modeling. This difficult and essential exercise is the same whether one has one, three, or three hundred children or students.

At our Chabad Center, just as at Chabad centers worldwide, we offer a full roster of rigorous, compelling classes, workshops, and semester-long courses. But the quotidian details of our lives and interactions are no less important to our mission.

There is a famous story of a Chassid who traveled a great distance to visit with his Rebbe. When asked why, he replied: "I wanted to see how he tied his shoelaces."

My colleagues and I are simple folk, pedestrian chassidim. We work each day on "how to tie our shoelaces." It is an ongoing journey.

---

16. Cited in *Hayom Yom, Teves 22*, compiled by Rabbi Menachem M. Schneerson (1943).

Chapter 8

TOUCH OF GRAY: AGING AS SPIRITUAL COMPLETION IN THE THOUGHT OF THE LUBAVITCHER REBBE

Shaul Wertheimer,[1] *Chabad on Campus of Queens*

Growing old is part of the human condition. In Western society, even though aging is commonly associated with the gradual atrophy of physical attributes, the hope is that this can be done gracefully and in the company of loved ones.

Perhaps surprisingly, although Judaism is a source of much of Western cultural thinking, its teachings on aging have not yet been fully appreciated or integrated into societal thinking. As will be briefly shown here, one finds rich insights on aging in Judaism's millennia-old teachings.

---

1. I would like to thank Prof. Philip Wexler and Rabbi Menachem Schmidt for the opportunity to speak and write on this important topic. Thank you to Prof. Boaz Kahana for his enthusiasm, and to Prof. Shnayer Leiman for reading the first draft of the paper. Thank you to Rabbi Michoel Seligson for help in clarifying some ideas, and thank you to Rabbi Zalman Dubinsky for his insightful questions and encouragement.

    Many thanks go to my father, Dr. Douglas Wertheimer, for his guidance throughout the research and writing process. Thank you to my wife, Tzipah, for her support and encouragement.

    I hope I have done justice to the Rebbe's views on aging and society; any mistakes or ambiguities are mine.

From the Talmud to Rabbi Menachem M. Schneerson, the Lubavitcher Rebbe, an appreciation of the Jewish outlook on aging can provide many benefits today, both personal and societal.

I

In the penultimate Mishna of the fifth chapter of *Ethics of Our Fathers*, we find a blueprint for the pattern of Jewish life.[2]

> Yehuda ben Teima used to say: The 5-year-old is the age for learning Scripture; the 10-year-old is the age for learning Mishna; the 13-year-old is the age for the obligation of the mitzvoth; 15 for the study of Talmud; 18 for marriage; 20 to seek livelihood; 30 for strength; 40 for understanding; 50 for giving counsel; 60 for old age; 70 for ripe old age; 80 for strength; 90 for a bent back; at 100, one is as if he were dead and removed from the world.

The first few statements discuss young ages, and the statements are presumably addressed to the parents.

Rabbi Menachem ben Solomon Meiri (1249–1306) writes: "In dividing a person's life into periods, the Mishna intends to encourage the parents to have their children receive their Torah education in their proper time."[3] Each stage seems to be a preparation for the next, one building upon the other. In effect, the Mishna can also be viewed as strategic goal setting.

In this context, we can note that the stages that are enumerated do not happen automatically or without effort. Old age is not something that "just happens," but—like the previous stages—invites our active participation. Moreover, life does not end with old

---

2. Irving M. Bunim, *Ethics from Sinai*, vol. 3, p. 222.
3. Beis HaBechirah on Pirkei Avos 5:24.

age, as the Mishna continues to list more advanced ages and their respective accomplishments.

The Mishna is cautioning us to take advantage of our time, as wasted minutes cannot be regained.[4] There is much to accomplish in life. One who has reached old age is included in this list and is expected to continue achieving.

Old age often brings with it physical weakening, and perhaps one should be expected to be less productive than when in one's younger years. Yet the exact opposite is true: With the weakening of one's physical capabilities comes the strengthening of one's intellectual capacity.[5]

It is notable that other versions of the Mishna exist, in which the age of sixty is said to be the age of wisdom, not old age.

Not only are these two versions—sixty as the age for being considered elderly or as the age for wisdom—not contradictory; they are complementary.[6]

The Talmud[7] states, "Rabbi Yosei HaGelili says: An 'elder' [*zakein*] means nothing other than one who has acquired wisdom." He interprets the word as a contraction of the phrase *zeh kana*, meaning: This one has acquired. Elsewhere the word *kana* (acquire) is used in reference to wisdom, "as it is stated that wisdom says[8]: 'The Lord acquired me at the beginning of His way.'"[9]

Yet is the connection of "elder" to wisdom merely a play on words? Rabbi Yosef Chaim of Baghdad (1832–1909) probes beneath the surface of this Talmudic passage, quoting a Mishna in Ethics:[10] "Who is wise? One who learns from every person." With the vicissitudes of life, one gathers wisdom from many people, and it can

---

4. Rabbi Shmuel ben Yitzchak de Uçeda, Midrash Shmuel 5:23.
5. Rabbi Judah Loew, Derech Chaim 5:21.
6. Rabbi Shmuel ben Yitzchak de Uçeda, Midrash Shmuel.
7. Kiddushin 32b.
8. Proverbs 8:22.
9. This paragraph is from the Koren Talmud Kiddushin, p. 173.
10. 4:1.

thus be considered as if they've lived longer than their biological years. Furthermore, Job wrote,[11] "I said, Days should speak, and multitude of years should teach wisdom." It is specifically over the course of time that one gains wisdom.[12]

Shortly after Joseph discloses his identity to his brothers, he prepares them to return to their father, Jacob. He promises to provide for them there, in Israel, and requests that they tell Jacob about all the great honor being accorded him in Egypt.

Pharaoh approves and sends gifts.

Then it is stated:[13] "And to his father, he likewise sent 10 donkeys, laden with the good things of Egypt."

What is "the good of Egypt"? The Talmud[14] comments:

"What are 'the good things of Egypt' [that are mentioned but not specified here]? Rabbi Binyamin bar Yefet says in the name of Rabbi Eliezer: He sent him aged wine, which the elderly find pleasing."

Why did Joseph send his father aged wine? Rabbi Shmuel Eliezer Edeles (Maharsha; 1555–1631) comments[15] that the elderly get cold easily, and wine warms them up. But Rabbi Yosef Chaim of Baghdad's comment goes beyond a physiological observation and includes a comment on the human condition, in writing[16] that wine is different from other liquids and foods. Unlike most food and drink, wine gets better with age.

In other words, Joseph was sending his father a coded message, as if to say, I know you have grown older since we've last seen each other, but I know that—like a fine wine—you have certainly developed and deepened your character. You've only become better with age.

---

11. 32:7; Gen. 45:23.
12. Rabbi Yosef Chaim of Baghdad, Ben Yehoyada on Kiddushin 32b.
13. 32:7; Gen. 45:23.
14. Megillah 16b; Rashi ad loc.
15. Ad loc.
16. Ad loc.

II

The Talmud[17] makes a puzzling statement about old age:

"Until Abraham, there was no old age. One who wanted to speak with Abraham, would speak to [his son] Isaac [since they looked the same]; one who wished to speak with Isaac, would speak to Abraham. [What did Abraham do?] He prayed for compassion and then he gained the appearance of old age, as the verse states, 'And Abraham was old, coming of days.'"

The commentaries ask: Old age did exist before Abraham, and is mentioned earlier in the Bible, even with regard to Abraham himself! Different answers[18] are given, including[19] that his facial hair had not turned white, despite his advanced age.

Why would a white beard be so important to Abraham that he would pray for it? In today's society, there is a multi-billion-dollar anti-aging industry. People dye their hair to look younger, and Abraham wanted to look old!

Why does one's hair turn white with age?

Biological facts notwithstanding, Chassidic sources[20] add a mystical twist to the whitening of one's hair. Hair represents Tzimtzum, the Kabbalistic doctrine of the diminishing of a G-dly flow of energy. Hair from the head can be seen to represent an "outgrowth" of the intellect, a sort of casual conversation from which one can learn profound concepts that may have been previously inaccessible.[21] The nature of this "outgrowth" is determined by the

---

17. Bava Metziah 87a.
18. Yefei Toar, Bereishis Rabba ch. 65.
19. Maharsha ad loc.
20. See Rabbi Shmuel Schneerson, *Toras Shmuel* 5627, pp. 25ff.; Rabbi Menachem M. Schneerson, *V'Avraham Zakein* 5746; Rabbi Shneur Zalman of Liadi, *Maamorei Admor HaZaken al maamorei Chazal*, p. 287.
21. A father may wish to teach an abstruse concept to his son, yet the son is unable to comprehend due to the profundity of the idea. In order to transmit the concept, the father utilizes a parable, which, at its core, encloses the depth of the concept. When the child eventually grasps the parable to its

place from which it is drawn—namely, the mind—and is thus limited by the constraints of the mind.[22]

In contrast, the beard represents a flow of intellect beyond the normal progression, known as *Yud Gimmel Tikkunei Dikna* (lit. the 13 corners of the beard). The beard draws its spiritual energy from *Atik Yomin* (lit. the Ancient of Days), a level that transcends the intellect and the natural order. The beard bypasses, so to speak, the mind, and represents a flow of intellect that transcends one's mind. Young people do not grow facial hair because their intellect is limited to what they can comprehend. As one ages, one's intellect matures, and one becomes capable of grasping more abstruse concepts.

Old age brings with it a transcendence of experience; the beard turns white, indicating that change in the flow of intellect. Concerning *Atik Yomin*, it is stated,[23] "The One of Ancient Days sat; His garment was white like snow and the hair of His head was like pure wool." The whiteness thus indicates the maturity of intellect, which is no longer fettered by the typical constraints of the mind.

Let us consider the life of Rabbi Elazar ben Azariah, known to many for his prominent place in the text of the Passover Haggadah. At the age of 18, he was appointed the head of the Sanhedrin, the Jewish court. His beard miraculously turned white overnight.

The sages who appointed R. Elazar certainly knew his age, but they nevertheless saw fit to appoint him the head of the Sanhedrin. Why did it matter what color his beard was? This miracle took place in order that his outer appearance would reflect his inner

---

fullest extent (Babylonian Talmud, Avoda Zara 5b states, "A person does not understand the opinion of his teacher until after forty years"), he will be able to trace it to the analog (Rabbi Menachem M. Schneerson, Vayedaber, etc., Acharei Mos, 5722, p. 265).

22. Rabbi Menachem M. Schneerson, *Derech Mitzvosecha, Mitzvas Tiglachas Metzora*, p. 104b.

23. Daniel 7:9.

sagacity, despite his young age.[24] The whitening of the beard represents the completion of the beard, that is, a revelation of the *Yud Gimmel Tikkunei Dikna*.

Avraham was known for his hospitality and kindness to all, and is seen as representing the Kabbalistic Sefirah of Chessed/Kindness. Chessed is the first[25] of the 13 Attributes of Mercy, which correspond to the 13 corners of the beard (*Yud Gimmel Tikkunei Dikna*). It is thus Abraham who unlocked the secret of the 13 Attributes, revealing them to the world.

Our sages therefore state that Abraham was the first to attain old age, which the mystics associate with advanced intellect and the 13 Divine Attributes of Mercy.

III

At the Chassidic gatherings (Farbrengens) in celebration of the 70th and 80th birthdays of Rabbi Menachem M. Schneerson, the Lubavitcher Rebbe, the Rebbe commented on prevalent ideas about growing old and offered his own interpretation of aging as spiritual completion.

In summary, the Rebbe noted that we often think of life as being composed of productive and non-productive periods. The first 20 to 30 years have little achievement, and are often seen as setting the stage for "the real world," when we will become productive. The next 30 to 40 years are years of achievement. Then comes retirement, enjoying the fruits of our labor, and trying to find ways to fill the time.

Yet the Torah does not distinguish in this manner; there are differences, of course, in the phases of life, but they are all productive.

---

24. Rabbi Menachem M. Schneerson, Sichot Kodesh 5741, Acharon Shel Pesach, vol. 3, chs. 67–73.
25. See Likkutei Sichos, vol. 4, p. 1348, regarding different opinions about the beginning of the 13 Attributes of Mercy.

As expressed in the aforementioned Farbrengens,[26] the Rebbe viewed retirement as a sort of *bal tashchis*, a wasting of resources and a tragedy of cosmic proportions.

There's nothing like the energy of youth; a young person may register physical accomplishments of great proportion, while an elderly person may have trouble walking short distances. But life isn't about physical accomplishments, the Rebbe noted. It's about making life on earth brighter and holier than before we were born.

To support this point, the Rebbe cited the Zohar,[27] which says that a weakness of the body is the strength of the soul, meaning that as one's strength and physical drives diminish with age, one achieves a spiritual maturity that more than compensates for any physical weakness.

When Job[28] said, "Man is born to toil," he expressed an essential fact of human nature. Just as a child thrives when challenged with responsibility, so too does an adult—and certainly a person of advanced age. Thus, the Rebbe argues, there is no such thing as a happy retirement; it is an oxymoron. G-d wants us to partner with Him rather than be passive recipients, and He therefore made the drive to achieve part of the fabric of our being.

IV

Notwithstanding the Rebbe's position, the fact remains that people will continue to retire, resulting in the destruction of many lives and a wasting of invaluable human resources.

The Rebbe strongly encouraged an effort to change the general societal view of aging by emphasizing the positive side of retirement. On a practical level, this would involve:

---

26. This passage is based primarily on Likkutei Sichos, vol. 29, pp. 263–271; see appendix.
27. Book I, p. 180b; ibid., 140b.
28. 5:7.

1. Not only changing the attitudes of the business and professional world, and of society at large, toward aging, but even more important, changing the self-perception of the elderly. As an example of the latter, I often tell nursing home residents that the very fact that they are still here is because they have something that only they can accomplish. On a regular basis, I share the very same idea with the college students with whom I work.
2. Opening Torah study centers for the aged, and, as the Rebbe put it, "the near-aged." The Rebbe also viewed these study centers as an opportunity for intergenerational relationships[29] and encouraged all[30] to participate.

---

29. It is noteworthy that when the Rebbe introduced the concept of creating Torah study centers geared to the elderly, he instructed that they should be referred to by the Hebrew term *kollel*. The Rebbe gave three explanations for this: (1) The term is commonly used to refer to centers of Torah study, and is therefore quickly recognizable; (2) The term Kollel is primarily used for Torah study centers for the newly married, and will thus help preclude the potentiality that a center for the elderly may generate a feeling of "I'm old"; (3) The word Kollel is more inclusive than *klal*. Whereas klal refers to one united group, kollel indicates an active inclusion of others (Likkutei Sichos, vol. 29, pp. 267–268).
30. The Hebrew word *kol* (all) can be viewed as a composite word that includes all the levels of the soul. The *chof* is numerically equivalent (gematria) to 20 and alludes to the two transcendent levels of the soul—*Chaya* and *Yechida*—which each comprise the 10 sefiros. The *lamed* is numerically equivalent to 30, and thus corresponds to the 10 sefiros of each of the three immanent levels of the soul (*nefesh* [physical awareness], *ruach* [emotions], and *neshama* [intellect]). See Ohr HaTorah, Haazinu, p. 1651, of Rabbi Menachem Mendel Schneerson (1789–1866). Additionally, the words *kollel, klal,* and *kol* share an etymological root. *Kol* means all; *klal* features the addition of the letter *lamed* (whose name itself means to teach) and hints to learning in order to teach (*lilmod al menas lelamed*); finally, *kollel* indicates the active pursuit to include others (see note 26). See Likkutei Sichos, vol. 21, p. 315, and footnote 6; Likkutei Sichos, vol. 29, p. 268, footnote 29.

The free time of the elderly presents an opportunity for them to continue being productive in a very meaningful way. By serving as mentors to young people, they create a bridge to the past and a link to our history. Spiritual growth ought not to end with old age, and the elderly should be given accessible ways to deepen their knowledge of Torah.

Together we can help the elderly—and dare I say, help ourselves in the process—reveal their true value to themselves, their families, and their communities.

Appendix

Translation of a talk by the Lubavitcher Rebbe, August 2, 1980 (20 Menachem Av 5740)

Due to the concealment [of G-dliness] and darkness in the world, a false perspective has been created, namely, that since old age brings with it the weakening of one's physical strength, the elderly are therefore no longer fit to work or to be productive, and therefore they should be dismissed from their position [of employment], relinquishing their work, etc.

It is self-understood that this thought alone generates a feeling of despondency and dejection: They will feel that they are now "old," and no longer able to accomplish anything of meaning; they are merely a burden on their family, G-d forbid....

According to the Torah of truth, the reality is exactly the opposite: Precisely in one's old age—despite one's physical weakening—one has an evident advantage: "the multitude of years should teach wisdom,"[31] and "the elders of Torah...as they get older, their knowledge settles within them."[32]

---

31. Proverbs 8:22.
32. Mishna, Kinim.

Even those who are not scholars also have the benefit of intellect and wisdom, which comes as a result of "how many experiences have occurred to these individuals...."[33]

Due to the wealth of experience and the challenges of life that an elderly person has weathered during their years, younger people should specifically come to them for advice.

And since, with regard to intellect, which is the primary quality of a person, old age actually generates the opposite of weakness—and, as mentioned above, the "multitude of years should teach wisdom"—it is understood quite simply that when it comes to matters that are connected to wisdom and intellect, the elderly should actually be more active.... [I]t is therefore understood that with regard to our general society, when a person reaches old age, they are pushed out—Heaven forbid!—partially, or even more so from their livelihood and so forth. This is damaging to the employer and damaging to them, even though the intention of the one who does it is good.

---

33. Babylonian Talmud, Kiddushin 33a.

Section III

LAW, LITERATURE, AND MYSTICISM

Chapter 9

DEMONIZATION AND TRANSFORMATION: LEGAL AND KABBALISTIC MYTHS OF SELF AND OTHER

Nathaniel Berman, Brown University

I. Two Grand Myths

All fundamental transformations—political, religious, economic, metaphysical—demand a regeneration of identity. Alongside its material dimensions, structural change cannot take place without the transformation of those who inhabit those structures. Revolutionary political ideologies invariably prophesy the advent of a "new man," a "new woman," even a "new humanity." This dimension is most salient in ideologies focused on specific groups: class, gender, nation, religion, and so on. Though some decry "identity politics" as a distraction from "real issues," profound transformation without the reconstruction of identity is unimaginable.

The rhetoric of "real issues," however, does point us, *a contrario*, to *myth* as a source of insight about identity-transformation—provided we understand "myth" not as delusion, but as imaginative narrative, above all tales of Self and Other, their conflicts, metamorphoses, even reciprocal transmutations. I examine here two grand myths of the dialectics of Self and Other. Both proclaim the emergence of a renewed Self from alienation, its liberation from the domain of the Other—a domain portrayed as "monstrous," even demonic. Nonetheless, they insist that the Self's emergence from alienation demands engagement with Otherness, even the transformation of the Other *into* the Self.

These two myths emerge from particular strands within two seemingly unrelated discourses, thirteenth-century kabbalah, especially the Zoharic literature,[1] and modern international law, especially after World War I. In kabbalistic myth, I discuss tales of the emergence of divine and human Selves from their alienation in the demonic, which Zoharic writers call the "Other Side," the *Sitra Ahra*. In international law, I discuss tales of "self-determination," the emergence of national Selves from their suppression by alien States. In both, one finds a diagnosis of an alienation of true selfhood, an etiological tale recounting the genesis of this condition, and an aspiration for the liberation of authentic desire and creativity. Both discourses portray Self and Other as irreducibly intertwined, forever fated to exchange places and shift roles. The ambivalences driving these myths find expression in the range of fates imagined for the Other, in the legal/political, existential, and metaphysical spheres.

Although the juxtaposition of these myths may seem startling, even implausible, their approaches to the regeneration of selfhood

---

1. I use this term for the texts printed in the sixteenth century as "*Sefer ha-Zohar.*" Recent critics have challenged the notion that the Zohar is a unitary book with a single author or even a unified group of authors. Elliot Wolfson summarizes these critiques while nonetheless arguing persuasively for reading the Zoharic literature together, in "Zoharic Literature and Midrashic Temporality," in *Midrash Unbound*, ed. Michael Fishbane and Joanna Weinberg (Portland, OR: Littman Library, 2013), 323–324. I have, throughout, emended the Zoharic texts in accordance with the critical edition established by Daniel Matt, Nathan Wolski, and Joel Hecker, available at www.sup.org/*Zohar*/?d=Aramaic%20Texts&f=index. Although I have made my own translations for the Zoharic passages discussed here, I have at times referred to the Matt, Wolski, and Hecker translation. See Daniel C. Matt, Nathan Wolski, & Joel Hecker, trans., *The Zohar: Pritzker Edition* (Stanford: Stanford University Press, 2004–17).

feature remarkable homologies. One might attribute these homologies to the participation of both in the oldest conundra of Western, Mediterranean, even world culture. There is also, however, a more proximate historical link between these two myths, or, more precisely, contemporary interest in them: the aesthetic/political/religious ferment of the early twentieth century known as "cultural-modernism."

Cultural-modernists were fascinated with so-called primitive sources of cultural energy—energy flowing from racial, geographical, or ethnic Others, or that intimate Other, the unconscious. Cultural-modernists, in a variety of fields, often created their masterpieces animated by a desire for a paradoxical "alliance" between such forces and advanced techniques of high culture. Picasso's *Les Demoiselles d'Avignon* (1907) is an iconic example of this "alliance."[2]

Cultural-modernists viewed their "primitive" forces with ambivalence. On the one hand, they desired them as indispensable sources of vitality for cultural renewal, for unblocking an ossified Western culture. On the other hand, they feared them as excessive and destabilizing. In 1926, the influential Protestant theologian Paul Tillich (1886–1965) highlighted this ambivalence by identifying the "primitives" of the artistic imagination with the "demonic" of the religious imagination.[3] Tillich shared his lifelong fascination with the demonic with his fellow Berliner, Gershom Scholem (1897–1982), who, like Tillich, emerged from the crucible of cultural-modernism.

---

2. See J.C. Middleton, "The Rise of Primitivism and Its Relevance to the Poetry of Expressionism and Dada," in P.F. Ganz, ed., *The Discontinuous Tradition: Studies in German Literature* (Oxford: Clarendon Press, 1971), 194. I have argued that such an "alliance" underlies the transformation of international law after World War I. See, e.g., "Modernism, Nationalism, and the Rhetoric of Reconstruction," *Yale Journal of Law and the Humanities*, 4 (1992), 351–380.
3. Paul Tillich, "The Demonic: A Contribution to the Interpretation of History" (1926), in *The Interpretation of History* (Elsa L. Tamley, trans., 1936), 85.

II. Law: From "Monstrous" States to Peoples' Self-Determination

In international law, the myth of self-transformation I discuss here concerns non-State, ethno-national groups. In the early twentieth century, such groups included European separatist nationalists aspiring to dismantle the Ottoman, Hapsburg, Hohenzollern, and Romanov empires, and, ever-increasingly, anti-colonial nationalists resisting the yoke of Britain, France, Spain, and Portugal. These were all groups perceived as peripheral, as Other, by the Western, State-centered international order bequeathed by the nineteenth century. These groups challenged the legitimacy of existing States, international law's foundational units, on the ground that they suppressed the ethno-national identities of those under their rule. From a Jewish perspective, these developments bore decisive historical consequences. Zionism emerged in the context of growing European ethno-nationalism; and, on a radically different note, the metastasis of that ethno-nationalism led to the greatest catastrophe in Jewish history.

In the nineteenth century, most international lawyers rejected such claims. In 1871, the Italian Guido Padelletti declared that, in contrast to "the concrete idea of the State," the idea of the "nation and the liberty of peoples" was "filled with contradictions."[4] This "other notion" was "vague and disintegrating," inevitably provoking the "dissolution of all political ties" and "chaos in public law."[5] Despite its ability to "overthrow the whole of Europe,"[6] its internal contradictions rendered it "impotent" to resolve territorial disputes.[7]

Paradoxically, despite its destructiveness, ethno-nationalism possessed the power to construct an alternative international or-

---

4. Guido Padelletti, "L'Alsace et La Lorraine, et le droit des gens," *Revue de Droit International et de Législation Comparée*, 3 (1871), 491.
5. Ibid.
6. Ibid., 478.
7. Ibid., 478–479.

der, a veritable demonic double of the existing State system. While multi-ethnic States like Belgium and Switzerland would no longer have "the right to exist," the "logical consequence" of nationalist claims would be the "formation of three or four monstrous States."[8] On the one hand, "disintegrating," and "filled with contradictions"; on the other hand, driven by an iron "logic" yielding fearsome "monsters": such was the paradox of ethno-nationalism. Those familiar with kabbalistic notions of the Other Side readily recognize this kind of paradoxical adversarial force.

This paradox was rooted in ethno-nationalism's twofold relation to alterity. On the one hand, the ethno-national Other sought to destabilize existing States—the Hapsburg Empire by the Czechs, the French Empire by the Algerians, and so on. On the other hand, this Other was internally fractured, due to the divergent elements within all collective identities, as well as the multiplicity of identities that cohabit all territories. Only in Italy, Padelletti declared, was there a convergence of "language, literature, geographical configuration, economic interests, race," and "the consciousness of belonging" to the same "nation and glorious historical traditions"[9]—unwittingly exemplifying the familiar "othering" of all nationalisms except one's own.

After World War I, jurists sought to embrace emerging ethno-nationalist Selves as indispensable to a new international order. Nonetheless, a new set of paradoxes arose. For the Alsatian Robert Redslob (1882–1962), nationalism was one of the "generating forces" of World War I,[10] but it had also "inspired the Peace Treaties."[11] It was to that paradox, the destructive and constructive dimensions of nationalism, that he devoted his 1930 study, *The Principle of Nationalities*.

---

8. Ibid.
9. Ibid.
10. Robert Redslob, *Le Principe des Nationalités* (Paris: Sirey, 1930), 36.
11. Ibid.

For Redslob, nationalism was "the pathos of an elemental force,"[12] an "ardent torrent of popular passion."[13] Redslob acknowledged that "the conservation of the existing State" was sometimes wiser than dismantling it in response to separatist nationalism, whose "unleashing of elemental passions" could be "difficult to master."[14] At the same time, in an almost exact reversal of Padelletti's associations, Redslob painted a gothic-horror image of merely "existing States." Such States, "devoid of ethnic personality," had no intrinsic vitality. As "incomplete, inorganic formations," they each sought "to destroy the other and assimilate its vital energies."[15] Again, those familiar with kabbalistic myth will readily recognize this imagery: essentially lifeless entities that have nonetheless gained destructive power through parasitically appropriating the vitality of others—a textbook definition of Lurianic *k'lipot*.

For Redslob, the international order founded on those false monsters must be overhauled by nationalist vitality. International law, stripped of its "artificial exterior," should "reflect the real movement of nationalities," indeed "model itself" on the "elemental force." Law would then not devote itself to preserving existing States, but to aligning itself with the "creative, emotional, passionate movement of people" striving for "a new constellation of their collective life."[16] The nationalist "torrent" unlocks the floodgates of human creativity, sweeps away the "inorganic" States, and regenerates collective identity and human history itself.

Nevertheless, due to nationalism's two-edged, vital/dangerous quality, progress cannot consist of a foundationalist substitution of Nation for State, Life for Law. Rather, the "élan of emancipation, the tumultuous flood," must "encounter" law—the latter revitalized by its own encounter with nationalism—and "make it its

---

12. Ibid.
13. Ibid., 36.
14. Ibid., 90–91.
15. Ibid., 86–87.
16. Ibid., 13 (emphasis added).

ally."[17] The "pact" between nationalism and law will domesticate the former, even while rejuvenating the latter. Once law has been revitalized by nationalist passion, the latter "will *discipline itself*" by reshaping itself in accordance with law.[18] Once the ossified State system has been overturned by nationalist energy, new legal forms can emerge to embrace, while "disciplining," that energy.

For jurists like Redslob, this double stance toward nationalism—embracing and disciplining—expressed itself in the new legal doctrines and institutions that emerged from the Versailles Treaty. The new legal order affirmed ethno-national energy while weaving it into that order, restraining its dangerous impulses.

Affirmation of nationalist claims seems to be most directly expressed in the right of self-determination: in its fullest form, entailing independence and thus the dismantling of an existing State. Self-determination addresses alterity through the *separation of different "Selves."* Nevertheless, while self-determination purports to directly translate nationalist identity into legal form, it always involves contestable acts of inclusion and exclusion. The secessionist claim of the American colonies shows this all too clearly, with its dubious assertion of a difference of "peoplehood" from the English and its immoral exclusions of indigenous peoples and enslaved Africans. But irresolvable conundra about who is included in the "Self" and who is excluded as "Other" attend the emergence of *every* collective or individual Self. All attempts definitively to resolve such questions inevitably involve domination and violence.

Two primary methods have been used to determine national "Selves": so-called objective and subjective self-determination. The Versailles settlement implemented "objective" self-determination by ratifying the establishment of new States in central and eastern Europe, purportedly founded on formerly repressed ethno-national Selves. It reserved "subjective" self-determination for disputed

---

17. Ibid., 36.
18. Ibid.

borderlands, such as Upper Silesia, where plebiscites were held to determine more murky "Selves."

The controversies involved in determining any ethno-national Self can be sketched through a series of questions. If we purport to determine that Self "objectively"—for example, through race, religion, or language—what is to be done with the alterities that undermine such criteria: racially mixed ancestry, religious heterodoxy or syncretism, and linguistic dialects or hybrids? What is to be done when "objective" factors cut in different directions—when racial and linguistic identity do not coincide, or when either clashes with religious identity? Should such cases be determined through plebiscites, the "subjective" method? But this method provokes its own conundra. For example, how does one determine the population to be consulted—all those living within the borders carved out by the incumbent State, or only those conforming to some "objective" definition of the nation, whose difficulties I have just outlined? Should émigrés and refugees be entitled to vote? The "subjective" method returns us to its "objective" counterpart, just as the latter did to the former. The challenge of alterity, which gives rise to the movement to form new national Selves, also renders them forever precarious.

A second set of legal/political regimes seeks to *affirm the identity of the ethno-national Other while integrating it into the State's citizenry.* After World War I, treaties protecting minority rights were imposed on the new States of eastern and central Europe—States themselves purportedly embodying the Selves of their ethno-national majorities. Often, particularly in relation to ethnic Germans in Poland and Czechoslovakia, the minorities granted protection were those who had formerly constituted the dominant ethnic group in the defunct empires. The minority Other to the new majority national Self was formerly part of the majority Self in relation to the erstwhile minority Other.

The minority protection system sought to safeguard cultural autonomy for ethno-national groups without infringing upon the new States' internal identity or international status: on the one hand, forbidding forcible integration into the majority culture; on the other, disallowing direct representation of minority groups in international fora such as the World Court and the Council of the League of Nations. The system diminished absolute sovereignty but did not transfer the prerogatives of States to ethno-national groups. While self-determination disciplined nationalism through legal procedures for determining selfhood, minority protection disciplined it by subjecting it to State sovereignty, albeit one subject to international scrutiny.

Controversy arose concerning the purpose of minority protection. Did it primarily seek to engender minorities' loyalty to the new States, or to protect their distinct cultural identity? If the former, the system could be temporary; if the latter, it would have to be permanent. The League hotly debated such issues for years, until the system's demise under fascist and Nazi assault. As the system collapsed, its ambivalences made it possible for some to accuse it of insufficiently protecting minorities and others to accuse it of encouraging minority disloyalty to the States of their citizenship.

Finally, a third option loomed throughout the inter-war period: the *effacement or extermination of ethno-national Others*. The temptation to expel minorities, deprive them of citizenship, or forcibly assimilate them beckoned to States eager to safeguard their precarious new national Selves. Such temptations eventually gave rise to the horrors of which we are all aware.

In every ethno-national struggle, decisions about inclusion or exclusion deeply affect the construction of the national Self. These decisions often prove to be provisional, as nationalist movements, like individuals, often oscillate, sometimes wildly, among a variety of stances toward the Other. Bounded selfhood on the national level, no less than the individual level, is always precarious because of the irreducible alterity in every Self. The energy of a nationalist Other may succeed in destroying an existing State, but the Self it seeks to embody in a new State will, in turn, be beset by its own Others.

III. Kabbalah: From Demonic to Divine Selfhood

The kabbalistic myths I discuss here also begin by diagnosing a monstrous condition: a Self that is distorted by its relation to an Other, a vitality blocked, an illegitimate political hierarchy. Dismantling this configuration unleashes creativity, liberates the true Self, and restores legitimacy. But this transformation demands that the Self engage with the Other that blocks it—an Other that often proves to be the Self in alienated form, vital energy lamentably reified, creative desire gone astray. These tales, precisely because of their overtly mythical quality, illuminate the ostensibly pragmatic legal discourse; the latter, in turn, highlights the stakes in kabbalistic myths. Political and legal tropes in kabbalistic discourse, as well as demonizing and spiritualizing tropes in legal discourse, heighten this reciprocal illumination.

The diagnosis of our world as ontologically and normatively inverted sets the stage for myths presented as etiologies of that condition. Divine power is the source of all existence, yet everywhere appears subordinated to adversarial forces; the divine is absolute unity, yet the world is violently divided; the divine is absolute goodness, yet evil reigns. Unlike much philosophical theodicy, thirteenth-century kabbalistic myths do not explain away these phenomena as subjective illusions, artifacts of limited human understanding. Rather, they portray them as ontological realities, however scandalous theologically and tragic existentially. Elements of theodicy appear in this discourse, but it is not these elements that give them their distinctiveness.

I draw my first kabbalistic myth from a number of thirteenth-century sources, including Zoharic and related texts. In thus assembling this myth, I follow Claude Lévi-Strauss's dictum that "a myth consists of all its variants."[19]

The first source, from the Zoharic literature, begins with its leading sage, Rabbi Shim'on bar Yohai, lamenting the distorted

---

19. Claude Lévi-Strauss, *Structural Anthropology*, trans. by C. Jacobson and B.G. Schoepf (New York: Basic Books, 1963), 206–231.

Demonization and Transformation

state of the world, prompting him to a tale that provides its secret explanation:

> One day, the Companions were walking with Rabbi Shim'on. Rabbi Shim'on said: "I see these nations are all elevated and Israel is the lowest of all. Why? Because the King has cast the *Matronita* [Queen] away and made the bondwoman enter in her place...." Rabbi Shim'on wept, and continued: "A king without a *Matronita* is not called a king. A king who cleaves to her bondwoman, where is his honor?"[20]

This tale is self-consciously etiological: the world's unacceptable political condition, which anyone can "see," provokes the mythical narrative of the divine king who has replaced his true consort with the bondwoman. The text identifies this bondwoman with the demonic: the "alien crown" and the "Other Side."[21] She is the counterpart, elsewhere called Lilith, of the divine Queen, the *Matronita*, a name for the Shekhinah, a divine female *persona*. The liaison is scandalous, even abject: the king "rides...in a place not his own, in an alien place, and suckles her."[22] The tale thus attributes the distorted world to deviant divine desire, causing royal disgrace ("where is his honor?"), indeed the loss of royal identity ("the king...is not called a king"). The myth provides the backstory of a world ruled by illegitimate sovereigns: a disqualified king, a demonic queen.

Our text refrains from justifying the king's improper desire. This silence implies, however shockingly, that the king's dalliance is due to overpowering lust for this Other woman. This motive is explicitly dramatized in a closely related tale by another thirteenth-century Spanish kabbalist, Joseph of Hamadan, who describes a

---

20. *Zohar* III, 69a.
21. Ibid.
22. Ibid.

divine king with two consorts, his public queen and the alluring "concubine" he visits at night.[23] Yet another thirteenth-century writer, Moshe of Burgos, describes the seduction of the divine phallus by Lilith, with the result that a "turban" encases it, blocking its proper creativity, causing the birth of demons.[24] These three tales are not identical, but constitute variants of an identifiable mythic pattern, the vicissitudes of divine desire.

Divine desire, the most powerful force in the cosmos, the creator of beautiful form, proves to be in continual danger of going astray, its power alienated by the Other, giving rise to a world of demons. In Joseph of Hamadan, the king's improper liaison co-exists with his rule alongside his proper consort; in Moshe of Burgos, it produces a demonic world; in our Zoharic text, illegitimate sovereigns rule a world marked by illegitimate hierarchies. The sovereigns' monstrous transmogrification is all the more horrifying because it is invisible except to those with esoteric knowledge.

In whatever variant, one may wonder: can divine desire, so powerful it overrides all norms, be devoid of redemptive potential? Joseph of Hamadan portrays the liaison with the Other woman as an ineluctable, if clandestine, feature of the divine king's intimate life. He even attributes to this liaison the kingship of the House of David, and thus eventually of the Messiah—for the origin of the royal line in the Other woman, the Moabite Ruth, is the price that the divine king's alien mistress exacted for their sexual relationship.[25] This shocking assertion is a mythical recasting of the various dubious liaisons that punctuate the Davidic genealogy.[26]

---

23. Published in Moshe Idel, "Seridim Nosafim Mi-Kitvei R. Yosef Ha-ba mi-Shushan ha-Birah," *Da'at*, 21 (1988), 47–48.
24. Moshe of Burgos, Ma'amar Al Sod, "Hasir Hamitsnefet Harim Atarah," in Gershom Scholem, "Le-Heker Kabbalat R. Yitshak ben Ya'akov Ha-Kohen," *Tarbiz* 5:1 (1933), 50.
25. Ibid.
26. See, generally, Ruth Kara-Ivanov Kaniel, *Kedeshot u-Kedoshot: Imahot Ha-Mashiah ba-Mitos Ha-Yehudi* (Jerusalem: Ha-Kibutz Ha-Me'uhad, 2014).

The liaison between the divine male and the demonic female, which explains distorted political hierarchies, is thus also the source of proper political rule, indeed of cosmic redemption.[27]

If the Zoharic king is a God lost in the Other, what of his improper consort, the bondwoman? When the king emerges from the "alien place," he will "have salvation" and will again be called "righteous."[28] But what of his consort? Might she be the alienated form of the divine *Matronita*? A number of Zoharic passages, indeed, portray the Shekhinah transmogrified into a terrifying figure, with distinctly Lilith-like characteristics[29]—often as a result of liaisons with the demonic male, attributed variously to seduction, capture, and rape. Indeed, the king-and-the-bondwoman passage is so striking because portrayals of sexual liaisons between the divine male and the demonic female are so much rarer than the converse. In one stark example, a liaison between the demonic male and the divine female leads to her physical transformation into a Lilith-like monster, with long hair and nails, wreaking violence upon the world.[30] Is the bondwoman in our passage, too, a transmogrified Shekhinah? Would the end of cosmic alienation, in which the king regains his honor and his name, bring about a similar transfiguration of the bondwoman? Will this Other woman regain her identity as a divine Self? Might the tale be one of the recovery of true selfhood by *both* illegitimate sovereigns? Is this a myth of the integration of the Other into a liberated State over which unalienated Selves preside?

Our king-and-the-bondwoman passage does not, however, give any indication in this direction. On the contrary, it twice identifies the "bondwoman" with she whose "first born the blessed Holy One killed in Egypt," seemingly relegating her to irremediable alterity. Despite divine desire for her, or perhaps as an overcompensation

---

27. "Seridim Nosafim," 48.
28. *Zohar* III, 69a, citing Zechariah 9, 9.
29. See, e.g., *Zohar* I, 223a–b; III, 79a.
30. *Zohar* III, 79a.

for it, this tale seemingly seeks the effacement or even extermination of the national and metaphysical Other.

A second myth, elaborated in a famous Zoharic passage from the *Idra Rabba* ("Greater Assembly") section,[31] more explicitly portrays the relationship between divine and demonic kingdoms, both national and metaphysical. It elaborates a seemingly superfluous passage in the Bible concerning the "kings who reigned in the land of Edom, before there reigned any king over the Israelites" (Genesis 36, 31). This biblical text enumerates seven kings who "reigned" and "died," apparently a succession of usurpers, and an eighth who reigned but whose death is not recited. Rabbi Shim'on proclaims that these banal verses contain the deepest cosmic secrets. Indeed, when Rabbi Shim'on began this discourse, the earth "shuddered" and his disciples "swooned."[32]

What is this unbearable secret that destabilizes the foundations of the cosmos and human subjectivity? It is the story of the instability of the divine Self and its ineluctable relationship to its demonic Other. The narrative begins by recounting the flawed initial creation of the cosmos by the Holy Ancient One, *Atika Kadisha*, the highest divine *persona* in the Zoharic literature. This ultimate deity prepared carefully for his doomed creative act: he "unfolded before Him a curtain and on it He engraved and measured kings." All for naught: "his *tikkunin*[33] did not endure"—and the "kings" died.[34]

"Kings," like "crowns," is a term that Zoharic writers use instead of the more common "Sefirot," the ten fundamental structures of all being, divine and demonic, cosmic and human. The creation of

---

31. The passage starts at *Zohar* III, 128a, and continues, with some digressions, for several folios.
32. *Zohar* III, 128a.
33. *Tikkun* (Aramaic plural: *tikkunin*) is a key term in the Zoharic and kabbalistic traditions. Its semantic range in Zoharic Aramaic includes: repair, rectification, preparation, arrayal, and adornment. Most often, the Zoharic texts seem to intend that the word evoke that full range of meanings. I leave it transliterated in this essay for the sake of brevity.
34. *Zohar* III, 128a.

the first seven "kings" alludes to the emanation of the seven lower Sefirot, associated with the seven days of Creation, as well as with the two divine figures about whom much of Zoharic drama revolves, the divine king and queen, the blessed Holy One and his Shekhinah/*Matronita*. Yet the passage also evokes the literal meaning of "kings," not only because the seven lower Sefirot govern the earthly world, but because the passage draws explicit political lessons.

The passage portrays the mythical "Edom" as the "place where all Judgments stand therein."[35] "Judgments" or "Laws" [*dinin*], in the Zoharic idiom, are associated with the left side of the cosmos, particularly with the Sefirah of Might [*Gevurah*]—by contrast with the right side of Grace [*Hesed*]. Despite Judgment's divine source, its dissociation from Grace causes it to metastasize and congeal into the demonic, often signaled by the plural form and by the adjective "fierce." The passage conveys the demonic nature of the first Edomite king by describing him as the "fiercest of the fierce decrees of Judgment."[36]

Such "Judgments" are paradoxical. On the one hand, they are hardened, untempered by Grace, forming a calcified legal system. An array of "kings" who reign in the "place where all Judgments stand": a veritable portrayal of a demonic international legal order, resembling Padelletti's "monstrous States" and Redslob's States of "inorganic personality," bent on war and dissociated from creative passion. "Edom" is the Zoharic name for such an order.

On the other hand, these "kings" lead precarious lives. Each of the usurpers violently seizes the throne and dies soon after. This paradox of the Zoharic "kings," like Padelletti's and Redslob's States, violent and fragile, stems from their dissociation from passion and compassion. Indeed, their demonic Otherness derives from this dissociation.

The defectiveness of the "kings" is foretold even when they only exist in *Atika Kadisha*'s imagination. When "it arose in His will to

---

35. *Zohar* III, 135a.
36. Ibid.

create," the Torah, figured here as something like a female consort of *Atika Kadisha*, "immediately said to Him: Whoever wishes to do *tikkun* and create, let him first do *tikkun* on his own *tikkunin*."[37] Attributing the defective creation to a flawed divine Self, the passage proclaims a political moral:

> From here we learn that unless a ruler of a nation receives his *tikkun* first, his nation cannot receive its *tikkun*.... How do we know this? From the Ancient of Days: until he received his *tikkun* in his *tikkunin*, all those who need *tikkun* did not endure—and all the worlds were destroyed.[38]

As Yehuda Liebes explains, it would take just one step further to identify "Edom" with this flawed, "pre-*tikkun*" state of *Atika Kadisha*. Although only an eighteenth-century Sabbatean work seems to have explicitly taken this shocking step,[39] it is implicit in the Zoharic narrative. The demonic Edom is the initial state of the ultimate God. And "the land of Edom" is his defective cosmos, figured as a system of "kings," a "monstrous" international order, an empire of the Other Side.

"Edom" is the great Other in Jewish tradition: first identified with Esau, Jacob's adversarial twin, then Rome, the destroyer of the Temple, and, finally, Christianity, the great political/theological enemy. The identification of Edom with the initial state of *Atika Kadisha*, and the "land of Edom" with his first creation, is breathtakingly bold. The great metaphysical, political, and religious Other is God-*as*-Other, an alterity that pre-exists his Selfhood.

---

37. *Zohar* III, 128a.

38. Ibid. The last clause relates the death of the Edomite Kings to the midrashic myth of the primordial worlds that were destroyed before our world was created. *Midrash Kohelet Rabbah* 3, 14.

39. Jonathan Eibeschütz, *And I Came This Day unto the Fountain*, ואבוא היום אל העין, ed. and introd. by Paweł Maciejko (Los Angeles: Cherub Press, 2014), 27.

Elliot Wolfson makes a closely related point regarding another Zoharic passage, portraying the relationship between metaphysical forms of Esau and Jacob as pre-*tikkun* and post-*tikkun* stages of the "same" personage, who passes from a demonic to a divine form.[40]

How does one effect metaphysical and political transformation, from the demonic to the divine order? The *Idra Rabba* prescribes two closely related requirements. The first is the transformation of the Self, the *tikkun* of *Atika Kadisha*, for it was his non-rectified subjectivity that created the defective cosmos. The "ruler of the nation," indeed of an entire international and metaphysical order, must transition from his defective, "Edomic" state to a rectified state, one in which, to cite the "king-and-the-bondwoman" passage, he can regain his honor and resume his name.

This *tikkun* is closely related to the second desideratum, the relationality of male and female *personae*. In Genesis, the surviving eighth kingdom is the only one of whom we are told the existence and name of its queen. The Zoharic text elaborates:

> These were not annulled like the rest, because they were male and female. Like the palm tree, which arises only as male and female. Therefore, now that they are found as male and female, "death" was not spoken of them as with the others, and they endured.[41]

This combination of sexual and arboreal imagery indicates that the flaw of the "Edomic" order was its dissociation from organic desire. The "Edomic" kings, to quote Redslob, are "inorganic personalities," who, for all their fierceness, are fundamentally lifeless. The flow of sexual desire and arboreal sap overthrows the lifeless kingdoms and replaces them with those nourished by vitality.

---

40. Elliot R. Wolfson, "Light Through Darkness: The Ideal of Human Perfection in the Zohar," *Harvard Theological Review*, 81 (1988), 81 n. 29.

41. *Zohar* III, 135a.

If Edom and *Atika Kadisha* are at once antagonistic Self and Other, and yet different stages of the "same" subjectivity, so are each of the "kings" within the two realms. The passage expresses this paradox in relation to their putative "death." On the one hand, with the Bible, it affirms this death. On the other hand, it declares: "and if you say, it is written, 'and he died...and he died,'...it is not so! But rather, anyone who descends from his former status, 'death' is spoken of in relation to him."[42] Once the overall *tikkun* has been established, the kings are rehabilitated—and, as in the "king-and-the-bondwoman" passage, they are then "called by different names."[43]

The "king-and-the-bondwoman" and "Edom" passages share key features. They each portray two political/metaphysical orders, one proper, one improper, with the shift between the two triggered by different states of the ruler's subjectivity and desire. The ruler is both the same in the two states *and* absolutely different. To be sure, the "Edom" passage concerns the initial divine emanations, while the "bondwoman" passage portrays an interruption of the proper state of the king. I would not, however, overestimate this difference, in view of the cyclical quality of Zoharic mythical time.

Both passages, moreover, express ambivalence about the Other's fate. The "Edom" passage declares not only that the "kings" died *and* that they were rehabilitated, but it also proclaims that "some became fragrant, some became fragrant and not fragrant, and some did not become fragrant at all."[44] In the "king-and-the-bondwoman" passage, the king appears completely rehabilitated, but is this rehabilitation not forever shadowed by his powerful, wayward desire? And, although the bondwoman seems condemned to banishment or death, must we not also imagine her rehabilitation as the Shekhinah, as other Zoharic passages instruct?

Moreover, how should we envision the relationship between the land of Edom, with its doomed bachelor-kings, and the land of

---

42. *Zohar* III, 135b.
43. Ibid.
44. Ibid.

tikkun, with its gender dimorphism and organic desire? At first these appear to be two radically separate lands, cultures, peoples, *cosmoi*. The resurrection of the "kings," however, implies that it is the same land, with the "Edomic people" eventually assimilated into the land/people/cosmos of *tikkun*. Nonetheless, in view of the fact that some of the "kings" did "not become fragrant at all," the tension between the two kingdoms persists—either in mortal combat, or, perhaps, as an irreducible alterity necessary for the continual re-consolidation of the always precarious divine, national, and personal Selves.

A third Zoharic myth, contained in the "desert hermit" passage, addresses such territorial questions directly. I will only sketch a few elements of this complex tale. The Zoharic sages encounter an old man who declares that he dwells year-round in the desert, for which he gives two paradoxically interrelated explanations. Portraying the "fierce desert" into which the Israelites fled Egypt as demonic, the "place and dominion of the Serpent, the wicked king, for it is literally his,"[45] he proclaims:

> We have separated ourselves from the settled area [*yishuva*] to the fierce desert, to study Torah there, in order to subdue That Side [i.e., the Other Side]. *And also*, because Torah only settles [*mityashva*] there—for there is no light except that which issues forth from darkness....[46]

This brief excerpt, including lines famously analyzed by Elliot Wolfson,[47] is rich with territorial paradox. The desert is the dominion of the Devil, "the Serpent, the wicked King." The "settled area," by contrast, is the territory of the "side of holiness."[48] Their relationship during most of the year is a political/metaphysical partition of

---

45. *Zohar* II, 184a.
46. *Zohar* II, 184a.
47. Wolfson, "Light through Darkness."
48. Ibid.

the land between two rulers, two distinct cultures, one divine, the other demonic.

However, these dominions are also irreducibly intertwined. On the one hand, the hermit dwells in the land of the Devil in order to subdue him, a saboteur behind enemy lines. On the other hand, he declares that it is only in the desert that "Torah is settled" [*mityashva*]. This verb plays on the term "settled area" [*yishuva*], the appellation of the region that is the *opposite* of the desert. It is, paradoxically, only in the "non-settled" area that the "settling" of Torah occurs. The separation of the two dominions thus cannot be permanent or impermeable because the demonic Other contains the key to the divine Self. "Settlement," the distinguishing characteristic of the divine side, can only occur in the domain of the Other. "Human perfection," in Wolfson's phrase, can only be achieved *not* by integrating the two sides but by continually engaging in dialectical struggle between them. True Selfhood, indeed the Torah itself, can only be constructed by dwelling in alterity. Without partition, the indispensable cross-border engagement would be impossible.

What is the ultimate fate prescribed for the Other in this passage? On the one hand, it might be the maintenance of its alterity, a reservoir of "unsettlement" through which Selfhood can be continually re-achieved ("settled"). The notion that there is "no light except that which issues forth from darkness" seems to require alterity as a foil against which the Self can continually reconsolidate itself. On the other hand, the passage also envisions the subjugation of the Other Side, even its annihilation. And, on the third hand (as it were), in the world in which we live, the world whose etiology the myth comes to provide, alterity seems irreducible. The scapegoat must be sent to the Devil every year, and the hermit lives his secret life in the land of the Other.

The passage thus suggests a perennial oscillation among separation, integration, engagement, and subjugation. To put it in all-too-familiar terms, the desert and the "settled area" oscillate among: partition between two sealed-off States; two States with citizens of each living in the other; one State that emerges through subordination or annihilation of the Other; a complex federation in which fraught cultural interchange is vital to the existence of each; and more still.

A final passage thematizes territorial and existential ambivalence toward the Other. This text concerns the *k'lipot*, "husks" or "shells," another key Zoharic term for the demonic. Two possible roles are attributed to the *k'lipot* in thirteenth-century kabbalah. Their proper role is to serve the divine realm, surrounding and protecting it, like the shell of a nut. When the cosmos is out of joint, they contaminate, dominate, or even destroy the divine. These two roles correspond to two opposite fates Zoharically envisioned for them. On the one hand, after protecting the divine while it gestates, they may be cast off or annihilated—a fate emphasized if they have improperly come to dominate the divine. On the other hand, they may, after serving their proper role, be integrated into the divine whole, their hardness melting into the flow of divine Grace.

Our Zoharic passage stages this ambivalence in the form of a debate between two sages, Rabbis Yitshak and Hamnuna Saba, about an entity called *nogah*, "brightness," one of the heavenly phenomena attending Ezekiel's vision of the divine Chariot. This *nogah* has a long history within post-Zoharic kabbalah, a liminal terrain where good and evil fight their battles. In this passage, it serves as the crux of a debate about the proper stance toward the *k'lipot* in general:

> Even though this side is nothing other than the side of contamination, there is "brightness [*nogah*] about it" [Ezekiel 1, 4]. Therefore a person should not cast it outside. Why? Because...it has a side of holiness, and one should not treat it with contempt. Therefore it should be given a portion in the holy side. Rav Hamnuna Saba: [the verse] meant as follows: "*could* there be a brightness about it?!"[49] And it should be treated with contempt.[50]

---

49. Reading the phrase as rhetorical sarcasm, rather than as a declarative statement.

50. *Zohar* II, 203b.

Ambivalence toward the Other thematized as a debate, with metaphysical, political, and existential consequences: *either* cast outside and treated with contempt, *or* given a place within holiness and treated with non-contempt (respect?). The territorial imagery of banishment/residence and affective imagery of contempt/non-contempt for the Other highlight the political and existential stakes.[51] Should the Other be integrated into the national or individual Self or banished to a separate territorial or psychic space?

Following others, such as Wolfson,[52] I have argued here that the demonic in kabbalistic myth is closely related to what we today again call "the Other"—that which teaches us about the unknown within, that without which we cannot consolidate our Selves, that which renders that consolidation ever precarious. Engagement with alterity promises the most vital creativity and renewal, as well as posing the gravest moral and existential dangers. These dangers include hatred, racism, violence, even exterminationism. Refusal to confront alterity, however, has its own dangers. It can bring (in ascending order of gravity): flattening of human diversity; sealing of wellsprings of cultural, political, or existential creativity; coercive assimilation to a dominant culture; and legitimation of pragmatist, as opposed to essentialist, forms of violence (Vietnam rather than Auschwitz). These dangers have been highlighted by a wide range of critical thinkers, including the Frankfurt School, post-colonial theorists, cultural feminists, and so on. Much of this thought has had a psychoanalytical dimension, the teaching that the repression of the Other is rooted in the denial of alterity within the Self, the denial of the unconscious, the denial that we are "aliens to ourselves."[53]

I conclude with a well-known passage by Scholem:

---

51. Both kabbalists and academics have long highlighted the political implications of kabbalah. Gershom Scholem, Elliot Wolfson, Yehuda Liebes, Haviva Pedaya, and Yonatan Garb are only some of the most prominent examples.
52. See, e.g., Elliot R. Wolfson, *Venturing Beyond: Law and Morality in Kabbalistic Mysticism* (Oxford: Oxford University Press, 2006).
53. Julia Kristeva, *Etrangers à nous-mêmes* (Paris: Gallimard, 1991).

> Removing the irrational stinger and banishing demonic fervor from Jewish history...this...is the original sin [of the nineteenth-century *Wissenschaft des Judentums*].... This terrifying giant—our history—is called to account...and this mighty creature, filled with explosive power, composed of vitality, evil, and perfection, lowers its stature, contracts itself, and proclaims that it is a nothing; the demonic giant is merely a simple fool...an average citizen....[54]

Scholem's "demonic giant" encapsulates cultural-modernist ambivalence toward the "primitive" that I described above. Scholem celebrates its "demonic fervor"—and yet, *or precisely therefore*, he also acknowledges its danger: its "vitality, evil, and perfection."

Scholem was a nationalist, as well as a scholar: a heterodox and protean Zionist fascinated by heterodox and protean kabbalah, especially its "demonic," Sabbatean form. This eloquent and startling passage brings together these two discourses, their promises, their dangers. It is this juxtaposition that, in a more prosaic way, I put before our project on Jewish spirituality and social transformation.

---

54. Gershom Scholem, "Mi-Tokh Hirhurim al Hokhmat Yisra'el" (1945), in *Devarim Be-Go* (Tel Aviv: Am Oved, 1976), 396. See David Biale, *Gershom Scholem: Kabbalah and Counter-History* (Cambridge, MA: Harvard University Press, 1982), 4.

Chapter 10

WALTER BENJAMIN'S MODERN-MYSTICAL THEORY OF YOUTH[1]

Yotam Hotam, Department of Learning, Instruction and Teacher Education, The Faculty of Education, University of Haifa

1. An Age of Youth

Between 1910 and 1917, Walter Benjamin composed a range of philosophical works and fragmented texts, including "The Life of the Students" (*Das Leben der Studenten*), "The Metaphysics of Youth" (*Die Metaphysik der Jugend*), "The Youth Is Still" (*Die Jugend Schwieg*), "Experience" (*Erfahrung*), "Socrates" (*Sokrates*), and "Dostoyevsky's 'The Idiot,'" all of which touch upon the concept of youth (*Jugend*) and its intersection with issues of modernity and theology, faith and political action, God and the world, and secularization and its discontents (Benjamin, 1991; Benjamin, 1996; Benjamin, 2011).[2] The trope of youth, the meaning of being young, the call for "youthfulness" (Benjamin, 2011, p. 56) and its success or

---

1. This paper is an adapted reprint of Yotam Hotam (2017), "Eternal, Transcendent, and Divine: Walter Benjamin's Theory of Youth," *Sophia* <https://doi.org/10.1007/s11841-017-0620-y> reprinted by permission of Springer, *Sophia*.
2. These texts were first published together in the German edition of Benjamin's writings (Benjamin, 1991). An English version of these texts is presented in Benjamin (1996) and Benjamin (2011).

failure, marked an issue with which Benjamin grappled in most of his early writings before and during the First World War. Benjamin, a member of what was then known as the "radical faction" of the German youth movement (Witte, 1991, pp. 22–23; Eiland & Jennings, 2014, pp. 39–40; Brodersen, 1990, pp. 50–51), "proclaimed the slogan of youth" (Benjamin, 1994, p. 23), which call was already rather widespread in the German cultural atmosphere of that time (Trommler, 1985; Janz, 1985; Hotam, 2009), making it an epicenter of his intellectual endeavors. "We are living in an age of Socialism, of the women's movement, of traffic, of individualism," writes the enthusiastic 18-year-old Benjamin. "Are we not headed toward an age of youth?" (Benjamin, 2011, p. 26).

What, then, is an "age of youth"? For Benjamin, such an "age" refers to a historical era and, more profoundly, relates to a particular human condition, pointing also to the distinction between the two. In relating to a human "individual time" (Benjamin, 2011, p. 242), an "age" is not equivalent to a particular biological phase (being 14, 19, or 35 years old), but rather to an inner spiritual essence. Thus, for Benjamin, the meaning of the word "youth" lies in the fact "that from youth alone radiates new spirit, *the* spirit" Benjamin, 2011, p. 136). Over and against a "philistine" experience "devoid of meaning and spirit," Benjamin draws an image of youth as "the voice of the spirit" (Benjamin, 1996, p. 4). Such a "voice" represents a site of independence and freedom. Thus an "intellectual autonomy of the creative spirit" denotes, for Benjamin, not just a resistance to particular social and cultural circumstances (that of bourgeois life, education, or morality), but, more radically, an independence from all forms of external social, cultural, educational, or political influences (Benjamin, 1996, pp. 43–44; Benjamin, 2011, p. 136). The point to note, then, is twofold: first, that an "age of youth" represents for Benjamin an inner human spiritual core—"the pure word for life" in an "inward, spiritual sense" (Benjamin 1996, p. 80); and second, that such an inner spiritual core lies beyond historical and societal conditioning: a site of "beyondness," to put it metaphorically.

This inner human spirituality is theologically articulated by Benjamin and, as such, composed of three characteristics: it is transcendent, eternal, and divine. It is transcendent because Benjamin conceptualizes youth as an unmalleable inner human essence, separated from all external demands. To put it differently, youth transcends worldliness (Wolin, 1982, p. 16; Steizinger, 2013, p. 60). Youth in this particular sense is dedicated to "faithfully serve the true spirit" (Benjamin, 2011, p. 133). Here the spirit (*Geist*) does not signify a particular culture or historical stage in some Hegelian sense, but rather an innate state of the human being. This point is important because, for Benjamin, "individual time" marks a distinct category that he wishes to advocate separately from any notion of the advancement of history and society.

Benjamin's short script "The Life of the Students" could serve as an example for this last point. The text opens with a clear differentiation between a "view of history" that concerns itself with the ways in which "people and epochs advance along the path of progress" and Benjamin's analysis of history, which aims at grasping a "metaphysical structure, as with the messianic domain or the idea of the French Revolution" (Benjamin, 1996, p. 37). Such a "metaphysical structure" underlines history and, in this sense, though embedded within history, lies beyond its different appearances and manifestations. It is separated from any notion of "progress" and advancement and contains a certain "spiritual" essence that points to a double meaning—the logic of history, but also, and more important, a differentiated inner core that transcends the social and historical.

This separation between history and its "spiritual" essence informs Benjamin's distinction between true and false education, central to his "The Life of the Students." Benjamin starkly distinguishes between an autonomous student "spirit" and "vocational training" (Benjamin, 1996, pp. 37–38).[3] True education, for Benjamin, is about an "erotic" and "creative" core that "cannot be captured

---

3. This particular text was based on a speech that Benjamin gave to the Berlin Free Student Group. See Witte (1991), p. 29.

in terms of the pragmatic description of details (the history of institutions, customs, and so on)" but rather "eludes them" (Benjamin, 1996, p. 37). Here the true "spirit" relates to an imagined human essence that escapes history and lies beyond historical conditions (Eiland & Jennings, 2014, p. 34; Witte, 1991, p. 24). What Benjamin then calls the "perversion" of the universities lies in their attempt to transform "the creative spirit into the vocational spirit" (Benjamin, 1996, p. 41). "All these institutions," argues Benjamin, "are nothing but a marketplace for the preliminary and provisional. . . . They are simply there to fill the empty waiting time, diversions from the voice that summons them to build their lives with a unified spirit of creative action, Eros, and youth" (Benjamin, 1996, p. 46).

Youth transcends existing social conditioning. It does so by means of a radical retreat to an inner human "spirit" (Benjamin, 2011, pp. 104–105). It also denotes Eros. As Benjamin explains in a letter to Carla Seligson, Eros for him combines the Platonic heavenly Eros with Christ's "Kingdom of God" (Benjamin, 1994, p. 92). It connects a passionate desire for self-cultivation (*Bildung*) with self-elevation to the realm of truth, beauty, and totality (Wolin, 1982, p. 6). Such an entwining of a modern concept of education (*Bildung*) with Platonic and Christian symbolism was a central theme in Benjamin's fragment "Socrates" (Benjamin, 1996, p. 52). Figuratively, self-cultivation (as denoted in the concept of *Bildung*) appears as a reenactment of the Socratic winged chariot in its trajectory of returning to the godly dominion, albeit in the Christian redemptive sense. Youth resonates a *theia mania* (divine madness), and human life is in this way re-enchanted.

Pedagogically, such a re-enchantment of human existence is not about learning a specific curriculum that prepares the young person for productive and meaningful life in a modern German society and culture; it is rather about transcending this curriculum. Socially speaking, over and against "bourgeois security" youth offers "the Eros of creativity" (Benjamin, 1996, p. 42). For Benjamin, this radical approach takes the Humboldtian kind of "freedom" (von Humboldt, 1966). with which Benjamin was familiar (Witte,

1991, p. 35) to its logical end—a *Freiheit zum Grunde* that is freedom from all types of limiting actions.

If transcendence denotes Eros and self-fulfillment, it also aims at the "Kingdom of God." This reference to the divine marks the second aspect of Benjamin's concept of youth. The human (youth) and the godly realm are interwoven. In this way transcendence aims at the divine. Youth taps into the divine element within the transcendent human (spiritual) essence. And it is this connection that Benjamin wished to capture by evoking the idea of "youth by the grace of God" (Benjamin, 2011, p. 102). There is a transcendent and divine "spiritual"—or youthful—core of the human being, an element that the human being incorporates, may experience, but that refers to God.

In following divinity, eternity is the last main aspect in Benjamin's conceptualization of youth. For Benjamin, youth-time is eternal because it lies beyond human experiences in the world (Benjamin, 1996, p. 37). Denoting *Kairos*, youth-time is also the "now" (*Jetztzeit*), or, better, represents the eternal-now moment (Levine, 2014, p. 27). Thus Benjamin reiterates a distinction between two concepts of time: the flow of time that characterizes this worldliness, and the other, removed, transcendent-eternal time of youth.

Understanding "the life of the students," for example, means for Benjamin transcending the particular social and historical reality and thinking in terms of the everlasting "metaphysical" nature of this reality (Benjamin, 1996, p. 37). Students as young people, according to Benjamin, embody such an eternal "metaphysical" feature. Here the distinction between two concepts of time makes an appearance in the form of a separation between the time of history and that of youthful eternity (Benjamin, 2011, pp. 41, 207). Such a distinction articulates the relations between eternity and temporality in a way that is starkly informed by a theological speculation. The suspension of world-time denotes for Benjamin the Christian true divine time that lies beyond historical linearity; it echoes a religious dualism between transcendence and immanence; and it is meant to play on the gnostic themes of redemption and fall (Steizinger, 2013).

2. "Young man, I tell you, stand up!"

Transcendence, divinity, and eternity point to the theological imagination invested in Benjamin's theory of youth. This imagination should be regarded more particularly as a mystical one. In order to make a case for Benjamin's reposing in mysticism, it is helpful to make sense of the type of mystical thought that informed Benjamin's symbolism. Meister Eckhart's mystical writings may provide us with a suitable example, not just because of their strong mystical tone, but also because of what could be viewed as Eckhart's own theory of youth. The importance of Eckhart's mystical writings for the discussion of Benjamin's theory of youth lies in their modern reception. As Ingeborg Dengenhardt's pivotal study has shown, Eckhart's mystical writings received particular attention within the intellectual environment of the turn of the nineteenth century, in which mysticism was once again "in the air" (Degenhardt, 1967, p. 226; Pfeiffer, 1857; Landauer, 1903; Büttner, 1903). Though a full analysis of Eckhart's mysticism is beyond the scope of this essay, it is possible at least to point to some of the main notions that characterize his take on youth.

Eckhart's mystical writings presented modern celebrators no less than Middle Ages excommunicators with a theologically explosive substance. His allegorical interpretations of biblical texts were rather central.

The birth of Christ, for example, is presented not as a historical affair, but as an allegory for the manner in which God can "awaken" his "son," potentially in every human soul. The "son" becomes an emblem for a transcendent ground or an essence of the soul that can be "awakened" from slumber by the "father" (Eckhart, 2009, p. 27; Kopper, 1955, p. 33). The point to note is that the image of an awakened "son" is also symbolically understood by Eckhart as young. Youth (*Jugend*) marks, then, an important aspect of the godly presence embedded within the human experience.

This last point is accentuated by numerous sermons[4] that were made available in Pfeiffer's collection and (in part) in Büttner's translation (Büttner, 1903, vol. 2, pp. 149–156). In three of these sermons, Eckhart focuses in particular on one episode from the gospels in which Jesus, who is approached by a "widow" whose son lies dead before her, cries: "Young man, I tell you, stand up!" (*Adolescens, tibi dico: surge!* Luke 7:14).

Eckhart's allegorical reading of this passage underlines the godly, transcendent, and eternal characteristics of being young to which Jesus supposedly refers. There are three points to note, the first of which is the charging of the text with a symbolic meaning. According to Eckhart, the widow represents the human soul devoid of God (Eckhart, 2009, p. 576). The young man stands for the "son," that is, the (godly) essence of the soul—"the highest intellect"—that "can receive the divine light" and thus can be awakened by God (Eckhart, 2009, p. 214). Youth is where the soul is "Godlike: *there* she is an image of God" (Eckhart, 2009, p. 396). In representing the godly within the soul, youth also transcends this worldliness. It connects the "now," the divine spoken word ("he says"), a command ("arise"), and youth—all are but elements of the human "soul" that "'arise' in herself" (Eckhart, 2009, p. 214).

A second point to note is how Eckhart's symbolism involves images of femininity and masculinity. The soul is a "widow," while the young core within it is a virile "son." In following this positioning, Eckhart underlines an intercourse between the masculine figure of youth and the feminine image of the soul. Thus the soul for him is "virginal" (*Jungfrau*—suggesting also a young woman) when it is free from "alien images" (Eckhart, 2009, pp. 77–78). It elevates itself to the position of "bearing fruit" and thus being a "wife," only on being incepted with the "young man" (Eckhart, 2009, p. 214). Youth represents, then, the "intellect" or the "citadel" of the soul, which is not only transcendent and divine, but also imagined as masculine— or better, masculine within the feminine (Eckhart, 2009, p. 77).

---

4. Eckhart, 2009, Sermons 8, 21, 37, 79, 80.

Finally, youth is eternal. In denoting the faculty of the human being that "touches neither time nor flesh," youth is underlined by Eckhart as the "eternal now" (Eckhart, 2009, p. 79). The "eternal now" also denotes being young, which corresponds to the "eternal life" of the soul (Eckhart, 2009, p. 148). It is where the soul is "free from time" (Eckhart, 2009, p. 394; Kopper, 1955, pp. 50–52). The dualism of the eternal-godly and the human-worldly, a central theological trope, is here suspended by the introduction of an eternal presence within the human experience. Here, it seems, human time and world-time are disconnected because the first—human—entails a godly presence, while the second—worldly—is discussed in the wake of its absence.

3. *The Metaphysics of Youth*

Benjamin probably became familiar with Eckhart's writings long before he enriched his personal library with a copy of Eckhart's sermons (Benjamin, 1994, p. 178). In using the pseudonym "Eckhart. Phil" for his 1912 essay "School Reform: A Cultural Movement," he made clear, at the very least, his awareness of Eckhart. The main issue, however, is not whether Benjamin was directly influenced by Eckhart's theory of youth, but rather in what manner he was precociously attuned to the type of mysticism that Eckhart's writings exemplified.

Perhaps the most striking text into which Benjamin engraved his reworking of mystical allegories was "The Metaphysics of Youth." The text was written between 1913 and 1914 and, according to Gershom Scholem, remained unfinished (Angermann, 2015, p. 46). As Steizinger (2013, p. 48) points out, the text aimed at explicating what should be understood under the concept of "youth" in a way that brought together the prevalent themes within a variety of the texts that Benjamin had written prior to this point. It does so, however, by employing a highly enigmatic style (Eiland & Jennings, 2014, p. 56) that resists systematic scrutiny. Its value to an understanding of Benjamin's philosophy, rather than poetics, remained heavily debated.

The style and content, nonetheless, seem to be rather useful to a more detailed analysis of Benjamin's mystical orientation as described above. Benjamin's obscure style relates to rather mundane experiences from his everyday life—dancing, conversing with friends, writing a diary, and addressing sexual desires in venues that were fairly common to members of the young bourgeoisie of the time. It does so, however, in following the call upon the readers—most probably the circle of friends among which the text was circulated—to decrypt the "uncomprehended symbolism" that "enslaves us" in our everyday life (Benjamin, 1996, p. 7). This opening statement resonates well with Benjamin's call to understand the student's life "as a metaphor, as an image of the highest metaphysical state of history" (Benjamin, 1996, p. 37). The reading of everyday life as a symbol, or "as a metaphor," presents here the issue to note. In suggesting such a symbolic turn, the text reflects a tension between the overly poetic description of mundane experiences characteristic of youth (dancing, writing a diary, conversing with friends) and the elevation of these issues to an allegoric and, for Benjamin, profound order. Benjamin reads life allegorically (Cowan, 1985; Steizinger, 2013), and such a reading means that mundane experiences are taken by Benjamin as reflections of more abstract, metaphysical themes.

Taking on Benjamin's call to engage with the text's symbolism seems to be particularly fruitful in gaining some insight into its play with mystical themes. The text has three sections, respectively labeled "Conversation," "Diary," and "Ball." Read allegorically, the first (conversation) takes on youth mainly in terms of language and gender; the second (diary) conceptualizes youth in reference to time and temporality; the third (ball) may be seen as focusing on space and transcendence.

Benjamin's "conversation" relates to language and gender because it is made of an interaction between a "speaker" (appearing rather bluntly as a "he") and a "listener" (addressed as a "she") who also stand, respectively, for masculinity and femininity (Benjamin, 1996, p. 8). Here Benjamin expands on a variety of rather challenging concepts, like "genius" and its counterpart, "prostitute" (*Dirne*), manhood (*Mannheit*) and its womanly (*Weiblich*) equal. These are, however, used as symbols of an inner human experience—partly carried over by Benjamin from German romanticism (Wetters, 2014, p. 124; Friedlander, 2012, p. 75)—and do not refer to individuals or to social categories. They point to what Paul North called "a silent conversation in the soul" (North, 2015, p. 12). As such, speaker and listener, masculinity and femininity, are aspects of the human soul, engaged in the elusive instigation of truth and meaning.

Thus, for example, the speaker "receives meaning" from the "silent" listener, who is "the unappropriated source of meaning" (Benjamin, 1996, p. 6). One should note how in this case the "source of meaning"—eventually what youth should stand for—is located in an experience (what Benjamin calls "silence") that cannot be appropriated or grasped by the language of the conversation. Benjamin terms this source "the internal frontier of conversation," which he relates to the eternal and the true spiritual and which corresponds also to the innate womanly essence of the masculine (*Sein Weiblich-Gewesenes*) (Benjamin, 1996, pp. 7–9). Because conversation cannot appropriate its source, it becomes a paean for the fall of language, that is, what has been "lost" through its operation (Benjamin, 1996, p. 6). Because of the reference to a feminine characteristic, it is possible to see the variety of propositions relating to the woman who "protects meaning from understanding," or referred to as "the guardian of conversation," as allegories for the unappropriated source of meaning that is innate in the human soul.

These are not random images. For Eckhart, the being mute (*ohne Laut*), for example, characterizes the "original experience" (*ursprüngliche Erfahrung*) beyond understanding (Büttner, 1903, p. 188). In Benjamin's adaptation, the focus on experiencing a moment beyond understanding is the decisive one. The enigmatic character of the text that Benjamin composes, for example, could be seen as intended to break with understanding and to make a case for experience and for poetics. As in Eckhart's mysticism, the source of meaning is not external to human experience (which the symbol "conversation" represents), but is rather internal, located within this experience: an embedded transcendence of sorts. It also plays with aspects of femininity and masculinity in a way that relates to two of the missions apparent in Eckhart's writings. On the one hand, Benjamin refers to a concept of a "prostitute," who echoes the human existence devoid of God (what Eckhart terms the "Widow"), and who stands in opposition to the so-called "virginity" of the spiritual soul (Benjamin, 1996, pp. 35–36, 53). On the other hand, as "womanly" (*weiblich*), the feminine aspect of the soul marks, concurrently, the possibility—the conditions, as it were—for the human touching upon its inner youthful and divine essence. Woman is where the human "receives the silence" (Benjamin, 1996, p. 9), representing thus "the guardian of conversation"—the structural conditions, as it were—for the rise of "the youth of mysterious conversation" (Benjamin, 1996, pp. 9–10).

The second section of Benjamin's text, the "Diary" (*Tagebuch*), explicitly aims to engage with the question "in what time men live?" (Benjamin, 1996, p. 10). It aims, then, at rethinking the same issues of youth, divinity, human existence, and transcendence in terms of time and temporality (Steizinger, 2013, p. 66). In his answer, Benjamin articulates two times in which "men live." The first stands for the past-future linearity of this worldliness, and whose human characteristics are "mortality," "emptiness," "hopelessness," and loss of meaning (Benjamin, 1996, p. 11). Living is articulated by Benjamin as a living toward death (McFarland, 2013; Steizinger, 2013). Death indicates for Benjamin not only finitude, but also being empty, hopeless, and devoid of meaning. Over and against this "emptiness of time," however, lies the second "eternal," "youthful," that is, "true" and "immortal" time: "That time, our essence, is the immortality in which others die" (Benjamin, 1996, pp. 11–12). Eternity marks here a characteristic of youth, and its "immortality" stands against the temporality of this world. In this way it may be argued that world-time (mortal, empty, moving toward death) and eternal-time (youthful, true, immortal) are contrasted by Benjamin.

As a "book of time," the diary points to the possible "act of liberation." Against the "calendar time, clock time, and stock-exchange time," where "no ray of immortality casts its light over the self," the diary embodies the potential for the emergence of its opposite when "an 'I' that we know only from our diaries stands on the brink of an immortality into which it plunges." Here, the "immortal" time stands on the other side of the world-time. It penetrates world-time in the form of an "interval" (*Abstand*—to be read also as "distance"). One of the points to note is that the interval represents for Benjamin "the diary's silence"—the source of meaning, the idea of youth, and that of internal frontier, put in temporal terms (Benjamin, 1996, p. 12). A diary stands, then, as a symbol for the eternal-present youth, and in this way Benjamin's accentuation of the interval as a "pure time" relates to his overall theory. As such a "pure time," it suspends temporality by the very experience of "timelessness" and "the birth of immortal time" (Benjamin, 1996, p. 15).

The stark distinction between the eternal/timeless and linear/worldly—life-time (*Lebenszeit*) and world-time (*Weltzeit*), to use Hans Blumenberg's terminology—should command our attention. Because of this distinction, dualism of the kind expressed by Eckhart remains here a sound basis for Benjamin's thoughts. As a "ray of immortality," the eternal may pierce into the world; as a suspending "interval," it cannot act through this worldliness—or, better, cannot act by its means. The image that Benjamin seems to evoke relates to a certain performance of penetration: eternity may erupt, disturb, or suspend the other temporality, but cannot be reconciled or combined with it. Benjamin seems, then, to reject rather than accept a Hegelian conceptualization of the cunning of history, in which the advent of the divine-eternal is fulfilled by the workings of the worldly. To put it more polemically, Benjamin advocates not the advent of transcendent reason through history but rather its reverse implosive eruption in history. The potential for salvation, though always present and possible, remains nonetheless out of human control and beyond historical reach.

It should also be noted how, at this point, the mystic theme of "awakening" (*erwachen*) becomes meaningful to Benjamin (Kirchner, 2009; Steizinger, 2011). As Ansgar Hillach (1999) points out, a concept of "awakening" is informed by a "utopian movement of the spirit" (p. 890). Within the context of the diary (that recalls Hölderlin's poem that Benjamin chose as a motto for his text), such a movement maintains for Benjamin the meaning of "resurrection" of the self, "for immortality can be found only in death, and time rises up at the end of time" (Benjamin, 1996, p. 16). Benjamin thus explicitly connects his concept of time with the "awakening" of the human being, in a way similar to Eckhart's redemptive awakening of the "son" embedded within each of us (Benjamin, 1996, p. 12). The trope of "awakening youth" seems to be here not just about being self-conscious. More profoundly, it represents for Benjamin the mission of the "new religion," in which "the spirit of youth will awaken in *all*," and as the mystical opening up of "a spiritual reality" (Benjamin, 1996, p. 133).

Shifting the focus from time to space, the "ball" could be seen as the succinct culmination of these discussions. This culmination is arrived at by taking a prom night to symbolize "a space for Elysium, the paradise that joins the isolated into a round dance" (Benjamin, 1996, p. 16). In Benjamin's allegory, this heavenly space of interaction between man and woman is where "we are truly in a house without windows, and a ballroom without world" (Benjamin, 1996, pp. 16–17). In a way, then, we are dealing here with a free space (i.e., free from the "external" worldliness) that is represented by the joining together of the different forces of our mental lives, and in which "time is captured" (Benjamin, 1996, p. 17).

To the extent that youth is associated in this way with freedom and implies—one could say—a room of one's own, it also denotes a singularity located not in the outer universe but rather within our inner experience—on the other side of the "outside world"

(Benjamin, 1996, p. 17). Described from a mystical perspective, this singularity depicts the numinous unity of opposites. In alignment with mystical symbolism, the mysterious unity of opposites is embodied in Benjamin's poetics by the joining together of the virile and feminine aspects of the human experience (Benjamin, 1996, p. 16). The "ball" culminates in such a unifying "dance" and thus dovetails with the potential of salvation—existing, but beyond reach, celebrated, but out of sight.

Read allegorically, the conversation, the diary, and the ball bear on Benjamin's play with mysticism. Jean-Luc Nancy pointed out—in quoting Meister Eckhart—that this type of mysticism brings the "nothing" into the center of "the world." For Nancy, then, it is about praying to God to make us "free of God" (Nancy, 2008, p. 36; North, 2015, p. 26). According to Nancy, the act of awakening affirms an inner freedom, a pure spiritual singularity, beyond the possible, and as an imagined limitless limit that only a nothing—a *nihil*—can represent (Collins, 2015, p. 332; North, 2015, p. 26). Similarly, an affirmation that affirms the nothing is what Benjamin seems to drive at. Youth, in this sense, depicts a pure, uncontaminated, not-of-this world, original, creating being. This being is truly transcendent to the extent that it contains no substance that could be captured by form, or by any articulation; it is truly divine if, while being the creative force of this world, it is fundamentally detached from the world; eternal only in being non-temporal; existing in its non-existence. To follow the notion of singularity, youth may be seen as the event horizon, representing for Benjamin a gravitational center of all that is. Such a gravitational center refers to "the potential for redemption" that is embedded, according to Benjamin, in every present moment (Benjamin, 1996, p. 85). It refers to a youthful "time of the now" that can occur only as an "extra-historical" event within history (Kohlenbach, 2002, p. 34)—a notion that is not so much about the transformation of eschatological time into historical progress, but rather about symbolizing the break from history, or else the possibility of a break/rapture within history (Khatib, 2013, p. 217; Jacobson, 2003, p. 28; Frisby, 1985, p. 220).

4. A Modern-Mystical *Theory?*

Benjamin's theory of youth depicts the most intimate stances of the mystical mystery: the fortress of the soul, the unity with the beyond, femininity and eternity, nothingness and self-contraction—all are part of the young Benjamin's enthusiastic—maybe too enthusiastic—imaginaries. In this particular way, Benjamin makes a case for what Paul North called "the *logos* of theology" (North, 2015, p. 4). Nonetheless, mysticism also undergoes transformation. This point is crucial to the understanding of Benjamin's modern adaptation of mystical imaginaries, and also for why it could be defined as modern-mystical.

Benjamin's theory of youth is mystical in its retreat to the mystery of the intimate unity with the divine, which Benjamin describes as an eternal-present moment of awakening and salvation. It is modern and secular because, in so doing, the human being encounters an alleged human inner true self—i.e., youthfulness—without, however, any reposing on a simple faith in a unity with God. Transcendence here denotes an innate human faculty rather than the presence of an almighty God; a spiritual trait that may be fulfilled in any mundane human action or simple communication (dancing, conversing, or composing a diary, as examples), yet which is not conditioned by godly providence. The "secular" characteristic stands for the transformation that is enclosed within Benjamin's play between religious symbolism and its modern adaptation, which brings the original religious meanings that were ascribed to divinity to bear on simple, unconditioned, human interactions.

Modern mysticism is thus also a form of secularization (*Verweltlichung*) in the sense that it reframes transcendence within independent human experience in the world (Wexler, 2007). Benjamin, in this sense, reframes mystical symbolism rather than simply reproduces it. When Benjamin, for example, discusses the "awakening" of the inner-transcendent experience, he does so by focusing on an exclusive human experience. In Benjamin's allegory, what "awakens" the humanity of the human being is the human being; a self-referring self, one might say, that stands for the former mystical "divine self-revelation" (Kohlenbach, 2002, p. 50). The traits that were associated with a divine sphere are absorbed into a definition of the humane in the form of an autonomous, self-referring, human experience. As in the case of the "Metaphysics of Youth," the notion of God is relocated (rather than disappearing—God is not "dead," in the strict sense) because transcendence is compartmentalized within a human experience with no excess beyond it (Fenves, 2010, p. 34). Put differently, an inherited mystical mechanism is restructured as an exclusive human experience—pointing, perhaps, to gnostic elements in Benjamin's thought (Steizinger, 2013; Hotam, 2013; Lazier, 2008). Such a restructuring, however, does not refer to an absorbing of an eschatological time into historical progress, because it is exactly this alignment that is negated by Benjamin's concept of time, or that of messianism.

The restricting of transcendence within an exclusive human experience may be seen as signifying a distancing from the original mystical endeavor—for example, the one that Eckhart's writings expressed. At the same time, the relocation of the godly still reverberates with the same mystical logic. Is it not possible, then, to argue that Benjamin evokes a mystical notion and turns against it at the same time? What is accentuated, in this sense, is Benjamin's mystical turn against mysticism. To follow this idea through, Benjamin's modern reworking of mysticism takes mysticism to its radical, heretical conclusion, signifying a break with the mystical tradition itself. Doing so, however, denotes a performance of consistency with this tradition's original message (that of a break with a tradition). As in the case of von Harnack's *Marcion* (von Harnack, 1924; Grainer & Schmidt, 2001) such a composition may be seen as being religious to a fault (to put it ironically), or going to the limits of a religious message, which takes an original doctrine so seriously as to break with it altogether.

References

Angermann, A. (Ed.). (2015). *Theodor W. Adorno, Gershom Scholem Briefwechsel, 1939–1969.* Frankfurt a.M.: Suhrkamp.
Benjamin, W. (1991). *Gesammelte Schriften.* II (1–3), ed. R. Tiedemann & H. Schweppenhauser. Frankfurt a.M.: Suhrkamp.
Benjamin, W. (1994). *The correspondence of Walter Benjamin.* Chicago: University of Chicago Press.
Benjamin, W. (1996). *Selected writings, vol. 1: 1913–1926.* Cambridge, MA: The Belknap Press of Harvard University Press.
Benjamin, W. (2011). *Early writings.* Cambridge, MA: Harvard University Press.
Brodersen, M. (1990). *Walter Benjamin: A biography.* London: Verso.
Büttner, H. (1903). *Meister Eckeharts Schriften und Predigten.* Leipzig: E. Diedrichs.
Collins, A. (2015). Towards a saturated faith: Jean-Luc Marion and Jean-Luc Nancy on the possibility of belief after deconstruction. *Sophia, 54*, 321–341.
Cowan, B. (1985). Walter Benjamin's theory of allegory. *New German Critique, 22*, 109–122.
Degenhardt, I. (1967). *Studien zum Wandel des Eckhartbildes.* Leiden: E.J. Brill.
Eckhart, M. (2009). *The complete mystical works of Meister Eckhart.* New York: Herder & Herder/Crossroad Publishing Company.
Eiland, H., & Jennings, M.W. (2014). *Walter Benjamin: A critical life.* London and Cambridge, MA: The Belknap Press of Harvard University Press.
Fenves, P. (2010). *The messianic reduction: Walter Benjamin and the shape of time.* Stanford, CA: Stanford University Press.
Friedlander, E. (2012). *Walter Benjamin: A philosophical portrait.* Cambridge, MA: Harvard University Press.
Frisby, D. (1985). *Fragments of modernity: Theories of modernity in the work of Simmel, Kracauer and Benjamin.* Cambridge, UK: Polity Press.
Grainer, B., & Schmidt, C. (Eds.). (2001). *Arche Noah: Die Idee der "Kultur" im deutsch-jüdischen Diskurs.* Freiburg: Rombach Verlag.
Hillach, A. (1999). Ein neu entdecktes Lebensgesetz der Jugend: Wynekens Führergeist im Denken des jungen Benjamin. In K. Garber &

L. Rehm (Eds.), *Global Benjamin. Internationaler Benjamin-Kongress 1992*, vol. 2. (pp. 873–890). München: Wilhelm Fink Verlag.

Hotam, Y. (Ed.). (2009). *Deutsch-jüdische Jugendliche im Zeitalter der Jugend*. Göttingen: V&R Unipress.

Hotam, Y. (2013). *Modern gnosis and Zionism: The crisis of culture, life philosophy and Jewish national thought*. London: Routledge.

Jacobson, E. (2003). *Metaphysics of the profane*. New York: Columbia University Press.

Janz, R.P. (1985). Die Faszination der Jugend durch Rituale und sakrale Symbole. Mit Anmerkungen zu Fidus, Hess, Hoffmannsthal und George. In T. Koebner, R.P. Janz, & F. Trommler (Eds.), *"Mit uns zieht die neue Zeit": Der Mythos Jugend* (pp. 62–82). Frankfurt a.M: Suhrkamp.

Khatib, S.R. (2013). *"Theleologie ohne Endzweck": Walter Benjamins Entstellung des Messianischen*. Marburg: Tectum Verlag.

Kirchner, S. (2009). *Walter Benjamin und das Wiener Judentum zwischen 1900 und 1938*. Würzburg: Königshausen & Neumann.

Kohlenbach, M. (2002). *Walter Benjamin: Self-reference and religiosity*. New York: Palgrave Macmillan.

Kopper, J. (1955). *Die Metaphysik Meister Eckharts*. Saarbrücken: West-Ost.

Landauer, G. (1903). *Meister Eckharts mystische Schriften*. Berlin: Karl Schnabel.

Lazier, B. (2008). *God interrupted: Heresy and the European imagination between the world wars*. Princeton, NJ: Princeton University Press.

Levine, M.G. (2014). *A weak messianic power: Figures of a time to come in Benjamin, Derrida, and Celan*. New York: Fordham University Press.

McFarland, J. (2013). *Constellation: Friedrich Nietzsche and Walter Benjamin in the now-time of history*. New York: Fordham University Press.

Nancy, J.L. (2008). *Dis-enclosure: The deconstruction of Christianity*. New York: Fordham University Press.

North, P. (2015). *The yield: Kafka's atheological reformation*. Stanford, CA: Stanford University Press.

Pfeiffer, F. (1857). *Deutsche Mystiker des Vierzehnjahrunderts: Meister Eckhart*. Leipzig: G.J. Göschensche Verlagshandlung.

Steizinger, J. (2011). Zwischen emanzipatorischem Appell und melancholischem Verstummen Walter Benjamins Jugendschriften. In

D. Weidner & S. Weigel (eds.), *Benjamin-Studien* (pp. 225–238). München: Wilhem Fink Verlag.

Steizinger, J. (2013). *Revolt Eros und Sprache*. Berlin: Kulturverlag Kadmos.

Trommler, F. (1985). Mission ohne Ziel: Über den Kult der Jugend im modernen Deutschland. In T. Koebner, R.P. Janz, & F. Trommler (eds.), *"Mit uns zieht die neue Zeit": Der Mythos Jugend*. Frankfurt a.M: Suhrkamp.

von Harnack, A. (1924). *Marcion: Das Evangelium vom Fremden Gottes*. Leipzig: J.C. Hinrichs'sche Buchhandlung.

von Humboldt, W. (1969). *The limits of state action*. London: Cambridge University Press.

Wetters, K. (2014). *Demonic history: From Goethe to the present*. Evanston, IL: Northwestern University Press.

Wexler, P. (2007). *Mystical interactions: Sociology, Jewish mysticism and education*. Los Angeles: Cherub Press.

Witte, B. (1991). *Walter Benjamin: An intellectual biography*. Detroit, MI: Wayne State University Press.

Wolin, R. (1982). *Walter Benjamin: An Aesthetic of Redemption*. Berkeley: University of California Press.

Section IV

MEDITATION, MORALITY, AND THE SELF: HABAD AND MUSAR

Chapter 11

CONTEMPLATION, MEDITATION, AND METAPHYSICS IN SECOND-GENERATION HABAD

Jonathan Garb, The Hebrew University of Jerusalem

Reception History

The second generation of Habad has a place of pride in the library of world mysticism, owing to the tracts dedicated to contemplation and meditation composed by its two major figures and protagonists, R. Dov Baer Shneuri (the *mitler* or median rebbe, 1773–1827), and R. Aharon ha-Levi Horowitz of Starosselje (1766–1828), the closest student of the founder of Habad, R. Shneur Zalman of Liadi (1747–1813), who contested the inheritance of the movement's leadership (and subsequently broke off from its main branch). In and of itself, this dispute brings together society, in the sense of sociology of religious movements, and spirituality, in what is perhaps its most universal form: the contemplative/meditative state and its effects. The controversy led to the sharpening of respective positions and to an innovation in genre—the first Hasidic texts devoted to contemplation/meditation and its effects.

It is hardly surprising, then, that these texts, which I shall soon enumerate, have enjoyed relatively extensive attention in the English-speaking world. The pioneer here was Rabbi Louis Jacobs (1920–2006), a colorful and controversial figure in his own right, who in 1963 translated the *mitler*'s *Quntres hi-Hitpa'alut* under the somewhat misleading[1] title *Tract on Ecstasy* and wrote a biography of R. Aharon entitled *Seeker of Unity: The Life and Works of R. Aaron of Starosselje* (1966). Though Rachel Elior's more detailed work on the second generation and its "theory of divinity" (based on her 1976 dissertation) remains in Hebrew, her *The Paradoxical Ascent to God: The Kabbalistic Theosophy of Habad Hasidism* (translated in 1993 from the Hebrew edition) includes two chapters on contemplation (and on the wider controversy in the first generation of Habad, to be discussed below). Yet earlier than the latter book, Naftali Loewenthal's study of the first two generations of Habad, *Communicating the Infinite: The Emergence of the Habad School* (1990), advanced a persuasive sociological thesis according to which, in response to the controversy, the *mitler* reserved his highly stratified and nuanced approach to meditation for the elite, offering simpler options for the wider following, including women.[2]

After a relatively dormant period in the last decade or so, there has been a reawakening of scholarly as well as internal interest in these texts. Without going into graduate work in Hebrew, one should surely mention Anthony J. Steinbock's *Phenomenology and Mysticism: The Verticality of Religious Experience* (2007), which grants almost two chapters to *Quntres ha-Hitpa'alut*, albeit entirely mediated through translation, and compares it to the writings of St. Teresa de Amhuda of Avila (1515–1582) and Rūzbihān Baqli (1128–1209)—all this as part of a wider phenomenological investigation of mysticism and of what Steinbock terms "verticality." To summarize Steinbock's thesis in his own words: "Religious experience is not immune to what we might call 'modalization' of that experience. In this case, one might undergo experiences of self-deception or self-delusion" (139). In this context, the *mitler*'s elaborate gradation of meditative practice and designation of some of its effects as undesirable or even demonic is transplanted from its polemical context of dynastic rivalry and

---

1. I do not see the utility of the term *ecstasy* in its original etymology or its rather vague prevalent use for translating the Hasidic term.
2. See esp. 120–138.

accorded a wider, theoretical significance in the study of religion. Again in his words, "my overall concern...is with the attempt to elucidate the nuances...[i]n what I am calling vertical experiencing" (88). Clearly, then, "vertical" denotes hierarchical distinction.[3]

Shortly after, in 2009, Elliot R. Wolfson's *Open Secret: Post-messianic Messianism and the Mystical Revision of Menahem Mendel Schneerson*, though focused on the seventh *rebbe*, broke new ground in claiming that all seven generations of Habad should be viewed as a whole, as well as devoting some important discussions to the *mitler*'s ontological thought (and one to R. Aharon).[4] Assisted by the great wave of publication of Habad texts from the 1980s onward (i.e., coming after some of the studies mentioned above), Wolfson has assembled a remarkable array of texts from the extensive corpus penned by the *mitler*. He was later (2010) joined by a comprehensive Hebrew-language book, Dov Schwartz's *Habad's Thought from Beginning to End*.

Far beyond the question of language, Wolfson's work is relevant to the global audience due to his profound comparative reflections, especially engaging the Mādhyamika stream of Buddhism.[5] Before wrapping up this brief survey of existing work, one should note the classes on *Quntres ha-Hitpa'alut* delivered by R. Eliezer Zvi Safrin, a direct descendant of the highly mystical Hasidic leader Yitzhak Eizik Yehuda Yehiel Safrin of Komarno (1806–1874), who actually critiqued early Habad writing. R. Safrin's classes were also

---

3. See my earlier article "Mystics' Critiques of Mystical Experience" (*Revue de l'histoire des religions* 221 [2004]: 293–315), not cited by Steinbock, which briefly addresses two of his case studies. A comparison to Pierre Bourdieu's use of the term "distinction" could be fruitful.
4. See, e.g., below, as well as E.R. Wolfson, *Open Secret: Post Messianic Messianism and the Mystical Revision of Menahem Mendel Schneerson* (New York: Columbia University Press, 2009), 108.
5. Compare to my online talk (in Hebrew): <https://www.academia.edu/10806487/Response_in_evening_in_honor_of_Evyatar_Shulmans_book_Rethinking_the_Buddha>. See also my *Shamanic Trance in Modern Kabbalah* (Chicago and London: University of Chicago Press, 2011), 76, 80–81).

attended by a couple of academics. One now-prominent figure who attended an earlier series of Safrin's classes (on different texts, yet constantly engaging Habad thought) was R. Yitzhak Meir Morgenstern, a *rebbe* and Kabbalist, whose teachings on R. Aharon's works are recorded and developed in *Yira'ukha 'im-Shemesh* (2012), a wonderfully erudite and lengthy work by R. Shmuel Ehrenfeld.

One should contrast the interest in these texts outside Habad to the scarcity of discourse inside Habad. Obviously, R. Aharon's breakaway texts are barely mentioned inside the movement[6] and are actually printed and distributed by the Satmar Hasidim, certainly no friends of Habad. Yet even the *mitler*'s writing is barely addressed in Habad teaching. The very term *mitler* signals his median and marginal role when compared to his predecessor and his successor, R. Menahem Mendel Schneerson (1789–1866), the *Tzemakh Tzedek*, namesake of the last *rebbe* (1902–1994), whose own equally massive œuvre has eclipsed all previous generations combined in contemporary Habad discourse.

In moving into thematic discussion, one must introduce one caveat regarding the seemingly natural comparative move. Cross-cultural terms (such as "ecstasy") occlude the interpretative and nomian context in which these texts were composed. The "treatise on contemplation" is a name found in manuscripts, but it was printed (also) as *Sha'ar ha-Yihud*, the gate of unity, along with *Sha'ar ha-Emuna*, clearly denoting its debt to *Sha'ar ha-Yihud ve-ha-Emuna*, gates of unity and faith, the second (or perhaps first) part of the classic *Tanya*, by the *mitler*'s father, the founder of Habad, R. Shneur Zalman of Liadi. Likewise, *Sha'arei ha-Yihud ve-ha-Emuna*, by R. Aharon Horowitz, is obviously intended to be an expansion on this foundational text. In other words, following Wolfson's intergenerational reading here, the writings of the second generation need to be read as commentary on those of the first. Furthermore, as we shall see at length, the *mitler*'s treatise on contemplation is in fact

---

6. Hardly accessible on Habad's marvelous contribution to online Jewish learning <www. Hebrewbooks.org>.

designed as a "short form" and Hasidic internalization of the same structure that guided the writing of his father, that of the founder of modern Kabbalah, R. Yitzhak Luria of sixteenth-century Egypt and Safed. In other words, prior to any etic reading, whether in the philosophical traditions of ontology and phenomenology or in a comparative arc, it is advisable to establish the emic base, namely the original setting, framing, and purpose of the texts.

As for the nomian domain, R. Aharon's companion volume, *Sha'rei 'Avoda*, gates of worship or work, deals with the intention of prayer, as in the *Sha'ar ha-Tefila* (gate of prayer; also published as a separate book and available online). *Quntres ha-Hitpa'alut* begins with the need to remove mistakes in *Avoda she-ba Lev* (work or worship of the heart),[7] the Talmudic term for prayer,[8] while *Sh'ar ha-Yihud* is a more anomian text, only mentioning prayer at the end of section 4 (see below). In other words, while contemplation and meditation are useful universal terms referring implicitly to a self-contained practice, *hitbonenut* and its effect *hitpa'alut* (which, if pressed to translate, I would render as affectedness in the sense of being affected) refer, at least in Habad, to states accessed in the course of daily set prayer. Here again, spirituality and society, for prayer in the traditional Jewish context, is not a private mode, but rather a public, vocal, and ritually orchestrated setting.

Following this historical and methodological preface, it is high time to dive into the texts and let them speak for themselves, yet with the aim of exploring the delicate relationship of metaphysics or ontology and meditative practice and experience, holding the cultural context in mind and searching to comprehend the nature of the dispute and divergence between the two masters. Jewish thought and life develop through controversy and polemic, despite constant attempts to create "party lines."

---

7. All quotes are from the fine Ma'ayanotekha edition, Jerusalem 2014, in this case 343–344.
8. Although the rare and typically Habadian term *avoda she be moah*, the work of the brain, is also used.

Text One:
R. Aharon ha-Levi Horowitz, Sha'arei ha-Yihud ve-ha-Emuna, *Gate 4, Chapter 26*

Before entering into textual analysis, one must caution that the seeming repetitiveness of the Habad texts is misleading, as repetition is already part of the process of contemplation. Our first text, translated by myself from R. Aharon's main work *Sha'arei ha-Yihud ve-ha-Emuna*, is part of a lengthy historiosophical discussion based on the classical trope of the four exiles. When discussing the present, or last, exile, the author assigns it to *Malkhut*, the tenth or lowest of the *Sefirot* or emanations (as in the classical Kabbalistic system), which he then interprets as the revelation of the infinite:

> Even in the aspect of the vessels of the *yesh* (existent), not in the aspect of the nullification (*bitul*)[9] through *Bina* [the third *Sefira*, associated in Habad thought with *hitbonenut*, or contemplation] or *middot* [Sefirot 4–9, associated with the emotions], as from the perspective of the Bina and *middot*, in the aspect of unification, indeed the nullification is not revealed through the essence of the existent in itself [one is tempted to use the Kantian term *an sich*], that is to say that his blessed divinity will be revealed even from the perspective of the manifestation (*gilui*) of the existent, but rather the nullification is through the contemplation of His blessed greatness and unity...[10] but the main in-

---

9. Loewenthal, for example, translates this term as "abnegation."
10. According to this historiosophical scheme, the exile in Egypt corresponded to the revelation of Bina, in a dialectical process of countering the *Bina* of the other side (the magical knowledge of the Egyptians), while the Babylonian exile corresponded to the lower level of the *middot* (and was thus characterized by the removal of prophecy), corresponding to *Bina* (see Gate 4, Chapter 25, fols. 143B–144A). As I have briefly indicated elsewhere (Garb, *Kabbalist in the Heart of the Storm* [Tel Aviv: Tel Aviv University, 2014], 323–324, n. 7, following Isaiah Tishby), here and in other texts it is quite

tention [of the creation] is that there shall be nothing else in heavens above and on earth below [based on Deut. 4, 39], that is to say that the nullification will be even in the aspect of the existent that is on the earth below, the nullification will be even in the aspect of the existent....

And this is termed the yoke of the kingdom of heaven, that is to say that the nullification will be specifically through the yoke and nullification of the will towards Him, blessed be He, without any understanding and *middot*, even though in this nullification it is necessary also to have contemplation of His blessed unity, and through contemplation to give birth to the aspect of nullification of the *middot*, for there is no distinction between the Holy One Blessed be He [*Sefirot* 4–9] and His *Sekhina* [*Malkhut*], for from the perspective of truthfulness (*mi-tzad ha-amitut*) all is in one unification, but nonetheless in the aspect of revelation it [the unification] is not revealed...however the revelation of nullification of now [the present exile], even in the aspect of understanding and *middot*, is all as if (*be me-'ein*) and a shining (*he'ara*), but all is deliberately in the mode (*ofen*) of the existent, and His blessed unification shines in the mode of the existent, except for the chosen (*yehidei segula*), the great of soul, who can experience the revelation of the *'etzem* (essential and core being) even in this time, but usually it is as if.

And after the existent will be clarified [a Lurianic term for rectification through the historical process] in complete revelation, through the labor of Israel in the aspect of trials and in nullification specifically in the aspect of the existent...through this the *'etzem* is revealed more, in nullification of the selffull (*ha-'atzmi*) than in nullification through understanding and *middot*, for this is

---

clear that R. Aharon's source is the eighteenth-century Italian Kabbalist R. Moshe Hayyim Luzzatto.

not such an innovation that the nullification is from the perspective of the revelation of His unity, but when the nullification is from the perspective of the concealment the nullification of the *'etzem* is revealed more from the perspective of the Godhead itself (*'atzmuto*)... and then there will be revelation of His unity[11] not in the aspect of enclothement [*halbasha*, a Lurianic term of concealment of essence in mediating levels], but rather there will be complete revelation, that is to say that His blessed unity will be revealed from the perspective of the existent without any concealment at all, through his equal power as explained above [Here R. Aharon is most likely referring to his discussion in Chapter 22, on the power of the Godhead/*'Atzmut* to equalize the existent and the *'ayin* or non-existent[12]] and then all aspects will be joined, vessels with lights, and the bounded (*gvul*) with that that is above bounds... and then the light of the moon [a symbol of *Malkhut*], which is the revelation in the aspect of the existent... will be as the light of the sun, which is the aspect of the Holy one Blessed be He.[13]

It would require an entire presentation in itself to unfold all of the riches of this text. Clearly it echoes Wolfson's reading of the

---

11. Here, too, the language is very close to that of Luzzatto. Nonetheless, R. Aharon is cautious in discussing the revelation of the Godhead itself, as he himself praises R. Hayyim Vital, Luria's main disciple, for not discussing the levels beyond the self-contraction of the divine (*Tzimtzum*), implicitly critiquing the alternative Lurian theosophy of R. Israel Sarug (Gate 1, Chapter 26, fol. 44A [in the medium-size format] and comparing to the gloss in Chapter 27, fol. 70A–B).

12. Fol. 138A. See the more detailed discussion in Gate 2, Chapter 28, fol. 72A, clearly influenced by Geronese Kabbalah, most likely mediated by sixteenth-century R. Meir Ibn Gabbai, whose formative effect on R. Aharon's thought is apparent throughout his writings.

13. Fols. 144B–145B. For a fuller discussion of *Malkhut*'s eventual ascent to the infinite, see Gate 2, Chapter 20, fol. 64A.

main Habad corpus in terms of a subtle dialectic of concealment and revelation, culminating, as in the poetic crescendo of our text, in the total revelation, which corresponds to the unification of the *Malkhut*, or female aspect, within the male aspect, known here as the Holy-One Blessed be-He (or possibly its attainment of an equal status).[14] There is also an entire historiosophical layer, differentiating here, in a semi-sociological move, between two levels or tiers. First, we have the point of view of the general Jewish population, who only experience the unity of the higher levels as a refracted shining and as-if (as in the philosophy of Hans Vaihinger[15]), and for whom accepting the yoke of the divine kingdom and law without understanding connects them to *Malkhut*, as the purpose of creation. For these, contemplation is by no means the royal road. Second, we have the aspect of the great of soul, who transcend history (see Chapter 24), and experience the complete unity of the levels of contemplation, emotion, and mere performance at all times.

I would like to amplify this text with four shorter quotations. One is from the polemical introduction to the book, where R. Aharon explicitly states that "unification is above understanding, but rather in the aspect of the grasping (*tfisat*) and feeling (*hargashat*) of His blessed unity in the divine soul of each and every one of Israel from the perspective of its root which is above wisdom and understanding."[16] In other words, contemplation is secondary to the direct, unmediated grasp of the soul itself. The second text is found in the polemical introduction to the companion volume *Sh'arei 'Avoda*, where R. Aharon castigates the "great mistake and lack of knowledge" of those who wish to set aside the feeling of the heart, as the idea is

---

14. Compare to Wolfson, *Open Secret*, e.g., 176–177 (which also discusses the question of the vessels, 209–210). R. Aharon's dialectic has been discussed at length in the above-mentioned study by Elior.

15. Here one is reminded of the philosophy of Hans Vaihinger (see Garb, *Shamanic Trance*, esp. 34, 181 n. 65). Compare to Sha'arei 'Avoda, Gate 1, Chapter 11, fol. 18A.

16. Fol. 9B.

actually to experience one's existence, in all of its emotional power, and then nullify it. R. Aharon goes on to say that all the entirety of the teaching of the founder of Habad, R. Shneur Zalman, was directed at confirming the *hitpa'alut* of each and every person, precisely because it involves self-feeling, and without being concerned about self-deception, but rather experiencing (as in the Zen saying) mediation as war, which inevitably involves defeat.[17] More radically, he goes on to say that, in any case, lack of self-feeling on one level can be deemed to be complete self-feeling relative to a higher level.[18] These moves demolish the entire edifice of differentiation between levels of attainment in the *mitler*'s treatise on *hitpa'alut* (as explicated by Steinbock). As is often the case, R. Aharon's approach is explicit in his later, exegetical work *'Avodat ha-Levi* (on the Torah). There he writes on the highest of the four worlds of classical Kabbalah, *Atzilut*, or emanation: "For the aspect of *Atzilut* is the revelation of the blessed unity that is above all intellect and there the nullification is in the *'etzem* as it is in truth, without needing any contemplation at all."[19] There he also takes the notion that the purpose is the revelation of God in the lowest level to its logical sociological conclusion: It is those who work for their living, engaged in the material world, who can reveal the essence of God.[20]

---

17. For spiritual warfare as conquest of the existent (*yesh*), see *Sh'arei 'Avoda*, Gate 2, Chapter 31, fol. 69A. Of necessity, this descent to the existent precludes purism as to meditative experience.

18. Fols. 7A–9B in this format. Compare to Tanya, I, 13. There are intriguing parallels, picked up on by R. Shmuel Ehrenfeld (and his teacher, R. Yitzhak Meir Morgenstern), to the Kabbalistic system of R. Shalom Shar'abi. Compare to the introduction to *Sh'arei 'Avoda*, fol. 9A, which appears to link this relativistic approach to his as-if philosophy (i.e., in any case each level of attainment is ultimately imaginary). One should also note later texts by R. Aharon that seem to point toward a different approach, far closer to that of the *mitler*. See, e.g., *'Avodat ha-Levi* (Jerusalem, 2004; reprint of 1842–1866), vol. 2, Liqqutim, 105A.

19. *'Avodat ha-Levi*, Devarim, vol. 2, A1. Compare this discussion to Elior, *The Paradoxical Ascent*, 201–218.

20. *'Avodat ha-Levi*, Liqqutim, 100A.

Text Two:
R. Dov Baer Shneuri, Shaʻar ha-Yihud

There is an advantage in general contemplation, through which one reaches the level of depth in general, that is the aspect of the essence of the divine light in general... which is the main purpose of revelation of divinity in the soul, etc., and there is an advantage in the detailed contemplation in particular from the point of view of bringing close the revelation of the divine light in his soul to a greater extent. For in a general contemplation one can deceive oneself until it appears to one that the matter [divine light] is very close [see Deut. 30, 14] and actually God appears to him from very far [see Jeremiah 31, 2], as it is only in a general manner, as opposed to contemplation in detail that each particular matter apprehended is fixed in his soul in the closest manner and from this he will come to the next higher specific matter gradually[21] until he comes to the general apprehension so that it is affirmed more without any self-deception at all.[22]

As when he begins with detailed contemplation of the immanent divinity in the quality of the coming to being of the root of the spiritual influx of the spheres and constellations, from nothingness to existence from the residues of the *Ofanim* [lowest level of angels],[23] and then contemplate in detail the *Ofanim* and *Hayyot* [next level of angels] until the aspect of *Malkhut* of *ʻAssiya* [the lowest of the above-

---

21. This formulation merits comparison to the Buddhist (especially Chan and Tibetan) distinction between "sudden" and "gradual" paths.
22. Compare to the similar formulations of R. Shneur Zalman of Liadi in *Ma'amrei Admor ha-Zaqen: ʻInyanim* (New York: Kehot Publication Society, 2008), 159–161.
23. On this topic see, e.g., *Imrei Bina* (New York: Kehot Publication Society, 1985), Gate of Qriyat Shema, 32B.

mentioned four worlds]...and after all of this thorough study of all the details, even though each detail in and of itself is not generally speaking divine and is only a subsidiary detail but when all the study is joined from the particulars to the general principle then the aspect of the general will be fixed more in the soul as is known and tested for all who are engaged in depth in contemplation....

But the restriction of the deepening of the *Da'at* [the psychic faculty related to in-depth thought] in each detail is the opposite of the deception and the distance, and to the contrary, through this the matter comes closer to him as he goes from detail to the higher detail until he includes them all, performing a general *yihud* [unification] and not a particular *yihud*.... [W]hoever does not deepen his *Da'at* in the particular *yihud* and begins from the general aspect even when it comes to him with great effort in many attainments...will not fix in his soul its true matter so much as in the case of good study of all details...and this resolves the question of those who ask on the meaning of the words of prayer in detail for those who know them, how do they not confuse the general thought, for actually the *Kavvanot* [intentions] of the meaning of the words according to the Kabbalah helps strengthen the depth of the general apprehension...as known to those who taste them.[24]

Here, too, there is much to be said, yet I will only list the following points. To begin with, besides the obvious polemic against the self-deception that lies in wait for those who follow R. Aharon in "general" contemplation, it is clear that the very vector of this contemplation is opposite to that found in his rival's teaching: rather than the lower world being the goal of practice, it is merely the starting point for a vertical ascension leading up to the highest levels of the divine. Actually, there is no advantage in any particular aspect of

---

24. *Sha'ar ha-Yihud*, section 4, 222–223.

the cosmos, for the goal is to grasp it all as simultaneously and apprehend its unity.[25] Thus, even non-divine details can be included. In this sense, the traditional Kabbalistic cosmology, with all its elaboration, is upheld, as is the practice of *Kavvanot* (as set out in the *mitler*'s work *pirush ha-milot,* the meaning of the words, hinted at here).[26] The only shift relative to Lurianic Kabbalah is the re-interpretation of *yihud* as realization of divine unity through contemplation rather than unification of the divine names. In other words, the critique of the detailed teaching of Kabbalah (on the part of the students of R. Menahem Mendel of Vitebsk, as we shall see now) is parried, at least when the elite are concerned. (Later on in the text, beginners are allowed to engage in general contemplation.)

Toward a Cross-Hasidic Comparison

In one of a series of groundbreaking articles (in *Qovetz Beit Aharon ve-Israel*), the Hasidic historian R. Avish Schor has already noted the similarities between R. Aharon's approach and that of the critics of Habad among the students of R. Shneur Zalman's teacher, R. Menahem Mendel of Vitebsk. As Schor has shown, figures such as R. Avraham of Kalisk claim that their approach goes back to R. Dov Baer of Mezeritch, the teacher of both R. Menahem Mendel and R. Shneur Zalman himself. Schor has demonstrated that R. Dov Baer deliberately taught in a multifaceted manner, expecting each disciple to absorb one dimension of his approach appropriate for him and for his cultural setting, in order for him to spread Hasidism in that

---

25. As we have seen, R. Aharon engages this argument, stating that our concern should not be with intrinsic unity but rather with its revelation. This is part of a wider debate that I cannot go into here. See, e.g., *Sha'ar ha-Tefila*, 35A–37B, contrasted to the *mitler*'s *Imrei Bina*, "Gate of Qriyat Shema," section 56, 54A–B.
26. See the explicit formulations in *Sha'ar ha-Yihud*, section 7, 227. Compare to the more reticent approach to the proliferation of Kabbalistic study and practice in the preface to R. Aharon's *Sh'arei ha-Yihud ve ha-Emuna,* fol. 3A–B.

setting, as indeed happened.[27] Nonetheless, I wish to argue that this is a strong current in the teaching of R. Dov Baer, as can be seen through the examination of a "control group," the teachings of R. Menahem Nahum Twersky of Chernobyl (1730–1787), a senior student of R. Dov Baer, who transplanted his teachings to the Ukraine. In his *Ma'or 'Enayim*, R. Menahem Nahum writes as follows: "One needs to include oneself in dealing with Torah or prayer or any commandment in the totality of all of Israel, and not necessarily amongst the totality of the *Tzaddikim* (righteous)…but rather one needs to include oneself in the totality of all of Israel, even those who are in the material, low, level."[28] Here, like R. Aharon (who unlike his teacher, R. Shneur Zalman, does not strongly emphasize either the distinction between the *Tzadik* and the *Benoni*, or everyman, or the related distinction between the divine and animal soul[29]), the goal is to connect to the lower level, here interpreted in the sociological sense.[30]

Like R. Aharon, R. Menahem Nahum espouses a strong sense of relativity, as he soon continues in this teaching:

---

27. See now his *Writings; Studies in the Doctrine and History of Karlin-Stolin* (Jerusalem: Makhon Beit Aharon ve-Yisrael, 2018), esp. 515–518.

28. *Ma'or 'Enayim*, Bereshit, p. 17 in the Ashdod 2008 edition (compare to p. 15). Some portions of this work have been translated in A. Green, *Upright Practices; The Light of Eyes: Homilies on Genesis* (New York: Paulist Press, 1982), yet for the present purposes I have opted for my own translation.

29. See *Sh'arei 'Avoda*, Gate 2, Chapter 2, fol. 42B, where R. Aharon states that from the point of view of equalization, there is no distinction between the two souls. I cannot go into the question, discussed at length in R. Ehrenfeld's above-mentioned study, of the relative level of loyalty of R. Shneur Zalman's two heirs to his teaching, and whether each adopted a different stage in the diachronical development of his thought (which is my own inclination; compare to my talk at <https://www.academia.edu/12079300/The_Early_Writings_of_Rashaz>).

30. On sociological dimensions of R. Menahem Nahum's thought, see the excellent Hebrew-language study by David Zori, *Not in the Hands of Heaven: The Limits of Human Action in the Teachings of Early Hassidic Masters* (Jerusalem: Magnes, 2016), esp. 256–257. On his doctrine of the *Tzadik* as including simple Jews, see 269–277.

> And it is known that every time the *Tzaddik* (righteous one) arrives at a greater level he considers himself more to be nothing, for he has attained more of the greatness of God.... And is not allowed to imagine that he is in that exalted level, for indeed his worship, Blessed be-He, is without end and limit, and the more he goes further and draws closer to his worship he sees several levels higher upon higher and higher yet above them in the aspect of the residing of the *Shekhina*, that according to his level, thus for him is the residing of the *Shekhina*, until he realizes that he has not yet attained anything.[31]

This relativistic *via negativa*, reminiscent of the thought of a later figure, R. Nahman of Bratzlav (1772–1810), is even more pronounced in another Torah:

> And after one studies the entire Torah one knows and understands that one doesn't know anything, for the goal of knowledge is not to know... and when one learns and knows that one has not attained anything one unifies lower wisdom with the higher wisdom... and if God forbid one imagines that one has attained something then one has not arrived at all at wisdom and is called "a troublemaker separates the leader" [Proverbs 16, 28; my translation echoes the usual Kabbalistic interpretation in terms of separating the *Sefirot*].[32]

In other words, the desired union of the higher and the lower is realized through realization of non-knowing. I would like to

---

31. *Ma'or 'Enayim*, Bereshit, 17. See also, e.g., 18–19.
32. Ibid., 20. I cannot here go into the question, broached by Schor, of the relationship between Bratzlav thought and that of the critics of Habad in its first generation.

amplify R. Menahem Nahum's epistemological humility with two quotes. The first is from Walt Whitman:

> *Darest thou now, O soul*
> *Walk out with me toward the unknown*
> *Region,*
> *Where neither ground is for the feet*
> *Nor any path to follow?*
> *No map there, nor guide....*
>
> —Leaves of Grass

And the second is from Richard Rorty's 1979 *Philosophy and the Mirror of Nature*, describing the role of philosophers:

> Preventing man from deluding himself with the notion that he knows himself, or anything else, expect under optimal description. (379)

Bibliography

Samuel Ehrenfeld, *Yira'ukha 'im-Shemesh* (Jerusalem: Makhon Yam ha-Hokhma, 2012).

Rachel Elior, *The Paradoxical Ascent to God: The Kabbalistic Theosophy of Habad*, trans. J. Green (Albany: SUNY Press, 1993).

Jonathan Garb, "The Early Writings of Rashaz" <https://www.academia.edu/12079300/The_Early_Writings_of_Rashaz>

———. *Kabbalist in the Heart of the Storm* (Tel Aviv: Tel Aviv University, 2014) [Hebrew].

———. "Mystics' Critiques of Mystical Experience," *Revue de l'histoire des religions* 221 (2004): 293–315.

———. "Response to Evyatar Shulman" <https://www.academia.edu/10806487/Response_in_evening_in_honor_of_Evyatar_Shulmans_book_Rethinking_the_Buddha>

———. *Shamanic Trance in Modern Kabbalah* (Chicago and London: University of Chicago Press, 2011).

Arthur Green, *Upright Practices; The Light of Eyes: Homilies on Genesis* (New York: Paulist Press, 1982).
R. Aharon ha-Levi Horowitz, *Avodat ha-Levi* (Jerusalem, 2004, reprint of Lvov 1826) vol. 2.
———. *Sha'arei ha-Yihud ve-ha-Emuna* (Jerusalem, n.d, reprint of Shklov 1820).
Louis Jacobs, *Seeker of Unity: The Life and Works of R. Aaron of Starosselje* (London: Vallentine Mitchell, 1966).
———. trans and ed., *Tract on Ecstasy: Dobh Baer of Lubavtich* (London: Vallentine Mitchell, 1963).
Naftali Loewenthal. *Communicating the Infinite: The Emergence of the Habad School* (Chicago and London: University of Chicago Press, 1990).
Richard Rorty, *Philosophy and the Mirror of Nature* (Princeton: Princeton University Press, 1979).
Avish Schor, *Writings; Studies in the Doctrine and History of Karlin-Stolin* (Jerusalem, 2018) [Hebrew].
Dov Schwartz, *Habad's Thought from Beginning to End* (Ramat Gan: Bar Ilan University Press, 2010) [Hebrew].
Dov Baer Shneuri, *Imrei Bina* (New York: Kehot Publication Society, 1985).
———. *Quntres ha-Hitpa'alut* (Jerusalem: Torat Habad le-Bnei ha-Yeshivot, 2014).
———. *Sha'ar ha-Yihud* (in *Ner Mitzva ve-Roah Or*] (New York: Kehot Publication Society, 2014).
Shneur Zalman of Liadi, *Ma'amrei Admor ha-Zaqen: 'Inyanim* (New York, 2008).
Anthony J. Steinbock, *Phenomenology and Mysticism: The Verticality of Religious Experience* (Bloomington: Indiana University Press, 2007).
Menahem Nahum Twersky of Chernobyl, *Ma'or 'Enayim* (Ashdod: Anak ha-Sefarim, 2008).
Elliot R. Wolfson, *Open Secret: Postmessianic Messianism and the Mystical Revision of Menahem Mendel Schneerson* (New York: Columbia University Press, 2009).
David Zori, *Not in the Hands of Heaven: The Limits of Human Action in the Teachings of Early Hassidic Masters* (Jerusalem: Magnes, 2016) [Hebrew].

Chapter 12

THE ROAD FROM RELIGIOUS LAW (HALAKHA) TO THE SECULAR: CONSTRUCTING THE AUTONOMOUS SELF IN THE MUSAR TRADITION AND ITS DISCONTENTS

Shaul Magid, Indiana University, Bloomington

Charles Taylor begins his *Sources of the Self* with the following assertion: "Selfhood and the good, or in another way selfhood and morality, turn out to be inextricably intertwined themes."[1] Tying theories of modern selfhood to morality—not only how we should act but, as important, the sources we draw from in determining how we should act and how these sources are, or should be, interpreted—stands at the center of my inquiry in regard to what is conventionally called modern musar, better known as the Musar Movement initiated by Israel Salanter (1810–1883) in nineteenth-century Eastern and Central Europe.[2]

---

1. Charles Taylor, *Sources of the Self* (Cambridge, MA: Harvard University Press, 1992), 3.
2. On the Musar Movement more generally, see Dovid Katz, *Tenuat Musar*, 5 vols. (Bnei Brak, 2006) [Hebrew]. On Salanter, see Hillel Goldberg, *Yisrael Salanter: Text, Structure, Idea* (Hoboken, NJ: Ktav, 1982); and Immanuel Etkes, *Rabbi Israel Salanter and the Musar Movement: Seeking the Torah of Truth* (Philadelphia, PA: JPS, 1993).

I argue below that musar offers an innovative theory of the self deeply embedded in traditional society (articulated through fidelity to *halakha*) yet introduces, or perhaps anticipates, a notion of human autonomy, and in doing so plants the seeds of a kind of secularism that later emerges in what is sometimes called the neo-musar movement in contemporary America. While law, or *halakha*, as the quintessence of Jewish life remains intact in classical musar, it co-exists with musar's autonomy in the construction of the fulfilled self. In the case of neo-musar, law becomes unmoored from the Jewish self, although it may still be practiced in various forms. The elasticity of law as obligation reaches its limit as musar is now refracted though non-traditional lenses. Deployment of terms such as secular, secularism, and secularization is loaded, and their mere mention arouses curiosity and at times consternation.[3] I am using the term *secular* here in a very narrow sense. By secular I do not refer to complex theories of secularism and secularization that include a multilayered mix of cultural, political, theological, and religious dimensions. Rather, I use "secular" in a very narrow sense to refer to ways of constructing the self as an autonomous agent who can, and must, determine proper behavior. This behavior is originally tied to, but not identical to, traditional authority structures, particularly the act of Torah study, the legislative acumen of the Torah scholar (*talmid hakham*), and the obligatory nature of halakha. Secular here needn't deny God by definition, but it does incorporate competing—sometimes even alternative—forms of agency in regard to human flourishing. In musar, I suggest that God's role is limited in the construction of the fulfilled self-accomplished through behavioral refinement (*tikun ha-midot*).

I want to illustrate this through an analysis of some of the musar teachings in *Hokhmat U Musar*, the collected teachings

---

3. There is a veritable library of work on these terms. For two examples, see M. Warner, J. Van Antwerpen, and C. Calhoun (eds.), *Varieties of Secularism in a Secular Age* (Cambridge, MA: Harvard University Press, 2013); and Charles Taylor, *A Secular Age* (Cambridge, MA: Harvard University Press, 2007), 1–24.

of Simha Zissel Zvi of Kelm (1824–1898), one of the prominent disciples of the founder of modern musar, and Israel Salanter. Further, I will contrast these with the anti-musar treatise *Emunah u Betachon* by Abraham Yeshaya Karelitz (1878–1953), better known as the Hazon Ish, the preeminent rabbinic sage in Bnei Brak, who, more than half a century after his death, remains a figurehead of *haredi* Judaism in Israel.[4] My contention is that the Hazon Ish's critique of musar (which is also expressed in his equally sharp critique of Lithuanian Talmudism) is precisely directed at the question of human autonomy, that is, the emergence of the self as an agent that can act independently of halakha, even as the individual remains bound by it. Finally, I will conclude with a brief foray into some of the more recent neo-musar circles that are blossoming in contemporary non-Orthodox Judaism in the United States, arguing that their very existence illustrates the extent to which the Hazon Ish's concerns found expression in non-traditional neo-musar circles.

The relationship between law and piety—or, as Isadore Twersky preferred, law and spirituality—in Judaism has a long history. Twersky's suggestion is that this relationship is best situated as

---

4. The definitive study of the Hazon Ish is Benjamin Brown's *Hazon Ish: Posek, Ha-Ma'amin u Manhig Ha-Marekha Ha-Haredit* (Jerusalem: Magnes Press, 2011). Other studies that have informed my views are Yakir Englander, "The Understanding of the Human and the Purpose of Halakha in the Writings of the Hazon Ish" [Hebrew], in *Reishit* 2 (2010): 183–201; Daniel Stein, "The Limits of Religious Optimism: The Hazon Ish and the Alter of Novordok on *Bittahon*," *Tradition* 43:2 (2010): 32–48; Lawrence Kaplan, "The Hazon Ish: Hasidic Critic of Traditional Orthodoxy," in *The Uses of Tradition: Jewish Continuity in the Modern Era*, ed. J. Wertheimer (New York and Jerusalem: JTS Press, 1993), 145–174; and idem., "The Ethics of Submission: Unification with the Spirit of Torah and Its Stature in Reference to Contemporary Challenges, R. Avraham Yeshayahu Karlitz, the Hazon Ish" [Hebrew], in *Ha-Gedolim: Leaders Who Shaped the Israeli Haredi Jewry*, ed. B. Brown and N. Leon [Hebrew] (Jerusalem: Magnes Press, 2017), 479–519. On Simha Zissel, see Geoffrey Claussen, *Sharing the Burden: R. Simhah Zissel Ziv and the Path of Musar* (Albany: State University of New York Press, 2015).

part of the medieval Jewish tradition that arose as Jewish thinkers grapple with the adaptation of Hellenistic ideas. In his essay "Religion and Law," Twersky writes as follows:

> A tense, dialectical relationship between religion in essence and religion in manifestation is at the core of the religious consciousness.... The tension flows from the painful awareness that manifestations and essence sometimes drift apart, from the sober recognition that a carefully constructed, firmly chiseled normative system cannot regularly reflect, refract, or energize interior, fluid spiritual forces and motives.... If halakha is a means for the actualization and celebration of ethical norms, historical experiences, and theological postulates, then external conformity must be nurtured by internal sensibility and spirituality.[5]

Twersky's claim here is that the tension between law and spirituality is healthy and necessary in any pietistic system and that relieving that tension, either by siding with a pure halakhic totalism common in some ultra-Orthodox circles, or a version of the liberal "ethical monotheism" common in progressive Jewish alternatives, undermines the core of the Jewish pious system. The modern musar movement and its discontents—in our case, the Hazon Ish—emerge from within this tension, whose elasticity is being challenged by the influx of modernity in numerous ways. Premodern musar, including pietistic literature at least from Bahya ibn Pakuda's tenth-century classic *Hovot Ha-Levavot* to the pietism of Safadean kabbalists and later the works of Moshe Hayyim Luzatto in eighteenth-century Italy, is part of a perennial meta-halakhism that argues that the halakhic system is best augmented by an inde-

---

5. Isadore Twersky, "Religion and Law," in *Religion in a Religious Age*, ed. S. Goeitin (Cambridge, MA: Harvard University Press, 1974), 69–70.

pendent yet not oppositional frame through which the individual could best cultivate the devotional life.⁶

One challenge of modern musar is how to act and cultivate correct inter-human behavior in a way that is not identical to the medieval philosophical claim of conjunction with the Active Intellect, the mystical claim of union with the divine (*unio mystica*), or the pietistic claim of self-effacement (*bitual ha-yesh*) that is common in pre-modern musar. It also seems, in my view, to relate to *devekut* as an idea in Hasidism that potentially creates an autonomous agent outside the system of halakha. (Buber develops this in interesting ways.⁷) That is, modern musar explores the vicissitudes of human conduct in a way that is not in direct relation to God, but is rather through the vehicle of Torah by way of study or rabbinic authority. Here musar's behavioral refinement (*tikun ha-midot*) and Hasidism's communion with God (*devekut*) share a common thread that traditionalists such as the Hazon Ish viewed as dangerous to the perpetuation of Torah.

I suggest that this is one of the central structural points of dispute between modern musar and its traditional critics. Thus modern musar, as opposed to pre-modern musar, may come closer to what we conventionally call "ethics" by drawing a distinction between relational and pietistic acts. This often-unspoken distinction, when examined closely, may be the wedge that creates the space for the secular to take root as cultural circumstances change—that is, as the larger project of secularization takes root in the Enlightenment and its aftermath. When human perfection becomes ethics enacted through a subtle severing of the connection between piety (one's relationship to God) and relational behavior (one's relationship to the human other), even when the latter claims fidelity to

---

6. On pietism in the sixteenth century, see Patrick Koch's *Human Self-Perfection: A Re-Assessment of Kabbalistic Musar-Literature of Sixteenth-Century Safed* (Los Angeles: Cherub Press, 2013).

7. See, for example, in Buber's *Hasidism & Modern Man* (Princeton, NJ: Princeton University Press, 2015).

the former, a shift occurs that undermines the very healthy tension that Twersky claims is the spine of Jewish devotional life.

In modern musar, the fledgling autonomous self begins to emerge and to function as the arbiter of *tikun ha-midot*, once deemed self-perfection and now better translated as ethical or behavioral refinement, and which, while still articulated as an extension of halakha, in its premise and even practice gives rise to something that, given different historical circumstances, enables that self to separate from the halakha to function in its place. While certainly not the intent of musar, it does not mean it is not a possible mutation.[8]

In my view, the crucial issue that stands between modern musar and anti-musar is the nature of the self, that is, the existence and extent to which autonomy functions as the vehicle of piety. How the Hazon Ish and musar thinkers construct the nature of the self in relation to the possibility of ascertaining certainty is an illustration of how a particular form of the modern self emerges once there is tacit acknowledgment that the individual can act as an autonomous agent with limited fidelity, albeit not unequivocal submission, to the vehicle of halakha. In some ways, both modern musar and Hasidism are founded on that very possibility—that is, the possibility for an individual to come to understand what is required in terms of human action in accord with divine will outside, but not necessarily in contradiction to, the orbit of mitzvot. A short excerpt from Israel Salanter's *Ohr Yisrael* makes this point quite succinctly:

> One should transform one's emotional forces and character traits for the good, until the power of evil is entirely uprooted from within oneself. In this area, it does not suffice to correct one's will in a general manner.... Rather, a person must seek out the way to correct

---

8. I do not mean mutation in a negative sense as distortion but rather in the biological sense of one thing becoming another through a variety of internal and external changes and circumstances.

each individual character trait and emotional force. This aspect of rectification refers to the rational mitzvot that are between a person and their fellow.⁹

The implication here is that we—or better, the autonomous "I"—can actually succeed in this act of rectification, and that this is not fully dependent upon the life of halakha, or at least not fully determined by it. In this sense, musar is a meta-halakhic enterprise, an instantiation of Twersky's "spirituality" not unlike Hasidism (which focuses on experience of the divine through *devekut*) and the Lithuanian act of Talmud study (focused on *hidush* as the quintessential act of Jewish creativity). Here Moritz Gudemann (1835–1918), an early Conservative rabbi who was likely the first to use the term *sifrei musar* (which became popular in ultraorthodox literature in the twentieth century as *sifrei mussar ve yerah*), openly states that musar must be distinguished from halakha, the former a complement to the latter, assuming that halakha alone was not sufficient to meet the ends of human perfection.¹⁰

It is well known that the Talmud Torah Yeshiva in Kelm, founded by Simha Zisel, was one of the first in Eastern Europe to establish a curriculum that included general studies as a norm (and not as a reluctant response to an edict, as we see in the Volozhin yeshiva, which ultimately chose to close its doors rather than incorporate mandatory study of the Russian language).¹¹ Of this innovation Simha Zisel writes:

> Let it be known, that all these studies are grounded in the path of reverence, the fulfillment of the Torah,

---

9. Israel Salanter, *Ohr Yisrael*, Letter #30.
10. Cited in Koch, *Human Self-Perfection*, 11, 13.
11. On this see Shaul Stampfer, *Lithuanian Yeshivas of the Nineteenth Century* (London: The Littman Library of Jewish Civilizations, 2014). The decision to close the Volozhin yeshiva was a bit more complicated than that, but the mandatory study of Russian in the Yeshiva curriculum added to the decision.

and this is done very wisely and carefully.... We have implanted in their hearts a fixed understanding that students should grasp these things as part of the fulfillment of the Torah... so that they not turn away from the awe of God.[12]

Focusing on the rabbinic dictum *"derekh eretz kadma le-Torah,"* Simha Zisel writes elsewhere:

[W]e can see with our eyes that he who is wiser regarding the human work of musar [*musar enoshi*], such musar being part of moral decency as is known among the philosophers, is closer to knowing the Torah. He who understands this will be astonished and aroused in the realization that applying one's reason to the wisdom of moral decency is part of musar.[13]

While this sounds close to a kind of modern Maimonideanism or the Neo-Orthodoxy of Samson Raphael Hirsch, I think it is different in a few ways. First, we are not talking about knowledge of God; we are talking about the cultivation of the ethical personality (*tikun ha-midot*), ethics here replacing the pre-modern pietist whose goal was being subsumed in the divine glory.[14] Second, this is not utilitarian in the sense of accommodating one's modern surroundings or in terms of halakhic progression and revision. While Hirsch focused on the rabbinic adage *"Torah 'im derekh eretz,"* which in modern Orthodoxy becomes *"Torah 'u Mada"* (that is, the co-existence of Torah with the secular), Simha Zisel focused on *"Derekh eretz kadma le-Torah,"* which suggests more of a distinction, perhaps even a hierarchy, than co-existence. In any case, even given

---

12. See Claussen, *Sharing the Burden*, 30, 31.
13. Ibid., 32.
14. On this see Diana Lobel, *A Sufi-Jewish Dialogue* (Philadelphia: University of Pennsylvania Press, 2006), 146–176.

its Eastern European traditional context, modern musar is really about modernity without openly saying so, as in the case with Hirsch, although Hirsch was much more open about his program.[15] Moreover, given that traditional context, I am suggesting that it is not about halakha, either. *Derekh eretz kadma le-Torah* here is not positing one as an extension of the other. Rather, musar *is* "torah" in the sense of divine truth, but is reached though the cultivation of the self through the training of musar, and not simply fidelity to *halakha* (although in this case it is certainly not opposed to it). And it is this behavioral refinement, or *derekh eretz*, that is the proper *condition* (*kadma*) for Torah. Even in Simha Zisel's moderate *Hokhmat u Musar* we find passages where the exclusive study of Torah as an end in itself is deemed detrimental to the cultivation of the true *ba'al musar*, which in many cases becomes an alternative heroic model to that of the *talmid hakham*.[16]

While the subtleties of musar's innovation in regard to the autonomy of the self may be undetected to the outside reader, the Hazon Ish was very attuned to the potential dangers of such an innovation were it to become the norm in the yeshiva world he shared with advocates of musar. In his *Emunah u Betachon*, published posthumously in 1953 because he did not want to engage in open warfare against musar, the Hazon Ish argued that musar had the potential to undermine the centrality of halakha and Torah study as the *sine qua non* of the religious life.[17] In *Emunah u Betachon* (and

---

15. Although we do know that Simha Zisel read some maskilic literature—for example, the works of Menachem Mendel Lefin. See Claussen, *Sharing the Burden*, 56.

16. The Hazon Ish spends considerable space in Part III of his *Emunah u Betahon* arguing against any legitimate comparison between the *talmid hakham* and the *ba'al musar*.

17. In a forthcoming essay devoted to the Hazon Ish, I develop this idea in numerous ways. See my "Beyond Faith and Reason: The Hazon Ish's *Emunah u Bitahon* on Certainty and Doubt, Love of the Law, and Constructing the Halakhic Self," in *Religion and the Emotions*, ed. A. Dailey, L. Levy, and M. Kavka (Philadelphia: University of Pennsylvania Press, forthcoming).

supplemented by many letters of correspondence collected in his three-volume *Kovetz Igrot*), the Hazon Ish posits what I call a theory of "halakhic totalism" as a counter to musar's meta-halakhic behaviorism. Halakhic totalism begins with a theory of the self, founded on the notion that the sin of Adam and Eve left the human being with evil and good inclinations so intertwined that the good (that which can serve as an agent for divine will separate from the law) can never extricate itself from evil, understood as the desire for self-interest. The Hazon Ish's reading of Adam and Eve constitutes, in my view, a type of non-kabbalistic Jewish doctrine of original sin. Reason is forever in a state of doubt, and human beings are forever fooled by themselves as a result of Adam's sin.[18] In fact, the "I" for the Hazon Ish is in a state of incommensurable doubt whereby all calculations (*shikul ha-dat*) are subject to error and uncertainty. Reason, too, however refined, can never free itself from the grip of self-interest. This contrasts starkly with some musar positions—for example, in Simcha Zissel, when he writes in his *Hokhmat u Mussar*, "But with God's help we will clearly demonstrate that most of the Torah is based on natural human reason, and from such [reason] we can understand the depth of what goes beyond human reason and is only known from being received at Sinai."[19]

Yet the Hazon Ish does not fall prey to a fideism whereby reason cedes to irrational faith. The Hazon Ish does not avow the view of Tertullian, Luther, his musar contemporary Yosef Yuzel Hurvitz of Novordok, or the Hasidic master Nahman of Bratslav.[20] Rather, for him the only option for the one who desires fealty to divine will is submission to an external system in its entirety (the halakha) and

---

18. On original sin in Judaism, see my *From Metaphysics to Midrash* (Bloomington: Indiana University Press, 2008), 34–76.
19. Simha Zissel, *Hokhmat u'Musar* 3:240, and Claussen, *Sharing the Burden*, 82, 83.
20. On Hurvitz and Nahman on doubt and certainty, see my "Doubt and Certainty in Contemporary Jewish Piety," in *Jewish Philosophy for the Twenty-First Century*, ed. Hava Tirosh-Samuelson and Aaron Hughes (Leiden: Brill, 2014), 205–228.

that one simply accepts the system as the product of divine will. For the Hazon Ish, that is the definition of *betahon* (trust). *Emunah* (faith) is a belief in the divine system as revealed law, and *bitahon* is the practical application of that *emunah*.

Once one submits to the law, reason becomes operative as the tool needed to ascertain that law in the form of halakhic adjudication, or *p'sak halakha*. Submission to the law—the Hazon Ish prefers "falling in love with the law"—sets the stage for reason's function as the essential tool of adjudication. The hero is the *talmid hakham*, an individual for whom reason is the tool of his trade. But reason never engages in the pursuit of certainty outside the law; reason's function is exclusively in the understanding of divine will in Torah, manifest in Talmud, and never functions autonomously, as it does, for example, in Maimonides. Therefore, reason for the *talmid hakham* is different than it is for Simha Zisel's *ba'al musar*. The *talmid hakham* is one who uses reason to decipher what is given as truth (the Talmudic text or its practical application). In Simha Zisel's view, the *ba'al musar* uses reason to ascertain the Torah of Sinai through the cultivation of human character and behavioral refinement (*tikun ha-midot*). When reason functions exclusively as the tool of law, the result of which the Hazon Ish claims is *p'sak halakha*, following the law in its practical application is as close as one can come to the certainty of correct behavior. For the Hazon Ish, the proper use of reason after submission to the law receives divine sanction precisely because it does not presume human autonomy. This is because reason is only reasoning *about* the Talmudic text, as opposed to reason as a self-assertive act more common in secular formulations of reason. In this regard, the question for the Hazon Ish is not whether this or that halakhic decision is or is not true in any ontological sense. Rather, it is true because it is the product of one who is absorbed and subsumed in a system whose truth is a given, but undetermined. The pious act, one that includes the rectification of human behavior—that is, the true *tikun ha-midot*—lies in the submission of the "I" to the divine system that dwells outside it (the law) and that one then examines through the use of reason to determine its applicability. Although the *yetzer ha-ra* remains, it is mitigated by the system imposed upon the self, resulting from the self's submission to it. The Hazon Ish claims that will help prevent the *yetzer ha-ra* from intervening for the sake of self-interest. That is, submission to the law will oftentimes force people to act against their self-interest. This is precisely its purpose.

In one place the Hazon Ish states that for a true *posek* or *talmid hakham* דיין ודין חד הוא literally, the judge and the law become one. I don't think he means this in any mystical way. Rather, I think he means that when the *talmid hakham* submits to the law, his "I" is reconstructed through that act of submission such that his reason can now be utilized to apply this new "I" (the fusion of self and the law) to different situations. It is not that the *talmid hakham* cannot err in his deliberations, but the error itself becomes divine will when it is made through reasoned examination of the sources.[21] Here, then, certainty is not about objective truth; rather, it is the product of submission of reason to a system accepted as true. Thus, the Hazon Ish's view of the law is without ontology as far as I can tell. Unlike Soloveitchik in *Halakhac Man*, the Hazon Ish makes no ontological claim about halakha, which is why, I think, his focus on the praxis of the law is void of any discernible theoretical construct. (He has a method, but that method is exclusively about understanding the words on the page and not the larger system it represents.) The *ba'al musar*, alternatively, uses reason to achieve *tikun midot* through a combination of Torah sources and autonomous deliberation. For the Hazon Ish, this too easily results in a distortion of the sources, since they are being evaluated without submission to the law as the sole criterion of determination. The act of submission to the law for the Hazon Ish is described by him as "falling in love

---

21. This supports his notion of *daas torah,* or the authority of the Torah sage in non-Torah matters. On this see the Hazon Ish, *Kovetz Igrot,* vol. 1–2, #194.

with the law" (*ahavat ha-halakha*), a locution I have rarely seen in classical sources. Deliberate or not, I see it as intended to promote an intimacy between the individual and the law cultivated through submission, an emotive exercise that cultivates a mentality whereby God is mediated through something quite tangible, requiring acts on the part of the lover.

From my reading of *Emunah u Betachon* and the Hazon Ish's correspondence, it is my view that he felt that the traditional way of life was endangered, not because of secularism *per se*. In fact, he had little interest in engaging with the larger secular Israeli society and by and large did not view it as a serious threat to his enclosed world. (He died in 1953.) Rather, the real danger was the infiltration of modern ideas in the name of Torah, not historical criticism which I think he may have thought was easily refutable on his terms, but the more subtle autonomy of the self developed through musar. As he saw it, once the fusion between self and halakha is severed, the deconstruction of what I call halakhic totalism is inevitable. Even though musar remains inside the yeshiva now, he understood that, given the proper circumstances, it can be adapted in place of, or outside of, the halakhic system. That is, musar can mutate into a "secularized" Torah whereby halakha plays no significant role in determining correct behavior.

I want to suggest that this is precisely what we see happening today in the rise of musar circles in many non-Orthodox communities. One of the main proponents of this neo-musar movement is Ira Stone, rabbi emeritus of BZBI, a Conservative synagogue in Philadelphia. I want to offer two brief examples from Stone's work to illustrate the way in which neo-musar may prove the Hazon Ish's fears to be justified that modern musar can yield a form of secular Torah. In Stone's 2006 book *A Responsible Life: The Spiritual Path of Musar*, he writes the following about pleasure:

> The theology that I have constructed embraces the enjoyment of pleasure as the core experience of being human. We do not deny our experience of the world, but rather

cherish it.... [W]e acknowledge that the enjoyment of pleasure is not only part of us, but the very engine of our existence, the essence of our very spirit, spirit itself.[22]

While it is true that Simha Zisel does offer a more positive assessment of pleasure than did pre-modern musar ascetics, his teachings remain deeply embedded in a larger view that still advocated a negation of the self as the act of pious devotion. His attempt to ameliorate that negation of self exists within that larger train of traditionalism. Stone's ostensible "theology of pleasure," requiring an autonomy of the self and taking pleasure in the self (as an expression of embracing pleasure), is a neo-musar example of the innovation of modern musar in regard to the autonomy of the self that Hazon Ish was so concerned about. Taking Simha Zisel's caveat into a secular context enables neo-musar to present itself as a kind of secular Torah. Later in the same work, Stone writes about the particular and universal:

> For Musar, Jewish particularity is a reflection of the conviction that each of us, as humans, is chosen. We are the particular agent of an infinite desire. To be a Jew is to be a human being.... Judaism—especially Musar—offers contemporary Jews a way toward discovering their own humanity. At this level, anyone who manages this discovery is a Jew—or better the distinction between the Jew and the non-Jew becomes moot.[23]

Here, too, Simha Zisel, Stone's major influence, does show an openness to the non-Jew and, in a very limited way, complicates the categorical distinction between Jew and non-Jew as traditionally understood. But Stone's adaptation is more than an extension

---

22. Stone, *A Responsible Life: The Spiritual Path of Mussar* (Eugene, OR: Wipf and Stock, 2006), 11.
23. Ibid., 100.

of Simha Zisel's progressive view. Here the determination of one as a "Jew" seems primarily the result of self-realization ("anyone who manages this discovery is a Jew"); it is the autonomous self that determines one's Jewishness. Whether we take this literally or heuristically, I think it illustrates precisely what the Hazon Ish feared, a secularized Torah utilizing musar where the self effaces the law entirely. This is not to say the halakha isn't practiced in these communities (some yes, some no). It is to say that halakha is no longer the primary vehicle of *tikun ha-midot*. *Tikun ha-midot*, or musar, has been severed from the obligatory nature of halakha. The origin of this severance (can we say its secularizing trajectory?) occurs the moment musar claims that the self has the capacity, when trained properly, to determine the truth independently, even if not against, the halakha. I think this move can be found subtly in the works of Salanter, Simha Zisel, and Eliyahu Dessler. Each was fully committed to the halakhic system, but each in his own way opened up the possibility for human autonomy in regard to behavioral refinement (*tikun ha-midot*). I believe that the Hazon Ish saw this potential and thus could not allow musar to be cultivated among the believers who seek fidelity to divine will.

I do not think that the Hazon Ish feared that only musar would undermine belief among the faithful (although that happened as well). He may have also feared that non-believers would find this development in the yeshiva world attractive and use it in a secular context, all in the name of Torah. The Hazon Ish makes his views on this matter quite explicit in *Emunah u Betahon*, where he writes:

> Maintaining the wish to cleave to God on the one hand and to neglect the study of the commandments on the other results in a fully formed system that would appear to the public to be self-sustaining. This system will declare about itself, and about those who adhere to it, as if they are saying, heaven forbid, "We accept upon ourselves the yoke of heaven outside the intricacies of halakha (*dikduk ha-din*)." This declaration is a

great departure from Torah; a person who declares such a thing is one who has thrown off the yoke of Torah. Even more so, that taking on such a thing is taking on a falsehood, one that is contaminated by the impurity of rebellion, a mixture that is both intentional and well-grounded, calculated and fundamental.[24]

Awareness of the dangers of musar without a deep and abiding commitment to normative halakha is not limited to the Hazon Ish. Here is a striking quote from the American Orthodox thinker Samuel Belkin that nicely captures what I take is the Hazon Ish's major concern. Discussing the survival of traditional Judaism in America in the 1950s, Belkin wrote: "The greatest danger to traditional Judaism lies in the philosophy of secular observance."[25] In a slightly different register, Immanuel Etkes argues in his book *Rabbi Israel Salanter* that musar served as a strong modernizing force in the Lithuanian yeshivot.[26] One could argue similarly regarding Hasidism, certainly according to the views of people like Martin Buber, Yosef Micha Berdyczewski, Hillel Zeitlin, and other proponents of first-wave neo-Hasidism.

The Hazon Ish (and Belkin) understood what was opened when musar served as the foundation of *tikkun ha-midot*, even as the musar the Hazon Ish was exposed to was deeply devoted to the halakhic life. For the Hazon Ish, when anything (e.g., *tikun ha-midot* through musar, or *devekut*) serves as a substitute, or even a dominant trope in one's devotional life other than *halakha*, the pillar of covenantal life is in danger. In this case, neo-musar has arguably proven him correct. Not speaking specifically of musar, Belkin understood that for the traditionalist, secular Jewish practice much more than secularism as the abandonment of practice poses traditionalism's greatest danger.

---

24. The Hazon Ish, *Emunah v Betahon* 4:19.
25. See Samuel Belkin, *Essays in Traditional Jewish Thought* (New York: Philosophical Library, 1956).
26. See Etkes, *Rabbi Israel Salanter*, 151–164.

I am not critical of the neo-musar project; in fact, I think it is quite valuable and creative and presents us with an alternative model to newer forms of neo-Hasidism. Whereas neo-Hasidism offers us a revision of Hasidic spirituality outside the social and even theological context of classical Hasidism, neo-musar does something similar with modern musar. Both are productive new forms of Jewish spirituality under Twersky's definition discussed above (though Twersky might not agree with such an assertion). In any event, I only want to demonstrate its genealogy as an illustration of Talal Asad's claim of the interdependence of religion and the secular, in this case suggesting how human autonomy as a central tenet of modern musar, and modern Judaism more generally, can yield secular piety in the form of neo-musar.[27] Neo-musar and, I would add, neo-Hasidism (both its first and second wave), have shown us how these new forms of Jewish piety are not continuations of the normative tradition but forms of secularizing deviance, mutations sharing more perhaps with certain forms of Jewish heresy in the past than conventional forms of Jewish religious practice today. And yet they continue to inform, inspire, and perpetuate the law/spirituality dichotomy that lies at the core of many forms of contemporary Jewish religiosity.

Taylor's claim that selfhood as the arbiter of the good stands at the center of the shift toward the secular is suggestive when turning to modern musar and then neo-musar as exemplars of selfhood and behavioral refinement in Judaism. Another practitioner of neo-musar, Alan Morinis, describes his neo-musar relationship to the past as follows:

> I am not trying to innovate on the authentic tradition, but rather to rearticulate the perennial truths in a more contemporary form. History shows that this is what the teachers of Musar have always done, as its sages told

---

27. See Asad, *Genealogy of Religion* (Baltimore, MD: The Johns Hopkins University Press, 1993), 27–82.

timeless lessons in language and in styles intended to meet up with the unique circumstances of their generation. In that way too, I strive to stay true to tradition.[28]

This study has argued that Morinis is being too coy in his claim that he is simply extending the teachings of modern musar. The tension between law and spirituality that informs the long trajectory of Jewish piety is tested when the self enters as an autonomous agent for the good. This begins inferentially in modern musar and becomes more overt in the neo-musar of Stone and Morinis. The Hazon Ish understood this well, perhaps better than the modern musar masters he criticized. Musar alone will not snap the cord that holds law and spirituality in tension. But when the autonomous self becomes operative in a modern register, even the piety and halakhic fidelity of modern musar may not be enough to keep the tension intact.

References

Asad, Talal. *Genealogy of Religions*. Baltimore, MD: The Johns Hopkins University Press, 1993.
Belkin, Samuel. *Essays in Traditional Jewish Thought*. New York: Philosophical Library, 1956.
Brown, Benjamin. *Hazon Ish: Posek, Ha-Ma'amin u Manhig Ha-Marekha Ha-Haredit*. Jerusalem: Magnes Press, 2011 [Hebrew].
Buber, Martin. *Hasidism & Modern Man*. Princeton, NJ: Princeton University Press, 2015.
Claussen, Geoffrey. *Sharing the Burden: R. Simhah Zissel Ziv and the Path of Musar*. Albany: State University of New York Press, 2015.
Englander, Yakir. "The Understanding of the Human and the Purpose of Halakha in the Writings of the Hazon Ish," in *Reishit* 2 (2010): 183–201 [in Hebrew].

---

28. Alan Morinis, *Everyday Holiness: The Spiritual Path of Mussar* (Boston and London: Trumpeter, 2008), 10. Cf. Morinis, *With Heart and Mind: Mussar Teachings to Transform Your Life* (Boston and London: Trumpeter, 2014).

Etkes, Immanuel. *Rabbi Israel Salanter and the Musar Movement: Seeking the Torah of Truth*. Philadelphia, PA: JPS, 1993.

Goldberg, Hillel. *Yisrael Salanter: Text, Structure, Idea*. Hoboken, NJ: Ktav, 1982.

Hazon Ish, *Emunah u Betahon*. Bnei Brak, 1953.

———. *Kovetz Igrot*. 2 volumes. Rav Hayyim Graineman ed. Bnei Brak, n.d.

Kaplan, Lawrence. "The Ethics of Submission: Unification with the Spirit of Torah and Its Stature in Reference to Contemporary Challenges, R. Avraham Yeshayahu Karlitz, the Hazon Ish." *Ha-Gedolim: Leaders Who Shaped the Israeli Haredi Jewry*, ed. B. Brown and N. Leon, 479–519. [Hebrew]. Jerusalem: Magnes Press, 2017.

———. "The Hazon Ish: Hasidic Critic of Traditional Orthodoxy," in *The Uses of Tradition: Jewish Continuity in the Modern Era*, ed. J. Wertheimer, 145–174. New York and Jerusalem: JTS Press, 1993.

Katz, Dovid. *Tenuat Musar*, 5 vols. Bnei Brak, Gittler Brothers, 2006. [Hebrew].

Koch, Patrick. *Human Self-Perfection: A Re-Assessment of Kabbalistic Musar-Literature of Sixteenth-Century Safed*. Los Angeles: Cherub Press, 2013.

Lobel, Diana. *A Sufi-Jewish Dialogue* (Philadelphia: University of Pennsylvania Press, 2006)

Magid, Shaul. "Beyond Faith and Reason: The Hazon Ish's *Emunah u Bitahon* on Certainty and Doubt, Love of the Law, and Constructing the Halakhic Self." In *Religion and the Emotions*, ed. A. Dailey, L. Levy, and M. Kavka. Philadelphia: University of Pennsylvania Press, forthcoming.

———. "Doubt and Certainty in Contemporary Jewish Piety." In *Jewish Philosophy for the Twenty-First Century*, ed. Hava Tirosh-Samuelson and Aaron Hughes, 205–228. Leiden: Brill, 2014.

———. *From Metaphysics to Midrash*. Bloomington: Indiana University Press, 2008.

Morinis, Alan. *Everyday Holiness: The Spiritual Path of Mussar*. Boston and London: Trumpeter, 2008.

———. *With Heart and Mind: Mussar Teachings to Transform Your Life*. Boston and London: Trumpeter, 2014.

Salanter, Israel. *Ohr Yisrael*. 1890.

Stampfer, Shaul. *Lithuanian Yeshivas of the Nineteenth Century*. London: The Littman Library of Jewish Civilizations, 2014.
Stein, Daniel. "The Limits of Religious Optimism: The Hazon Ish and the Alter of Novordok on *Bittahon*," *Tradition* 43:2 (2010): 32–48.
Stone, Ira. *A Responsible Life: The Spiritual Path of Mussar*. Eugene, OR: Wipf and Stock, 2006.
Taylor, Charles. *Sources of the Self*. Cambridge, MA: Harvard University Press, 1992.
———. *A Secular Age*. Cambridge, MA: Harvard University Press, 2007.
Twersky, Isadore. "Religion and Law." In *Religion in a Religious Age*, ed. S. Goeitin, 69–70. Cambridge, MA: Harvard University Press, 1974.
Warner, M., J. Van Antwerpen, and C. Calhoun (eds.), *Varieties of Secularism in a Secular Age*. Cambridge, MA: Harvard University Press, 2013.

Section V

JEWISH SPIRITUALITY AFTER MODERNITY: DEATH AND RENAISSANCE

Chapter 13

HOLOCAUST MEMORIES AND MEMORIES OF DEPRESSION: THE INFLUENCE OF MY PARENTS ON MY SCHOLARSHIP IN THE SOCIOLOGY OF EDUCATION[1]

Alan R. Sadovnik, Rutgers University-Newark

I was born and spent my first nine years in the Boulevard Housing Project in the East New York neighborhood of Brooklyn, a working-class section of New York City. Both my parents were Holocaust survivors, and the Holocaust became a major theme of my childhood. As I grew into adulthood, I learned a sense of social justice from my parents, which would come to shape much of my work as a sociologist.

My mother, Ruth Haas Sadovnik, left Berlin at the age of 11 on the Kindertransport. She lived in Hull, England, until 1945, when she was reunited with her parents and sister, who escaped Nazi Germany in 1941. Her difficult childhood left her with a sense of moral obligation, duty, and social justice, which she exhibited for the rest of her life.

---

1. Adapted from A.R. Sadovnik and R.W. Coughlan, "Holocaust Memories: Honoring My Mother Through Applied Scholarship and Building Programs," in *Leaders in the Sociology of Education* (Rotterdam, Netherlands: Sense Publishers, 2016), 201–216. With permission of the publisher.

She was married for 50 years to her beloved husband, Morris, who, with his half-brother, were the sole survivors of their family from Warsaw.

My mother's childhood was difficult, to say the least. I cannot imagine what it was like to be 11 years old and have to flee to another country on a train, speaking no English and to arrive in another country, never knowing if you would see your parents and sister again. My mother had to leave school at age 14 to work full-time at Hammonds Department Store in Hull. She would continue to work full-time until her retirement 48 years later at the age of 62. One story in particular captures my mother's determination and spirit. At the age of 13, after she had been evacuated to the countryside because of the nightly bombing of Hull, a local benefactor donated pork chops to the boarding school she attended. Being kosher, my mother ate only her potatoes, leaving the pork chops. Her teacher scolded her for not eating them. When my mother informed her that she could not eat them due to her religion's rules, the teacher demanded that she eat them and said that she would force her to remain in the cafeteria until she did. My mother told her that she would have to wait forever, as she did not escape the Nazis to be forced to eat pork in England. Finally, at midnight, when another student reported to the headmistress what was happening, the latter intervened. She allowed my mother to return to her room and, to her credit, immediately fired the teacher.

Twice during her time in England my mother cheated death. Once a bomb fell into the shelter and landed right next to her. Miraculously, it did not explode. Then, upon hearing the news that her parents and sister had made it safely to New York City, she begged Mrs. Levine, her foster mother, to allow her to make the dangerous trans-Atlantic voyage to join them. After numerous attempts to convince her, Mrs. Levine agreed, and they took the train to Southampton for the journey. At the last minute, Mrs. Levine decided against allowing her to go. My mother was devastated. It turned out that a U-boat sank the ship and, fortunately for her (and especially me), she was not among its passengers, all of whom perished.

My mother was one of the fortunate 10 percent of the 10,000 kinder who were reunited with their parents. Ninety percent perished in one of Hitler's concentration camps. Shortly after coming to New York, she met and fell in love with my father, a Polish immigrant, who came to the United States in 1937 and served with the Army Corps of Engineers in the Pacific. Soon after their marriage in 1948, when my mother was just 21, my father began to exhibit symptoms of the severe manic-depression that would haunt him until his death in 1998. When my father was in the manic stage of his illness, he was charming, loving, and totally devoted to my mother. When he was depressed, he was angry and unable to function, and railed against a God who would allow six million Jews, including most of his family, to perish. During my parents' 50 years of marriage, my father was hospitalized numerous times, including spending his last five years in a psychiatric nursing home. Although some could not understand her staying with him, my mother loved him deeply and took seriously her vows to care for him "in sickness and in health, till death do us part." For me, his mental illness became another theme of my life.

Some of my most cherished memories came when my mother and I returned to her childhood homes. In 1987, when I was lecturing at the Universities of London and Nottingham, she met me in London, where we sojourned back to Hull. We met four of the surviving Levine sisters, whom she had not seen in 42 years and who were now in their 80s. Nonetheless, as they entered her cousin Lotte's home, she immediately recognized each one of them. We went back to her childhood home on Beverly Road and sat together, hugging each other in tears as we sat in the bomb shelter. She took me to Hammonds, where at age 14 she had exhibited the traits of diligence and perseverance that would make her an exemplary legal secretary.

For years, I asked my mother to return to Berlin with me and to show me her childhood homes. She always refused, saying that England, not Germany, was her childhood home. She was forever grateful to the British for saving her life. It pleased her greatly that

I have spent so much time over the past 20 years at the University of London, to the point that it is like my second home. However, in 1995, when I was giving a paper in Bielefeld in western Germany, I told my mother a little white lie: that I had bought her a non-refundable ticket so that she could accompany me on a one-week trip to Berlin. (Although it was non-refundable, if she had not gone, I would have received a credit.) She agreed to go, and I often joked with her by asking, "How do you get my Jewish mother to get on a plane? Buy her a non-refundable ticket." It was, along with our trip to Hull, among the most important trips of my life. We visited her home in Shlasenzee, where for the first time I came to understand what the Nazis took from her family. Their house was not modest; rather, it was large, elegant, and expensive. They went from German-Jewish bourgeoisie to working-class refugees in a matter of years. We went to their apartment in Charlottenburg, the Park Avenue of Berlin, right off Kurfürstendamm, the city's Madison or Fifth Avenue. We visited the site of her synagogue, but all that was left of it was the plaque commemorating its burning on Kristallnacht. Her German, which she had not spoken since her parents' death two decades earlier, came back immediately. And she used it to tell everyone and anyone that she had been born in Berlin, had left on the Kindertransport, and that I was her son. She was saying to everyone that you did not kill us all.

As a child, I always knew that like my grandfather I would receive a Ph.D. In some way, without ever explicitly telling me this, I understood that it was my role to restore our family's level of educational attainment. Although my mother left school after the 8th grade, it was evident to all who knew her that if it weren't for the Holocaust, she would have continued her education and excelled.

My father's reaction to the Holocaust resulted in atheism and anger. On the eve of my bar mitzvah, after we came home from my singing the Friday evening Kiddish, he screamed unrelentingly at my mother for having a bar mitzvah for me. He kept saying, "How can we celebrate God when he permitted the killing of six million

Jews and lots of members of our families?" My earliest memory of my father was visiting him in the Fort Hamilton, Brooklyn, Veterans Administration Hospital, where he was hospitalized in the psychiatric unit from the time I was three to when I turned five. At this point, he was given a partial service-connected disability designation for his time in the Pacific during World War II for what today would be classified as PTSD. For the rest of his life (he lived to be 76), he was in and out of VA psychiatric wards, and by age 55 had received a 100 percent service-connected disability. A few months after my bar mitzvah, I watched in horror as he was taken out of our house in a straitjacket. When I was in graduate school, I visited him in the ICU after he took an overdose of his antidepressant medication, which he admitted was on purpose. By the end of his life, he had spent the last five years in a VA psychiatric nursing home in Westchester County. Throughout all of these hospitalizations, my mother stood by him and visited him at least twice a week when he was in the Manhattan VA and once a week when in Westchester. Given that it took an hour to get there from her apartment in Queens by car and she did not drive, I drove her every Saturday or Sunday. When numerous family and friends asked my mother why she stayed with him, she responded that she survived the Holocaust to take care of him.

When my father was in the manic state of his illness, he was funny, theatrical, loving, and argumentative, especially when it came to the causes of mental illness. An early proponent of biochemical explanations, he believed that his condition was genetic and hoped it would not be passed on to me. As a social scientist I argued with him about this, as I believed his condition was caused by "Holocaust survivor guilt." Since I, too, have suffered from recurring bouts of depression as an adult, I have come to agree with my father on the genetic pathways, although I also recognize that growing up in such a dysfunctional environment could also be a cause. I suffered my first bout of depression in 1997, when I was Interim Dean of the School of Education at Adelphi University. At that time the President and Board of Trustees had been removed by the New York State Board of Regents for fiscal and managerial malfeasance, and it was a very stressful period as the university tried to rebuild after a decade of faculty-administration civil war. I resigned as Dean and was given a six-month sabbatical in which to recover. During a time when it was often difficult to get out of bed, I finally understood what my father had gone through and how it had been unfair of me to think he could have willed himself out of bed. When I visited him in the nursing home before his death, I cried and apologized to him for being so judgmental about his many bouts of depression, but by this time he was too demented to understand. I continued to suffer from more bouts of depression over the next 20 years, always at times of extreme stress, mostly brought on by my administrative responsibilities.

In 2007, my mother died at the age of 79 after a brief illness. In the year before her death, she had worked hard to prevent the merger of her Conservative synagogue with a neighboring Orthodox one. She feared that if the merger were to occur, the men and women would be separated. She told me she did not survive the Holocaust to be told she could not sit next to her son in synagogue. It was characteristic of her spirit and life; unfortunately, she would not live to see the outcome. As an only child I had to handle everything myself, including cleaning out her apartment and selling it. It was again a very stressful time, and, combined with the difficulty of mourning, it resulted in another bout of depression. I am currently stable, and my medications seem to be keeping the depression at bay. The fact that I no longer have any administrative activities certainly has helped. Nonetheless, I live in fear that the next one is but a cycle away and hope that whatever genetic, biochemical causes are responsible will stay away.

These two themes—the Holocaust and mental illness—formed the basis of my childhood and continued into adulthood. Watching as my father was carried off in a straitjacket when I was 13 years old left a permanent imprint in my mind. Visiting him in psychiatric wards many times until his death, when he was 76 and I was 45, also has stayed with me permanently.

Changing Neighborhoods

We lived in the city housing project in East New York, Brooklyn, until I was 9. The neighborhood was integrated but was becoming increasingly African American and poor. The junior high school I was scheduled to attend in a few years had a reputation for being dangerous. My parents' American dream was to have their own home, so they bought a two-family house in the Rockaways, an integrated, lower-middle-class and middle-class beach community in the southern part of New York City in Queens, near JFK Airport.

Growing up near the beach, about 1.5 hours from Manhattan, was like living in a small town, not New York City. When I was 12, I learned to surf and was one of the early East Coast surfers in the Rockaways. When I was in college, I decided that I would become a college professor and teach at the University of Hawaii. Shortly thereafter, I broke my wrist in a skateboarding accident, which permanently ended my surfing career and my dream of living in Hawaii.

My parents had the misfortune of choosing changing neighborhoods to live in. A few years after moving to the Rockaways, a city edict turned two middle-income city projects into low-income ones, and an additional low-income project was built. Our house was thus surrounded by three low-income projects, with two others within a few miles. In a few years, the housing project population consisted of low-income African Americans and Latinos. At the same time, real estate blockbusters came to the families in our community and offered to sell their houses for a fair price and told them if they did not accept, once the block was more than 50 percent African American, the values would plummet. My parents refused to sell, saying they would not give in to this racism. However, within a few years they were one of only three white families left on the block.

There had once been summer bungalows on the surrounding blocks, but they soon were abandoned and often became drug dens. My mother became President of the Frank Avenue Civic Association and worked diligently to get them torn down.

My parents stayed in their house for 25 years and finally sold it after my father was mugged for the fourth time. It represented an end to their working-class dream of owning their own home, as it had turned into an urban nightmare. Although my father still did not want to leave, my mother and I made the decision, and my parents bought a cooperative apartment in Little Neck, Queens, the last town in New York City before the Nassau County line. The Rockaways have yet to recover, with significant sections home to low-income projects and nursing homes. Little Neck is largely middle-income and upper-middle-income white and Asian. My parents lived in a naturally aging community within a large cooperative development, and they enjoyed living there until their deaths.

Both in the Rockaways and in Little Neck my mother exemplified a life of public service. As President of the Frank Avenue Civic Association she worked tirelessly to improve a decaying neighborhood overridden by drugs and crime. Before we moved away, she was honored by the Rockaways Planning Board for her dedication to the community. In Little Neck she was active in a variety of organizations, including the Samuel Friedman Y and the North Hills League for Retarded Children, where she served as President and was honored with a Distinguished Service Award. She always said that surviving the Holocaust made her committed to social justice and public service. And it was her commitment to social justice that has influenced my own scholarship, teaching, and service.

Education

The elementary, junior high, and high schools that I attended were all integrated. However, although the schools were racially and socioeconomically integrated, my classes were almost all white and middle class. In elementary school I was in the IGC (Intellectually Gifted Children) program. This tracking system grouped most of the students in the same classes year after year. In junior high school we were in SP (Special Progress), and in high school we were in

Honors or AP (Advanced Placement). My own education illustrated the powerful effects of within-school tracking, as those in my track all went on to colleges that were, for the most part, competitive.

Far Rockaway High School had over 4,000 students when I attended, so large that it was forced to operate on split session. My graduating class had 1,070 students, but I probably knew only about 100 of them. These were students from the SP classes in all of the peninsula's junior high schools. Of the 100, the students were largely white and middle class. The Honors and AP classes were fairly rigorous, especially when compared to the regular classes. I decided to take regular English classes in order to devote more time to mathematics and science. The level of the English classes was very low, and to this day I regret not taking more advanced English classes, as my education in literature was deficient. It represented my first experience with the effects of tracking on both high- and low-track students.

Far Rockaway High School had no college counselor, only a few guidance counselors who could give advice on college choices but rarely did. Even though I had a 92 average and graduated 43rd out of 1,070, I did not have a sufficient understanding of the college application process. Nor did my parents, neither of whom went to college. So I went to *Barron's Profiles of American Colleges* and selected mostly local colleges, as going away did not even enter my mind. I wanted to stay near the beach and the waves. I was admitted to all of the colleges I applied to: Adelphi, Brooklyn College, Columbia, and SUNY New Paltz. The decision came down to Brooklyn and Columbia. My parents said they would find a way to pay for Columbia, but the free tuition at the City University of New York (CUNY) made Brooklyn more attractive.

I transferred to Queens College after three semesters because the student population at Brooklyn seemed too conservative. But in my first semester at Brooklyn, I had taken an introduction to sociology course that changed the trajectory of my education. Up to that point I thought I wanted to be a lawyer, but the sociology course made me decide to major in it. In that first semester, I also discovered how ill prepared I was. I received a C- on my first English Composition paper and had to work very hard to catch up. I discovered that what I thought had been a rigorous high school education was not that rigorous. In my third semester, I took a sociological theory course and for the first time read Marx, Weber, Durkheim, Goffman, and Mills. The Queens College Sociology Department had a strong reputation, so my decision to transfer seemed a solid one.

I was in the last class that received free tuition at CUNY, and I always say it was the best education money did not buy. At the time, Queens enrolled more than 25,000 students on a commuter campus, so developing a community was difficult. I spent most of my out-of-class time working at a part-time job and with my girlfriend, who also went to Queens, and whom I would marry upon graduation. Queens represented the mission of CUNY: it consisted of working- and middle-class students striving to move upward. They were smart and hardworking, and my class has done exceptionally well in life. In addition to majoring in sociology, I minored in secondary education/social studies. I decided to obtain my teaching license so that in the event that I did not get a fellowship, I would be able to teach and go to graduate school part-time. In my final semester, I student-taught at the new Beach Channel High School in the Rockaways. The school served the students in the western part of the Rockaways, who used to attend Far Rockaway High School. While student teaching, I learned another lesson about tracking. During the first quarter I taught an honors course in behavioral sciences. The students were largely white and middle class. In the second quarter, I taught a regular-level course in criminology. The students were largely African American and Latino and poor. When I asked my cooperating teacher why the two groups had different subjects, he replied that those taking criminology would need to know their rights and the ins and outs of the system. The lesson was that one group was being prepared for college and the other for jail.

I graduated from college in 1975, during New York City's fiscal crisis. Teachers were being laid off, and there was a hiring freeze, so I decided to go to graduate school in sociology full-time. Since I was getting married in July and my wife would be in her senior year at Queens, I applied only to New York City programs. I was accepted to all the programs I applied to, but only NYU gave me financial aid—a fellowship that included full tuition and a stipend. After my wedding in July, I began graduate school as a full-time doctoral student in September. I had a difficult adjustment. We lived in the Rockaways, so the commute was difficult, averaging about 1.5 hours each way. This made it difficult for me to spend long hours in the library or to become part of the student community, although I tried my best to do so. The courses were far more demanding than undergraduate courses. The students, who came from more privileged backgrounds and had graduated from Ivy League and elite liberal arts colleges, seemed more prepared than I was. The graduate school world that I was assimilating into was different than the world with my wife, which put a strain on our marriage, one that would eventually lead to its demise, although not for another eight years.

The Sociology Department at NYU was world-class. The faculty included Eliot Freidson, Edwin Schur, Dennis Wrong, Wolf Heydebrand, Richard Sennett, and Caroline Persell, among others. But the highlight of my doctoral career was the Visiting European Scholars program, where visiting professors would teach an eight-week course. During my three years of coursework, I studied with Anthony Giddens, Basil Bernstein, Michael Mann, and Jock Young. It was during my course with Bernstein that a lifelong friendship and colleagueship began, one that would blossom in the 1980s and last until his death in 2000. Bernstein taught me to connect sociological theory to empirical research and solidified my interest in the sociology of education. After I finished my coursework, I taught and worked on my dissertation.

Faculty Positions

In 1979 I secured a full-time instructor position in the Division of Education Opportunity (DEO) at the State University of New York,

College at Purchase (SUNY Purchase). The DEO was a compensatory higher education program consisting largely of working-class and poor African American and Latino students. We were supposed to teach both content and skills. I was hired to teach two sociology courses and one English composition course per semester, which turned out to be a heavy, labor-intensive load, given the need to teach underprepared students skills as well as content.

During this time I was looking for a dissertation topic. In the course of my first year at Purchase, I discovered that the students were unhappy with the separate nature of their program (they did not mainstream for two years). The effects of what was a racialized tracking system seemed an ideal dissertation topic, especially since I could get access to the site. Studying a program that I was a part of would prove to be a challenge, as I constantly had to step back from what occurred and try to be as objective as possible. There were many times I had to analyze my own behavior or position as a researcher and a member, not an easy task.

Writing a dissertation and teaching full-time proved difficult and slow. In 1983, I passed my thesis defense and received my Ph.D. in October. Given the length of my dissertation (651 pages) and the administrative responsibilities I would soon undertake, it took me 11 years to revise it for publication as a book (Sadovnik, 1994). At my May graduation, my mother was exceptionally proud, and my father was characteristically low-key.

All of this was done under the specter of pending unemployment, as my appointment had been terminated due to fiscal crisis, and 1983–84 would be my final year. I looked unsuccessfully for academic positions the entire year, and as late as August I was prepared to teach three courses per semester as an adjunct at NYU's School of Continuing Education, where I had taught one course while at Purchase. The most important thing for me about NYU's School of Continuing Education is that it is where I first met Susan Semel, who in later years would become my collaborator on a number of books—and, most important, my wife. But in August, while I was in San Francisco, I received a message from a friend at

NYU that I had gotten a call from Adelphi University about an administrative job, and I subsequently became Assistant Dean of Evening and Weekend Programs.

I spent 16 years at Adelphi where, having moved to the faculty in 1986, I went from Assistant to Full Professor. From 1996 to 1998 I served as Interim Dean of the School of Education. In 2000, I moved to Rutgers University-Newark, where I have served as Chair of the Department of Urban Education, the Co-Director of the Institute on Education Law and Policy and the Newark Schools Research Collaborative, and the Director of the Urban Educational Policy doctoral program. In 2010 I was named a Board of Governors Distinguished Research Professor.

My mother's involvement in civic engagement and social justice activities, as well as my parents' having survived the evils and horrors of the Holocaust, resulted in my choosing a scholarly path that revolved around social and educational justice. From my dissertation forward, my research has investigated issues of race and social class inequality and how they are reproduced by the educational system in the United States, as well as how educational reforms may ameliorate these inequalities to interrupt this reproduction. Given my experiences growing up in a rapidly decaying urban environment in the Rockaways, where all of the public schools I attended have been closed down by the New York City Department of Education for poor performance, I concentrated on urban education.

My scholarly accomplishments during the Adelphi years were limited by my significant administrative responsibilities. Nonetheless, I published a number of important pieces, including a social foundations textbook (Sadovnik et al. 1994), a book on the history of progressive education, and a book on Basil Bernstein that won an American Education Studies (AESA) Critics Choice Award (Sadovnik, 1995), and an article on Bernstein that won the American Sociological Association Willard Waller Award (Sadovnik, 1991). The latter two pieces established my reputation as the leading Bernsteinian sociologist in the world. The book on the history of progressive education, a successful collaboration with Susan Semel and fellow academics, established our reputations as leading scholars of progressive education (Semel and Sadovnik, 1999). Given the constraints of my administrative responsibilities, I did little original research, but rather wrote textbooks and edited collections. Nonetheless, it was my application of Bernstein's theories to U.S. education that became the foundation for my research on educational inequality.

In 2000 I moved to Rutgers University-Newark as chair of the Department of Education. Here I have produced a significant amount of applied urban educational research aimed at reducing inequality. But Rutgers-Newark proved to have its own challenges. On the positive side, it was part of a large research university, which made it easier to get grants. On the negative side, I found myself running an underfunded department with little capacity. After three years, the stress again got to be too much, so I resigned as chair. After a one-semester sabbatical, I came back to run the Ph.D. program and to work with Paul Tractenberg as Associate Director of his Institute on Education Law and Policy (IELP), which would define my original research for the next decade or so. This enabled me to engage in research aimed at understanding and reducing educational inequality for low-income African American and Hispanic students.

I worked on IELP's first major report on state takeover of local school districts (Tractenberg et al., 2002). Over the next decade, we wrote over a dozen research reports. In 2009, we founded the Newark Schools Research Collaborative (NSRC), which I co-directed. We wrote a number of major reports on education in Newark and Elizabeth, but struggled to keep afloat. When the new Newark Superintendent gave us access to data, we embarked on fresh research in Newark. In our examination of both Newark and Elizabeth, our focus has been on the attempts of these low-income urban districts to provide better educational opportunities and outcomes for their students.

In 2009 I received the Chancellor's Award for Applied Research for my research on Newark. It represented recognition of the type of research I believed in and which, I hoped, would have an impact on the schools and social justice. It also represented recognition of my working with the community. The Chancellor nominated me for the Board of Governors Distinguished Service Professor award, which I received in 2010. This major university-wide honor recognized my applied research and work with the community. In my acceptance speech I stated that the award honored my mother and the distinguished service she had done, as well as her being my role model.

During my years at Rutgers I continued to publish a number of different types of scholarship. In addition to applied research reports, I published articles, chapters, and books. Susan Semel and my book on women and progressive education won another AESA Critics Choice Award (Sadovnik and Semel, 2002). It cemented our reputation as experts on the history and sociology of progressive education. I published three editions of a sociology of education reader (Sadovnik, 2007, 2011; Sadovnik and Coughlan, 2016), four more editions of our textbook (Sadovnik, Cookson Jr., and Semel, 2001, 2006, 2013; Sadovnik, Cookson, Jr., Semel, and Coughlan, 2018), and a second edition of our history of progressive education (Semel, Sadovnik. and Coughlan, 2016). The major themes of all of these works have been educational inequality and social justice and have been inspired by my mother's life.

Looking Forward: Trumpism and Educational Policy

With the election of Donald Trump and the appointment of Betsy DeVos as his Secretary of Education, progressives face significant challenges in the area of educational policy. The president's education budget slashed billions of dollars from public education, most extensively from Title I programs for low-income children, including after-school programs. These funds are largely being transferred to give block grants to states to support charter schools and voucher programs for independent private and private religious schools.

What, then, is the role of educational research in such an administration? As always, we need to conduct careful empirical research on these new reforms so that they can be used by advocates to lobby against them, if this is what the evidence concludes. However, given the current administration's denial of scientific research on climate change and other social issues, there is no reason to believe that educational research, no matter how well designed, and no matter how compelling, will have an effect. Instead it will probably be denied as ideological "fake news." Nonetheless, educational researchers must continue to do good work and then collaborate with advocates to support policies that promote social justice and educational equality. Coming at the last stage of my teaching and research career over the next decade, I am working diligently to provide research, particularly on Newark and Elizabeth, to help promote greater equality.

"Why Can't I Live at Home? I Wouldn't Be a Problem"

My most recent book, written with my wife, Susan Semel, and my 49-year-old stepdaughter, Margaret (Mags) Semel, is based on Mags's 626-page diary about her life at a group home for the developmentally disabled in Red Hook, New York (Dutchess County), her strong desire to live at home with us, and why she does not understand that she cannot. She spends almost every weekend with us in our country home in Hudson, New York, about 25 minutes north of her group home.

This book is extremely difficult, as it brings up a lot of issues related to my father's and my own depression. Although Mags has been very stable for the past two years, she has suffered from anxiety, depression, and aggressiveness on and off since she was sent to the Devereux Foundation at age 17. She has been hospitalized in psychiatric wards at least three times and has made numerous visits to psychiatric ERs. I have become incredibly close with Mags, especially since her father died in 2009. But her psychological issues, especially her hospitalizations, have brought back difficult memories of my father's illness.

Holocaust Memories and Jewish Spirituality and Social Transformation

My parents had very different approaches to Judaism and to spirituality and social transformation. As an angry atheist, my father did not practice and had no inner spiritual life other than bemoaning his depression. One Passover, when he discovered I had invited a German friend to our Seder, he burst out angrily and demanded he leave, saying Jew killers were not welcome at his table. We calmed things down and my friend stayed, but it exemplified my father's anger. He grudgingly participated in Seders, but never went to synagogue. My mother remained a practicing conservative Jew her entire life, went to synagogue regularly, and was active in its Sisterhood, where she performed good works. She was contemplative and spiritual and remained committed to doing community engagement for social change: to improve her community and society.

I inherited from my father his skepticism about God and his avoidance of organized Judaism. I have rarely gone to synagogue since my bar mitzvah, except for other bar mitzvahs and funerals. But I inherited from my mother a strong commitment to social justice and social transformation and have used my teaching and research toward these ends.

Holocaust Memories and Memories of Depression

Looking back, my life and career have been affected greatly by my parents' lives. My mother spent her adult life doing good works in the civic arena, while my father spent his adult life in and out of mental hospitals, suffering from depression. The choices I made to run programs and to conduct applied civic research were always influenced by my mother's life. My father was an early proponent of a biochemical explanation for depression, and he believed it was genetic. Unfortunately, he may have been right as, since 1997, I have suffered five cycles of depression. These have helped me to better understand my father's suffering and the effect his illness has had on me. When he was alive, I was angry at him for his inability to function. Now I forgive him and understand how difficult depression is. And I will always be grateful to my mother for being a role model for working for social justice.

Bibliography

Sadovnik, A.R. (1991). "Basil Bernstein's Theory of Pedagogic Practice: A Structuralist Approach." *Sociology of Education* Volume 64, Number 1: 48–63.

Sadovnik, A.R. (1994). *Equity and Excellence in Higher Education: The Decline of a Liberal Education Reform.* New York: Peter Lang.

Sadovnik, A.R. (ed.). (1995). *Knowledge and Pedagogy: The Sociology of Basil Bernstein.* Ablex Publishing Corporation.

Sadovnik, A.R. (2007, 2011). *Sociology of Education: A Critical Reader.* New York: Routledge.

Sadovnik, A.R., Cookson, P.W., Jr., and Semel, S.F. (1994, 2001, 2006, 2013). *Exploring Education: An Introduction to the Foundations of Education.* Allyn and Bacon.

Sadovnik, A.R., Cookson, P.W., Jr., Semel, S.F., (2018). *Exploring Education: An Introduction to the Foundations of Education* (Fifth Edition). Routledge.

Sadovnik, A.R., and Coughlan, R. (eds.). (2016). *Sociology of Education: A Critical Reader.* New York: Routledge (third edition).

Semel, S.F., and Sadovnik, A.R. (eds.). (1999). *"Schools of Tomorrow," Schools of Today: What Happened to Progressive Education* Peter Lang Publishers.

Sadovnik, A.R., and Semel, S.F. (eds.). (2002). *Founding Mothers and Others: Women Educational Leaders During the Progressive Era.* Palgrave Macmillan.

Semel, S.F., Sadovnik, A.R., and Coughlan, R. (eds.). (2016). *"Schools of Tomorrow", Schools of Today: Progressive Education in the 21st Century. Second Edition.* New York: Peter Lang Publishers.

Tractenberg, P., Holzer, M., Miller, J., Sadovnik, A.R., and Liss, B. (2002). *Developing a Plan for Local Control in the State-Operated School Districts.* Trenton: New Jersey Department of Education

Chapter 14

JEWISH SPIRITUALITY IN ISRAEL AS LIVED RELIGION: A NEW PERSPECTIVE FOR THE STUDY OF CONTEMPORARY JEWISH LIFE

Rachel Werczberger, Ariel University and Holon Institute of Technology

In the last fifty years, the notion of "spirituality" has gained widespread acceptance in the West. From a term almost exclusively owned by the theological language of traditional religions, it has become a popular idiom found in the most unexpected folds of contemporary society and culture (Giordan, 2016). In tandem, the idea of "Jewish Spirituality" has also become prevalent among Jewish communities and individuals. Today, various cultural initiatives, institutional modalities, and individual practices are lumped under the label of "Jewish Spirituality," or "New Age Judaism," as they are sometimes called (Salkin, 2000; Werczberger, 2016). From the Jewish healing movement, through the transdenominational Jewish Renewal movement, to local grassroots, extra-institutional community-based groups such as the independent *minyanim*, Jewish spirituality has become a buzzword in the contemporary Jewish "spiritual marketplace" (Roof, 1999), especially in North America.

Parallel developments have emerged in Israeli Judaism, both in the Orthodox and the non-Orthodox world, such as Jewish spiritual renewal communities or neo-Hassidic Karlibach *minyanim* (Werczberger, 2016). Although not all of the participants would necessarily describe them as Jewish spirituality, these type of communities, events, and rituals share some of the traits of their North American counterparts, especially their de-institutionalized, individualized aspects. Observed broadly, these developments reflect "the lived creative struggle to arrange life—one's own, or that of others, inside and around an inherited religious tradition" (Ochs, 2005).

This chapter seeks to survey some of the Israel-based developments of Jewish spirituality, among them the women-only Amen Meals, neo-Hassidic prayer services, and contemporary pilgrimages, through the concept of "lived religion" (Hall, 1997; Orsi, 1997). Emerging from the social study of religion, the study of lived religion focuses on the everyday realities of religious people and the "everyday thinking and doing of lay men and women" (Hall, 1997, p. vii). Attempting to overcome binary oppositions such as that of "popular religion" vs. "official religion," the concept has become recognized among scholars trying to make sense of the perseverance of religion in contemporary times as well as of the immense diversity, multiplicity, and complexity of present-day spiritual and religious forms.

In this essay I suggest turning our sociological gaze from the accepted socio-religio-political categories of Israeli sociology to what people really *do* in their everyday religious life, with a special focus on practice and ritual. Doing so allows us not only to overcome the prevalent, binary ethnic and religious categories of Israeli Jewish society ("religious" vs. "secular" or *Ashkenazi* vs. *Mizrachi*) (Goodman & Yonah, 2004), but also to discover the multitude of ways in which a Jewish person's life and practice are realized in everyday situations and how this is related to mundane personal experiences such as family and social life, finances, or health. Furthermore, this focus illuminates the creativity embedded in the everyday practices that take place outside the walls of the formal Jewish religious institutions—the synagogue or the *beith*-midrash. This aspect is particularly important when studying the gendered aspects of contemporary Jewish worship.

A Personal Ethnography of Lived Judaism

A few years ago I participated in a Yom Kippur service that took place in Vertigo eco-art village, in Kibbutz HaLamedhe in the Ha'Ella Vally (Vertigo, n.d.). I had received a personal invitation to the event from a friend, a professional dancer, whose sisters (most of whom are also dancers) were deeply involved in this project. This friend, whom I will call Maya, was raised in a modern Orthodox family. Of her four siblings, she is the only one who is still observant. The rest of her siblings parted ways with the Orthodox lifestyle, yet if asked, would say that they remain emotionally attached to their tradition.

Founded by Maya's siblings and several other core members of the Vertigo dance company, the village aims, according to its website, to "generate social change and to promote an alternative model of sustainable living through comprehensive art and environmental educational programs for the public." In practice, the community comprises a small group of artists and dancers living in the Kibbutz, a mud-built dance studio and a few guest rooms reconstructed from an abandoned chicken coop. An additional space (another deserted chicken coop) hosts environmental mud-building workshops. Since 2012, the village has held Jewish holiday events, usually during the holidays of Rosh Hashana (the Jewish New Year), Yom Kippur (the Day of Atonement), and Shavu'ot (Pentecost). The events are organized and facilitated by the members of the village and a few guests.

The demographics of the participants in these events is rather varied. It includes both families and singles, some of whom appear secular (no head covering for the men, pants and short-sleeved tops for the women). Some of them are self-defined *datlashim* (acronym for *datiyim le'she-avar*, or ex-religious), and some clearly belong to the National-Religious sector, identified by the *kippot* (skullcap) on the men's heads and scarves wrapped around the women's.

The event I participated in on the eve of Yom Kippur began with a meal (vegetarian) before the fast and ended with the meal breaking the fast, and its rituals vacillated between the conventional Yom Kippur and alternative forms of Jewish prayer and devotion. It included the more-or-less traditional prayer service of the holiday with the prayer clearly oriented toward the Orthodox liturgy. The studio in which the prayers were held was gender-separated by a curtain that divided the space between the men and the women. Only men led the prayers, and the texts were indistinguishable from that of an Orthodox Yom Kippur prayer.

Yet some elements were decidedly nonconventional for an Orthodox event. Aside from the unusual venue and sleeping accommodations—the participants camped by the studio or slept on mattresses on the studio floor—as well as the meditation and movement sessions offered to the participants, the service itself had some unusual features. For instance, often during the long singing parts of the service the participants would clap their hands, stomp their feet, or even break into dance. In the prayer space itself, couches, mattresses, and large pillows were laid on the floor to allow the participants to lie down, rest, and even fall asleep during the prayer—which indeed some of them did.

Clearly, those involved in the planning of the event drew inspiration from different religious sources, both Orthodox and neo-Hassidic, as well as non-Jewish ones. The devotional style combined the non-egalitarian form of Orthodox prayers with the embodied ecstatic style of neo-Hassidism (Weissler, 2006; Persico, 2014). At the same time, by offering meditations and Tai-chi sessions, it resembled the hybrid concoction typical of New Age Judaism and spiritual festivals (Werczberger, 2016).

Having studied Jewish Renewal and New Age Judaism for a while now, I was intrigued by this mélange that combined "the Orthodox" and the "non-Orthodox." I questioned one of Maya's sisters on the rationale of the event: why did they make these specific choices—for instance, holding a non-egalitarian service and at the same time offering Tai-chi and meditation sessions? Much to my disappointment, my question was answered by a shoulder shrug. When I asked her why they made these choices, she answered that "it suited them," because "this [Orthodox] sort of prayer service was the sort of service they, and the Orthodox guests, felt comfortable with" or because "some people looked for spiritual practices beyond the traditional service." Seemingly, at least on the part of the organizers, there was no coherent theological rationale behind the event. Other participants I talked to, especially those who came from an Orthodox background yet were no longer observant, expressed their satisfaction with the ambiguous orientation of the event. Many of them told me that after long years of not attending synagogue service on Yom Kippur, they finally felt spiritually "at home."

The Yom Kippur event I witnessed in the Vertigo eco-art village, so it seems, was neither part of a formalized, institutionalized tradition (neither Orthodox nor liberal), nor a deliberate, organized attempt at Jewish renewal (cf. Werczberger, 2016). Much like the participants in other contemporary practices of Jewish spirituality, the attendees were looking for a personal spiritual experience of the holy day. To attempt to affiliate them, or the event, with any of the available socio-religious categories or with the established Jewish streams is both futile and unhelpful. Instead, I would suggest that it is another reflection of the variety, complexity, and "messiness" of contemporary Jewish everyday life in which individuals create, renew, and invent practices and rituals outside of their institutional settings.

Lived Religion and Lived Judaism

Over the last three decades, the study of religion took a cultural turn, as scholars began paying attention to personal religious discourses, identities, and rituals, looking especially at the way religion is embedded in the practices of everyday life (Edgell, 2012). The turn to lived religion arose out of a widespread recognition that the sociology of religion had gotten itself mired in the endlessly debated question of whether the modern world was, or was not, secularizing. This cultural turn in the study of religion has transformed the classic sociological questions regarding belief, doctrines, affiliation (or lack of), and authority into the inquiry on "what religion is and where it occurs" (Ammerman, 2016). New issues such as material culture—for instance, food and clothing as an expression of identity; spontaneous shrines and home altars, rituals of birth and death; and rituals of healing—have gained attention (Ammerman, 2016).

The term "lived religion" is widely credited to the historian of American religion David Hall, who first convened a conference and later published a book of essays titled *Lived Religion in America* (1997). In his introduction, Hall calls upon scholars to turn their attention to "the everyday thinking and doing of lay men and women" (p. vii). The chapters, mostly written by social historians and a few sociologists, examine aspects of practices of ordinary people's lives. The focus on the everyday religious practices of ordinary people suggested by Hall and his fellow historian David Orsi (1997) was fully realized in sociological scholarship almost a decade later with the publication of Meredith McGuire's book *Lived Religion* (2008) and Nancy Ammerman's edited collection *Everyday Religion* (2006).

So, what is lived religion? According to Penny Edgell (2012), lived religion is related to everyday practices of sacralization that may or may not coincide with institutionalized or collective definitions of the sacred. The focus, claims Edgell, is on the religious person and on contexts that are not traditionally religious, rather than on doctrines. According to Ammerman (2016), one way of understanding the concept of lived religion is by contrast—that is, what it is not. Lived religion is about ordinary people, *not* religious professionals, and it is about everyday life, *not* what happens in institutionalized settings.

The corollary to the non-institutional, non-dogmatic, non-elite focus is an implicit argument about practice. Defining religion in personalized, individual terms implies a shift toward what individuals *do*. Put differently, lived religion is first and foremost about "practices." As the scholarship teaches us, these practices tend to be creative and hybrid, as the actors freely adopt practices both from their own religious traditional origins and from others. Through these everyday practices centered on emotions, embodiment, narratives, and materiality, participants produce, encounter, and share sacred experiences (Ammerman, 2016). Hence, the study of lived religion points toward experiential domains through which to investigate religious and spiritual practice.

Importantly, while these rituals and ways of living are "everyday," they are not necessarily disconnected from religious institutions and tradition. Yet it is their de-institutionalized, personalized aspect that stimulates the question of the relationship between the category of lived religion and that of spirituality. Recent years have seen myriad efforts, both academic and popular, to distinguish between religion and spirituality. Typically, religion is associated with institutionalized, organized, authoritative, and collective beliefs and expressions, and spirituality with non-institutionalized, decentralized, and autonomous assortments of beliefs and practices. This binary distinction undergirds most of the popular and academic discourse on contemporary spirituality (Heelas & Woodhead, 2005; Fuller, 2001).

Yet scholars such as Ammerman (2013) argue that in everyday experience there is a great deal of overlap between the religious and the spiritual. In her study on the discursive categories people use when discussing religion and spirituality, Ammerman argues that "spirituality... overlaps significantly with what those people take to be religion" (2013, p. 259). In fact, most of her participants inhabit a world that "is both spiritual and religious at the same time.... For a large majority, spirituality is defined by and interchangeable with the experiences their religious communities have offered them and taught them how to interpret" (p. 273). Mary Joe Neitz, however, offers a different perspective on these issues. According to Neitz (2011), spirituality can be distinguished from lived religion in that it (spirituality) is about a personal subjective experience, while lived religion comprises the actual practices that take place in public.

Jewish spirituality, broadly defined, challenges these distinctions. While the practitioners of Jewish spirituality strive for inner spiritual experience, much of the actual practice takes place in public and in a collective setting, be it a synagogue or an informal weekend retreat. Even the most New-Agey, alternative forms of Jewish spirituality such as Jewish meditation (Niculescu, 2013) or Jewish healing (Rothenberg, 2006a, 2006b) take place in group settings. Like most Jewish practice, Jewish spirituality tends to blur the boundaries between the personal and the collective (Prell-Foldes, 1980).

Moreover, Judaism, more than a belief-based religion, is based on practice. Jewish law (*halacha*) and its practical implementation (*mitzvot*) form the core of Jewish tradition. This might serve as a preliminary hint as to the question of the lack of research on Judaism as a lived religion, an issue to which I now turn. Generally speaking, there is very little scholarly work on contemporary Jewish life that engages with the concept of lived religion (cf. Ochs, 2005; Sered, 2006). Sociological studies of North American Jewry tend to pay attention to questions of behavior, belonging, and belief, formulated through the categories of religion and ethnicity. While these issues have long functioned as useful and reliable ways of describing patterns of Jewish life, their utility in describing Jewishness as it is *lived* is limited (Kelman et al., 2017). Ethnographies of Jewish life observe the actual everyday practices of Jews. Yet they are inclined, as most ethnographies are, to focus on specific ethnic and religious communities (for instance, Werczberger, 2016; Leon, 2010; El-Or, 1994; Kugelmass, 1988). The exceptions to this rule seem to be the nascent works on Jewish material culture (for instance, Koltun-Fromm, 2015), and especially those that study its gendered aspects (Sered, 2006; Eichler-Levine, 2007). While these works do not explicitly employ the concept of lived religion, they do observe and comment on the everyday lives of Jews.

In the Israeli sociology of religion, the absence of the concept of lived religion is even more apparent. Here, Jewishness is typically explored through the lenses of religiosity, ethnicity, and nationality (Goodman & Yonah, 2004). Admittedly, new perspectives "beyond" the rigid binary categories of affiliation—that is, religious (*dati*) vs. secular (*hiloni*)—have recently been suggested. Yet most studies are still conducted within the accepted socio-religious categories of Jewish Israeli society: *Haredi* (Ultra-Orthodox), *Dati-Leumi* (National-Religious), *Mesorati* (traditionalist), and Secular (cf. Yadgar, 2010), and avoid looking at religious practice across affiliations and in a more nuanced way. For instance, Hagar Lahav's work explores the religious perceptions of women she identifies as "secular believers" (Lahav, 2016) and Tamar El-Or's ethnography of the separation of the *Challah* women's ritual (*hafrashat hallah*) (1994) does so in terms of the *Mizrachi Teshuva* (back to the fold) movement (cf. Sered, 2006).

The present study will attempt to challenge these analytical boundaries by exploring several new spiritual rituals that have recently emerged in Israel as forms of lived religion: the emergent neo-Hassidic communities and prayer services, the women-only "Amen Meal," and contemporary saint veneration. The three cases differ significantly from each other. The first engages primarily young adults from a secular or National-Religious background who are inspired by Hassidism and are actively seeking spiritual experiences. The second is a newly minted, women-only ritual, popular mostly (though not exclusively) among Orthodox women. And the third is the outgrowth and expansion of the North African–based folk tradition of saint veneration. All three, however, attest to the changes taking place in the Israeli religio-scape, whereby individuals of different affiliations autonomously re-create their everyday religious practices outside formal religious institutions and without regard to religious authorities.

Lived Religion in Everyday Jewish Practice

TRANSIENT NEO-HASSIDIC COMMUNITIES AND PRAYER SERVICES. In recent years, new forms of prayer services and communities have emerged both in Israel and in North America.[1] In Israel, young people are searching for alternative, more spiritual forms of Jewish devotion. They do so by creating informal prayer services and transient communities, much like the Yom Kippur service at the Vertigo eco-art village in the ethnographic vignette above. The most prominent example of these sorts of prayer events are the Jewish New Age prayer services I describe in my work on New Age Judaism in Israel (Werczberger, 2016; see Yzraely, 2014, for a discussion of non-Jewish prayer and song circles), as well as the secular (or cultural) forms of Jewish renewal prayer communities (*Batei-Tefilah*) (Azulay & Tabory, 2008).

Generally, Jewish prayer services are formalized in time and space. Traditional Jewish prayer takes place in a quorum of ten (men if Orthodox, men and women if not), three times a day, and in a designated space—the synagogue. Based on years-long routine participation, the attendees and their families form a community, which may or may not be formally affiliated with one of the existing denominations: Liberal or Orthodox.

In the transient communities discussed here, the prayer events do not take place inside the walls of the formal synagogue. Instead, they are convened in mundane, everyday venues: a dance studio, a large room in a community center, and often outside the confines of a four-walled room—out in nature. Not affiliated with any of the institutionalized Jewish denominations, they emerge in a bottom-up or grassroots process (Forman, 2004), initiated by individuals who seek to create their own personal spiritual prayer service. The resulting services are produced through the negotiation with the Jewish tradition mediated by personal outlook, values, sensibilities,

---

1. The North American equivalents of this trend are the "independent minyanim." These new spiritual communities display considerable diversity in location, religious ideology, aesthetic style, mission, and constituency. Yet they all tend to avoid the terms "synagogue" and "congregation," and seek to create intentional, authentic, and spiritual experiences, whether these are defined in terms of greater liturgical virtuosity or in terms of deeper meaningfulness (Cohen et al., 2007).

and adherence to the *Halacha*. As such, these prayer services are as often idiosyncratic as not.

Notwithstanding these differences, the participants share the desire for a personal, subjective, embodied, unmediated spiritual experience. Consequently, the traditional Jewish prayer is modified and transformed in order to generate an intense, immersive, often ecstatic, experience (Werczberger, 2016). Another feature of these types of events is that they are often declaratively experimental, allowing the participants to play creatively with different elements of the Jewish liturgy, including text and music. In the more New-Agey kinds, this may result in the hybridization of the Jewish ritual and the amalgamation of Jewish and non-Jewish practices, such as meditation or chanting (Werczberger, 2016).

THE "AMEN MEAL"/"BLESSING (BERACHAH) PARTY." Our second example is allegedly more traditional and Orthodox than the prayer services described above, yet it is no less creative or personal. The Amen Meal is a new women's ritual that emerged in Israel at the beginning of the millennium and later spread to the United States and England (Taylor-Guthartz, 2016; Neriya-Ben Shahar, 2015). While the roots of this new ritual are unclear, together with the *hafrashat* challah ritual,[2] it has become exceedingly popular among women across a wide spectrum of age, socioeconomic backgrounds, ethnic origin, and degree of religiosity. The stated goal is to achieve a maximum recitation—up to one hundred blessings—of "amen" in response to the blessings said over various kinds of food. The participants believe the more blessings and "amens" said during the meal, the greater the power of the prayer and the likelihood that it will be fulfilled. Moreover, each one of the blessings is associated with a specific *segulah* (charm)—some for a specific issue related to the life of Orthodox women, such as fertility or finding one's

---

2. *Hafrashat* challah ceremonies are another new women-only group ritual based on the obligation to separate and burn a portion of the dough before braiding and baking the challah (El-Or, 2011).

match, and some for general concerns such as livelihood and/or healing. During the ritual, the women recite the designated blessing over different categories of food (baked goods, fruit, vegetables, wine, etc.) in a pre-structured order and respond with an "Amen!" A prayer composed especially for this ceremony—*yehi ratzon* (May it be God's will that [...]), which emphasizes the associated *segulah* of the blessing, that is, livelihood, marriage, fertility, health, and personal and collective deliverance—is also recited (Neriya-Ben Shahar, 2015).

The Amen Meal may be gauged in several ways. First, as Neriya-Ben Shahar (2015) convincingly argues, it creates a feminine space for Jewish women, endowing them with a sense of spiritual empowerment and practical achievement. Unlike traditional masculine Jewish everyday practice, such as Torah study, it is not based on textual scholarship. Instead, like similar women's everyday rituals, it is centered on a traditionally feminine domain: the preparation and consumption of food (Davidman, 2007; El-Or, 2011). Thus, it offers Jewish women an alternative, domestic way to practice their religion and allows them to experience the sacred and offer healing to their loved ones in a palpable way. In a feminist perspective, one may speculate that in the Orthodox community, where women are generally barred from formal public ritual roles, the Amen Meal provides a space and time in which women regain their agency and become the wielders of feminine spiritual power (Neriya-Ben Shahar, 2015; Avishai, Jafar, & Rinaldo, 2015; Sered, 2006).

CONTEMPORARY SAINT VENERATION. The third example is also partially rooted in women's lived religion. Never assuming the role of obligatory ritual, these sorts of practices belong to the "little tradition" (Redfield, 1956), which takes place outside the formal, institutionalized forms of religious life and allows women to take part in a religious practice in a public space (Goldberg, 2003). Developing out of Jewish North African traditions of saint veneration as well as the Hassidic veneration of the *tzaddik*, this is a classic ritual of lived religion that in recent years has regained its popularity.

Traditionally, Jewish pilgrimages to gravesites of venerated saints, known as the *hillula*, took place on the anniversary of the saint's death and included storytelling, praying, eating, and drinking. In recent years, Israel has seen an unprecedented upsurge in pilgrimages to sacred gravesites, most of them located in Israel but some abroad. As anthropologist Yoram Bilu notes, this is the result of the work of specific individuals, or "impresarios" in Bilu's eloquent terms, who "imported" these rituals from North Africa to contemporary Israel, as well as of various state agents who engage in the discovery and mapping of old-new gravesites of sages and saints (Bilu, 2010; Ben-Ari & Bilu, 1997).

These sites now draw throngs of pilgrims who go there to appeal for the saint's intervention on their behalf. For instance, in Amuka, at the gravesite of R. Yonatan Ben Uzi'el, a late first-century Talmudic sage who has become renowned as the patron of "good marriage," single men and women gather, hoping to find a match within a year. These pilgrimages have become popular among new groups and individuals who are not necessarily *Hassids* or of North African descent and include Jews of Mizrachi and Ashkenazi origins who may be religious, traditional, or secular (Sarfati, 2004; Collins-Kreiner, 2007).

A similar crossover of socio-religious boundaries is evident in the mass pilgrimage to Uman in Ukraine, to the gravesite of the late eighteenth-century Rabbi Nachman of Breslav, at Rosh Hashana (Jewish New Year). This men-only pilgrimage, traditionally undertaken by Breslav Hassids, has become exceedingly popular today, with estimated tens of thousands of Jewish Israelis visiting the site every year. Among the multitudes who flock to Uman are individuals who are "part-time" Breslav, non-*Hassids*, of Mizrachi background or National-Religious, all of whom are seeking an uplifting spiritual experience (Bilu & Mark, 2012; Weinstock, 2011). During the pilgrimage they pray at the gravesite and hold various rituals that are related both to the holiday's liturgy and to specific Breslav rituals and prayers.

So, what can be learned from these three cases of everyday religious/spiritual practices of Israeli Jews? First, they bear witness to the fact that in real life the social boundaries between different religious groups in Israel are far more blurred than depicted in the reigning socio-political and public discourse. In the transient neo-Hassidic prayers, individuals who normally affiliate themselves with the National-Religious community, or are allegedly secular, traditional, or former-Orthodox, meet and pray together. The Amen Meal brings together women from an Orthodox and traditional background so that they can, through the recitation of the blessing, actively work toward the shared goal of emotional and physical healing. The pilgrimages, too, coalesce disparate groups of Israeli Jews in common prayer toward a venerated saint, asking for a specific request or searching for a spiritual experience.

Second, these cases remind us that the religious life of contemporary Jews is aligned not only according to formal legal texts, doctrines, or authorized persons and traditions, but is also constantly inspired, re-created, and even invented by everyday necessities, obligations, and physical or emotional hardship. Thus, a single woman who might ordinarily think of herself as secular might find herself joining an organized pilgrimage to Amuka to pray for a match. The same might be said of a woman with a sick child or parent, who participates in the Amen Meal, hoping that the hundred blessings and "amens" will bring her and her loved ones the relief they pray for.

Third, and connected to this aspect, these three cases illuminate the potential creativity embedded in the everyday religiosity of ordinary Jews. When observed from below, at the individual level, Jewish practice is revealed as a dynamic, "ever-changing, multifaceted, often messy—even contradictory—amalgam of beliefs and practices that are not necessarily those religious institutions consider important" (McGuire, 2008, p. 4). These practices tend to be creative and hybrid, as the actors freely adopt practices both from their own traditional religious origins and from those of others. The most obvious example of this sort of ritual is the Amen Meal, in which the traditional Jewish blessings over foodstuff and the saying of the "amens" are combined with folk beliefs regarding the charms present in different food (*segulah*) and realized in a women-only group ritual.

Finally, the different rituals described here all take place in ad hoc communities and informal groups. Yet unlike some of the contemporary forms of spirituality, these "new modes of sociality" (Laplantine, 2003; qtd. in Meintel, 2014) do not replace the lifelong commitment to established denominations and synagogues. Instead, they transpire in parallel and at times even complementary traditional affiliations. Individualized Jewish spirituality, it seems, does not necessarily stand in opposition to institutionalized Judaism, but rather as a corresponding track through which Jews make sense of their everyday lives, beliefs, and practices (cf. Neitz, 2011). Accordingly, Jewish spirituality, understood broadly, is neither a diffused individualized phenomenon nor a single cultural alternative to institutionalized Jewish tradition. Instead, it is an additional way for Jewish individuals to sacralize their daily lives and arrange them around their traditions. While small, heterogeneous in size, and ephemeral, these new associative "bunde" and elective "tribes" indicate the important role that collectivity still plays in contemporary Jewish life.

Lived Judaism: New Perspectives on the Everyday Lives of Jews

This chapter has offered a brief survey of contemporary Jewish life in Israel through three cases of lived religion. Drawing on the notion that lived religion is about ordinary people in everyday life and not about religious professionals or what goes on in institutionalized settings, these cases serve as examples of new personal forms of Jewish practice that have recently evolved in Israel. It goes without saying that each one of these cases deserves an in-depth exploration, yet the preliminary analysis offered here reveals that these everyday practices center on emotions and embodied practices, allowing participants to produce, encounter, and share sacred experiences.

These transformations in the Israeli Jewish religio-scape, as well as in the North American one, are of course related to wider global processes taking place in the early twenty-first century. For instance, consumer society, which furthers the individualization process of modernity by redefining life and society as arenas of *choice,* reshapes religion in a context of cultural deregulation by opening a vast range of new possibilities for new religious knowledge, practices, leaders, organizations, and forms of political action (Gauthier and Martikainen, 2013). Concurrently, in the Jewish world, more and more Jews from different localities and affiliations choose autonomously from the wide array of cultural practices and construe new and personally meaningful spiritual forms of Jewish engagement (Cohen & Eisen, 2000) and in turn expand the Jewish spirituality marketplace. When the institutionalized practices are deemed insufficient, new practices emerge to fulfill the spiritual needs of the individuals.

As a conclusion, I would like to suggest that in order to understand the meanings and sensibilities of Jewish life in the early twenty-first century, more research that focuses on the everyday spiritual experiences of Jews is necessary. If we want to understand what it means for people to be Jewish in this day and age, we need to stop "looking under the lamp" and instead observe the experiences that take place in settings outside of official religious bounds, in this-worldly, mundane realms of life, and in non-formal and non-institutionalized settings. We need to listen carefully to the narratives of individual Jews from various social and religious settings, the experiences they consider most important, and the concrete practices that make up their religious experiences and expressions. This will allow us to trace the intricate interweaving of the mundane, the religious, the sacred, and the spiritual of everyday Jewish experiences, outside and across institutionally and denominationally based groups and synagogues.

References

Ammerman, N. (Ed.). (2006). *Everyday religion: Observing modern religious lives.* New York: Oxford University Press.

Ammerman, N. (2013). Spiritual but not religious? Beyond binary choices in the study of religion. *Journal for the Scientific Study of Religion, 52*(2), 258–278.

Ammerman, N. (2016). Lived religion as an emerging field: An assessment of its contours and frontiers. *Nordic Journal of Religion and Society, 29*(2), 83–99.

Avishai, O., Jafar, A., & Rinaldo, R. (2015). A gender lens on religion. *Gender and Society, 29*(1), 5–25.

Azulay, N., & Tabory, E. (2008). A house of prayer for all nations: Unorthodox prayer houses for nonreligious Israeli Jews. *Sociological Papers, 13,* 22–41.

Ben-Ari, E., & Bilu, Y. (Eds.). (1997). *Grasping land: Space and place in contemporary Israeli discourse and experience.* Albany: State University of New York Press.

Bilu, Y. (2010). *The saints' impresarios: dreamers, healers, and holy men in Israel's urban periphery.* Boston: Academic Studies Press.

Bilu, Y., & Mark, Z. (2012). Between tsaddiq and messiah: A comparative analysis of Chabad and Breslav Hasidic groups. In P. Wexler & J. Garb (Eds.), *After spirituality: Studies in mystical tradition* (pp. 47–78). New York: Peter Lang,

Cohen, S.M., & Eisen, A.M. (2000). *The Jew within: Self, family, and community in America.* Bloomington: Indiana University Press.

Cohen, S.M., Landres, S.J., Kaunfer, E., & Shain, M. (2007). *Emergent Jewish communities and their participants: Preliminary findings from the 2007 national spiritual communities study.* <http://www.synagogue3000.org/files/NatSpirComStudyReport_S3K_Hadar.Pdf>.

Collins-Kreiner, N. (2007). Graves as attractions: Pilgrimage-tourism to Jewish holy graves in Israel. *Journal of Cultural Geography, 24*(1), 67–89.

Davidman, L. (2007). The new volunteerism and the case of unsynagogued Jews. In N. Ammerman (Ed.), *Everyday religion* (pp. 51–67). New York: Oxford University Press.

Edgell, P. (2012). Cultural sociology of religion: New directions. *Annual Review of Sociology, 38*, 247–265.

Eichler-Levine, J. (2007, December). *"I Made it a Jewish quilt": Crafting Judaism, telling stories.* Lecture given at the 49th Annual Conference of the Association of Jewish Studies, Washington, DC.

El-Or, T. (1994). *Educated and ignorant: Ultraorthodox Jewish women and their world.* Boulder, CO: Lynne Rienner Publishers.

El-Or, T. (2011). A temple in your kitchen: Hafrashat Hallah—The rebirth of a forgotten ritual as a public ceremony. In R.S. Boustan, O. Kosansky, & M. Rustow (Eds.), *Jewish studies at the crossroads of anthropology and history: Authority, diaspora, and tradition* (pp. 271–293). Philadelphia: University of Pennsylvania Press.

Forman, R.K.C. (2004). *Grassroots spirituality: What it is, why it is here, where it is going.* Charlottesville, VA: Imprint Academic Press.

Fuller, R.C. (2001). *Spiritual, but not religious: Understanding unchurched America.* Oxford: Oxford University Press.

Gauthier, F., & Martikainen, T. (Eds.) (2013). *Religion in consumer society: Brands, consumers and markets.* Burlington, VT: Ashgate Publishing Company.

Giordan, G. (2016). Spirituality. In D. Yamane (Ed.), *Handbook of religion and society* (pp. 197–216). London and New York: Springer International Publishing.

Goldberg, H.E. (2003). *Jewish passages.* Berkeley: University of California Press.

Goodman, Y., & Yonah, Y. (2004). Introduction: Religiousness and secularity in Israel: Possibilities for alternative views. In Y. Yonah & Y. Goodman (Eds.), *Maelstrom of identities* [Ma'Arbolet HaZe'Uyot] (pp. 3–37). Jerusalem: Kibbutz HaMeuhad and Van Leer [Hebrew].

Hall, D. (1997). *Lived religion in America: Toward a history of practice.* Princeton, NJ: Princeton University Press.

Heelas, P., & Woodhead, L. (2005). *The spiritual revolution: Why religion is giving way to spirituality.* Oxford: Blackwell.

Kelman, A.Y., Belzer, T., Horwitz, I., Hassenfeld, Z., & Williams, M. (2017). Traditional Judaism: The conceptualization of Jewishness in the lives of American Jewish post-boomers. *Jewish Social Studies, 23*(1), 134–167.

Koltun-Fromm, K. (2015). *Imagining Jewish authenticity: Vision and text in American Jewish thought.* Bloomington and Indianapolis: Indiana University Press.

Kugelmass, J. (1988). *Between two worlds: Ethnographic essays on American Jewry.* Ithaca, NY: Cornell University Press.

Lahav, H. (2016). What do secular-believer women in Israel believe in? *Journal of Contemporary Religion, 31*(1), 17–34.

Leon, N. (2010). *Gentle ultra-Orthodoxy: Religious renewal in oriental Jewry in Israel.* Jerusalem: Yad Izhak Ben-Zvi [Hebrew].

McGuire, M.B. (2008). *Lived religion: Faith and practice in everyday life.* New York: Oxford University Press.

Meintel, D. (2014). Religious collectivities in the era of individualization. *Social Compass, 61*(2), 195–206.

Neitz, M.J. (2011). Lived religion: Signposts of where we have been and where we can go from here. In G. Giordan & W.H.J. Swatos (Eds.), *Religion, spirituality and everyday practice* (pp. 45–55). London and New York: Springer.

Neriya-Ben Shahar, R. (2015). "At 'amen meals' it's me and God": Religion and gender: A new Jewish women's ritual. *Contemporary Jewry, 35*(2), 153–172.

Niculescu, M. (2013). "Find your inner god and breathe": Buddhism, pop culture, and contemporary metamorphoses in American Judaism. In F. Gauthier & T. Martikainen (Eds.), *Religion in consumer society: Brands, consumers and markets* (pp. 91–108). Burlington, VT: Ashgate Publishing Company.

Ochs, V.L. (2005). Waiting for the messiah, a tambourine in her hand. *Nashim: A Journal of Jewish Women's Studies & Gender Issues, 9*(1), 144–169.

Orsi, R. (1997). Everyday miracles: The study of lived religion. In D. Hall (ed.), *Lived religion in America: Toward a history of practice* (pp. 3-21). Princeton, NJ: Princeton University Press.

Persico, T. (2014). Neo-Hasidic revival: Expressivist uses of traditional lore. *Modern Judaism, 34*(3), 287–308.

Prell-Foldes, R. (1980). The reinvention of reflexivity in Jewish prayer: The self and community in modernity. *Semiotica, 30*(1–2), 73–96.

Redfield, R. (1956). *Peasant society and culture: An anthropological approach to civilization.* Chicago: University of Chicago Press.

Roof, W.C. (1999). *Spiritual marketplace: Baby boomers and the remaking of American religion.* Princeton, NJ: Princeton University Press.

Rothenberg, C.E. (2006a). Hebrew healing: Jewish authenticity and religious healing in Canada. *Journal of Contemporary Religion, 21*(2), 163–182.

Rothenberg, C.E. (2006b). New Age Jews: Jewish shamanism and Jewish yoga. *Jewish Culture and History, 8*(3), 1–21.

Salkin, J.K. (2000). New Age Judaism. In J. Neusner & A.J. Avery-Peck (Eds.), *The Blackwell companion to Judaism* (pp. 354–370). Malden, MA: Blackwell.

Sarfati, L. (2004). *Imported rituals: Zaddiq veneration in Israel.* Unpublished paper.

Sered, S.S. (2006). *Women as ritual experts: The religious lives of elderly Jewish women in Jerusalem.* Oxford: Oxford University Press.

Taylor-Guthartz, L. (2016). *Overlapping worlds: The religious lives of Orthodox Jewish women in contemporary London.* Unpublished PhD dissertation, University College, London.

Vertigo eco-art village, Kibbutz HaLamedhe. (n.d.). <http://vertigo.org.il/en/ecological-art-village/>.

Weinstock, M. (2011). *Uman: The Israeli journey to the grave of Rebbe Nachman of Bratslav.* Tel Aviv: Yediot Acharonot and Chemed Books.

Weissler, C. (2006). "Women of vision" in the Jewish renewal movement: The Eshet Hazon ["women of vision"] ceremony. *Jewish Culture and History, 8*(3), 62–86.

Werczberger, R. (2016). *Jews in the age of authenticity: Jewish spiritual renewal in Israel.* New York: Peter Lang.

Yadgar, Y. (2010). *Masortim in Israel: Modernity without secularization.* Jerusalem: The Shalom Hartman Institute.

Yzraely, Y. (2014). Kumbaya in Zion: Secular and religious elements in Israeli sacred singing circles. *Alternative Spirituality and Religion Review, 5*(1), 132–148.

NOTES ON CONTRIBUTORS

PHILIP WEXLER is Executive Director of the Institute of Jewish Spirituality and Society and Professor of Sociology of Education and Unterberg Chair in Jewish Social and Educational History at the Hebrew University of Jerusalem (emeritus). His research interests include critical social theory, the sociology of education, and the sociology of religion. His most recent book is *Mystical Sociology: Toward Cosmic Social Theory* (Peter Lang, 2013).

DON SEEMAN is Associate Professor in the Department of Religion and the Tam Institute for Jewish Studies at Emory University and serves as rabbi of the New Toco Shul in Atlanta. He is the author of numerous works in the anthropology of religion and Jewish thought, including Hasidism. He is the recipient of a research grant from the Social Science Research Council's New Directions in the Study of Prayer Initiative.

ELLIOT R. WOLFSON is Marsha and Jay Glazer Endowed Chair in Jewish Studies and Professor in the Department of Religious Studies at the University of California, Santa Barbara. His comparative research on Jewish mysticism and Hasidism intersects with philosophy, literary criticism, feminist theory, postmodern hermeneutics, and the phenomenology of religion. His most recent books are *The Duplicity of Philosophy's Shadow: Heidegger, Nazism and the Jewish Other* (2018) and *Heidegger and Kabbalah: Hidden Gnosis and the Path of Poiesis* (forthcoming 2019).

ELI RUBIN is an editor and research writer at Chabad.org, and a graduate research student in the Department of Hebrew and Jewish

Studies, University College London. His research focuses on Chabad's intellectual, social and cultural trajectories from the movement's origins to the present day. He is also a consultant at the Institute of Jewish Spirituality and Society.

NAFTALI LOEWENTHAL lectures in Jewish Spirituality in the Department of Hebrew and Jewish Studies at University College London, where he teaches courses on Hasidism and modernity, and on Maimonides. He is the author of *Communicating the Infinite: The Emergence of the Habad School* (University of Chicago Press, 1990), and a forthcoming academic book is *Hasidism Beyond Modernity: Essays in Habad Thought and History* (Littman Library). He is also the Director of the Chabad Research Unit, which promotes Chabad teachings in daily life through study sessions and publications such as the popular 'Friday Night,' a discussion of the weekly Torah reading. In addition, for many years he has taught Religious Studies at the Lubavitch Senior Girls' School in London, seeking to convey the art of communicating Judaism in contemporary society. He is married to Professor Kate-Miriam Loewenthal and they have a large family.

KATE MIRIAM LOEWENTHAL is Emeritus Professor of Psychology at Royal Holloway, University of London, and Visiting Professor at NYU in London, and Glyndwr University, Wales. Her most recent book is *Religion, Culture and Mental Health* (Cambridge University Press, 2006).

RIVKAH SLONIM is Educational Director at the Rohr Chabad Center for Jewish Student Life at Binghamton University. She lectures widely on the intersection of traditional Jewish observance and contemporary life and is the author of *Total Immersion: A Mikvah Anthology* (Jason Aronson 1996, second edition: Urim Publications, 2006) and *Bread and Fire: Jewish Women find God in the Everyday* (Urim Publications, 2008).

Notes on Contributors

SHAUL WERTHEIMER is the founder and Executive Director of Chabad On Campus of Queens. He wrote the monthly Torah column for the Chicago Jewish Star, and has also been published in the New York Times, Chabad.org, Huffington Post, and Moment Magazine. His weekly dvar Torah essays and broadcasts are enjoyed by hundreds. Shaul holds a degree in Philosophy from Northwestern University and is a graduate of the Rabbinical College of America. In his free time he enjoys biking, and spending time with his family.

NATHANIEL BERMAN is Rahel Varnhagen Professor of International Affairs, Law, and Modern Culture at Brown University. He is the author of *Passion and Ambivalence: Colonialism, Nationalism, and International Law* (Martinus Nijhoff Publishers, 2011) and *Divine and Demonic in the Poetic Mythology of the Zohar: the "Other Side" of Kabbalah* (Brill, 2018).

YOTAM HOTAM is a Senior Lecturer at the Faculty of Education at the University of Haifa. He is the author of *Modern Gnosis and Zionism: The Crisis of Culture, Life Philosophy and Jewish National Thought* (Routledge, 2013) and a co-editor of *New Social Foundations for Education: Education in Post Secular Society* (Peter Lang, 2015).

JONATHAN GARB is Gershom Scholem Professor of Kabbalah in the Department of Jewish Thought at The Hebrew University of Jerusalem. His most recent books are *Yearnings of the Soul: Psychological Thought in Modern Kabbalah* (Chicago University Press, 2015) and *Modern Kabbalah as an Autonomous Domain of Research* (Cherub Press, 2016).

SHAUL MAGID is Jay and Jeanie Schottenstein Chair in Jewish Studies and Professor of Religious Studies at Indiana University and Kogod Senior Research Fellow at The Shalom Hartman Institute of North America. His scholarship focuses on Kabbalah, Hasidism, and modern Jewish life and thought. His most recent books are *Hasidism Incarnate* (Stanford University Press, 2014) and *Piety and Rebellion: Essays in Hasidism* (Academic Studies Press).

ALAN SADOVNIK is Board of Governors Distinguished Service Professor in the School of Public Affairs & Administration at Rutgers University-Newark. He is the editor, author or co-author of numerous books, including *Exploring Education: An Introduction to the Foundations of Education*, Fifth Edition (Routledge, 2018), *"Schools of Tomorrow", Schools of Today: Progressive Education in the 21st Century*, Second Edition (Peter Lang, 2016) and *Leaders in the Sociology of Education: Intellectual Self-Portraits* (Sense Publishers, 2016).

RACHEL WERCZBERGER is a cultural anthropologist at Ariel University. Her works on New Age Jewish Renewal and Jewish spirituality are published in various journals and edited volumes. Her book *Jews in the Age of Authenticity: Jewish Spiritual Renewal in Israel* was published with Peter Lang (2016).

www.ingramcontent.com/pod-product-compliance
Lightning Source LLC
Chambersburg PA
CBHW030108010526
44116CB00005B/156